Giftedness in the Early Years: Informing, Learning and Teaching

Giftedness in the Early Years: Informing, Learning and Teaching

Edited by Valerie Margrain,
Caterina Murphy and Jo Dean

NZCER PRESS

NZCER PRESS
New Zealand Council for Educational Research
PO Box 3237
Wellington
New Zealand

© Authors, 2015

ISBN 978-1-927231-55-5

This book is not a photocopiable master.
No part of the publication may be copied, stored or communicated in any form by any means (paper or digital), including recording or storing in an electronic retrieval system, without the written permission of the publisher. Education institutions that hold a current licence with Copyright Licensing New Zealand may copy from this book in strict accordance with the terms of the CLNZ Licence.

A catalogue record for this book is available from the National Library of New Zealand

Designed by Book Design Ltd, www.bookdesign.co.nz

Cover art work: Flowers (1997), by Jordan Murphy, an acrylic painting completed at the age of 7.

Distributed by NZCER Distribution Services
PO Box 3237
Wellington
New Zealand
www.nzcer.org.nz

Whakataukī

Iti noa ana, he pito mata.
With care, a small kumara will produce a harvest.

Artwork by Isabella Dean (age 9) and Alexandria Dean (age 7).

Dedication

This book is dedicated to:

- all early years children who are gifted—may their potential be noticed, recognised and responded to
- Valerie's children, family and loved ones (especially Bergie), who all support her to be a lifelong learner
- Caterina's children and grandchildren, in their pursuit of lifelong learning
- Jo's children and extended family, nieces and nephews, flying high with their learning.

Contents

Foreword	x
Preface	xiii
Acknowledgements	xvi

PART 1: KEY CONCEPTS OF GIFTEDNESS IN THE EARLY YEARS

Chapter 1: Introduction and definitions of giftedness in the early years — 1
Caterina Murphy and Deborah Walker

Chapter 2: Identifying characteristics of giftedness in the early years — 14
Caterina Murphy and Sue Breen

Chapter 3: Through the lens of play: Complexities of giftedness — 38
Caterina Murphy

PART 2: PURPOSEFUL AND AUTHENTIC ASSESSMENT PRACTICES

Chapter 4: Assessment for learning with young gifted children — 57
Jo Dean and Valerie Margrain

Chapter 5: Looking at learning: Narratives of young gifted children — 75
Jo Dean, Carola Sampson, Annette Preston and Emma Wallace

PART 3: SUPPORTING QUALITY PRACTICE

Chapter 6: The myth busters: Fearless, inclusive teaching for young gifted children — 105
Melanie Wong and Valerie Margrain

Chapter 7: Social and emotional issues for young gifted children — 128
Carola Sampson

Chapter 8: Opening the treasure chest: Differentiation for young children who are gifted — 142
Caterina Murphy

Chapter 9: Talking together: Supporting gifted children and positive transitions to school — 163
Monica Cameron and Valerie Margrain

Chapter 10: Liam's story: At risk of underachievement — 181
Carola Sampson

PART 4: POSSIBILITIES FOR EMPOWERMENT

Chapter 11: Supporting the advocates of young gifted children: Weaving connections and inspiration — 200
Valerie Margrain and Jo Dean

Author biographies 217
Appendices 222
  Appendix A: Two models of giftedness 223
  Appendix B: Characteristics of giftedness in the early years 224
  Appendix C: Peer nomination form for use with 3- and 4-year
    old children 226
  Appendix D: Parent reflection statements 227
  Appendix E: Play patterns of young children who are gifted 228
  Appendix F: Myths and responses: Gifteness in the early years 230
  Appendix G: 'Excitabilities' and strategies 232
  Appendix H: Differentiation, metaphor and practice 234
  Appendix I: Applying a taxonomy to differentiation in the early years 235
  Appendix J: Teacher reflective questions 236
  Appendix K: School communication strategies valued by parents 237

Figures
  Figure 1.1. Gagné's Differentiated Model of Giftedness and Talent
    (DMGT) 5
  Figure 1.2. Three-Ring Conception of Giftedness 6
  Figure 5.1. Documenting the physical capabilities of a young toddler 78
  Figure 5.2. Jackson's teachers support literacy skills and technology
    interests 81
  Figure 5.3. Jackson's parents share his interests from home with his
    teachers 82
  Figure 5.4. Dereck's intense interest and understanding of Māori legends 86
  Figure 5.5. Dereck learning about the legend of the stingray 88
  Figure 5.6. Emma shares her interest and knowledge of plants 91
  Figure 5.7. Showing a strong sense of creativity 93
  Figure 5.8. Developing a plan for Emma 96
  Figure 5.9. Demonstrating the concept of distance 98
  Figure 6.1. Becoming fearless in supporting gifted children:
    an illustrative model 119
  Figure 10.1. Gagné's Differentiated Model of Giftedness and
    Talent applied to Liam 191
  Figure 11.1. Children role-playing the story of *The Three Billy
    Goats Gruff* 213
  Figure 11.2. Textile board created by children in a kindergarten 213
  Figure A.1. Gagné's Differentiated Model of Giftedness and Talent
    (DMGT) 223
  Figure A.2. Three-ring Conception of Giftednes 223

Tables

Table 4.1. Dispositions and curriculum connections	65
Table 7.1. Excitabilities and support strategies	138
Table 8.1. Differentiation, metaphor and practice connections	147
Table 8.2. Bloom's Taxonomy applied to young children and zebra learning	158
Table 9.1. Teacher communication strategies valued by parents	168
Table 11.1. The child's questions connected to considerations for gifted education in the early years	204
Table 11.2. Four national gifted education organisations and selected aims	207
Table F.1. Common myths about giftedness in the early years, with suggested responses	230
Table G.1. 'Excitabilities', behavioural indicators and useful support strategies	232
Table H.1. Differentiation, metaphor and practice connections	234
Table I.1. Bloom's Taxonomy applied to young children and zebra learning	235
Table K.1. Categorised school communication strategies valued by parents	237

Index 238

Foreword

Among the delights of teaching are the opportunities it brings to observe learners grow and flourish, ultimately developing independence and autonomy in their pursuit of knowledge. Seldom does a teacher also get the chance to watch her students become creators, leading and mentoring others as they develop and share new ways of knowing and thinking. Having taught the editors, Valerie, Caterina and Jo, as well as most of the contributing authors, during their studies in gifted education at Massey University, it is a great privilege to have been asked to write the foreword for this book, *Giftedness in the Early Years: Informing, Learning and Teaching*. It is one of those moments as a teacher when you step back, let go and feel a sense of awe and admiration for those you had the great joy to teach.

This book is one I wished for on my bookshelf back in the 1990s and early 2000s when I was attempting to teach the authors, who were each inquisitive, passionate and, dare I say, sometimes challenging, early years teachers. It is a book I think we imagined and hoped would come into existence during their studies. It didn't. But over time, the authors actively sought ways of differentiating materials developed for young children in other lands or for older children in our own country, researching and developing methods and materials, creating journal articles and conference presentations to share their ideas, and advocating to anyone who would listen to their cause. From the sidelines, I cheered!

Developing a book out of sheer necessity and based simply on practice is something any of the contributing authors could have done individually, for they each bring a wealth of practical and personal experience working with young gifted children. Yet, what this team of authors has provided for you, its readers, is a strong evidence base to support practice. Each chapter in this book is underpinned by relevant, credible, and authoritative sources of evidence, which move beyond theory and research by also encompassing and valuing the experiences, skills and knowledge of the young child, their teachers and families/whānau. Within an Aotearoa New Zealand context, research evidence is limited in gifted education, and policy for young gifted children is non-existent, making the creation of a supporting evidence base for practice all the more challenging, but, as you will learn, not impossible.

The book is structured around a central principle of gifted and talented education in this country, as first expressed by Associate Professor Don McAlpine in the textbook, *Gifted and Talented: New Zealand Perspectives*. Don described the interrelationships between how we define giftedness, the behavioural, cultural and personal characteristics of gifted learners, methods of identification, a continuum of provisions and their evaluation. Similarly, this book takes its readers through key concepts which contribute to authentic assessment and quality practice, with each chapter based on critical evaluation of practice through the authors' own research and their analysis, synthesis, application and evaluation of others' investigations.

Exploring these key concepts and ideas in the early years of education is critical. From birth to age 8, children who are gifted share unique characteristics: advanced language, a quirky sense of humour, early developmental milestones, deep curiosity, asynchronous development and so on. Recognition of these characteristics requires a response in order for potential to be developed, and, yet, we have evidence in Aotearoa New Zealand, as outlined in this book, that shows gifted children in early childhood settings and those first few years of primary school are not being identified. Importantly, by considering the early years of education, the bridge between early childhood education and schooling is crossed, aiding in the transition across systems with similar aims—but different ways of meeting those—for young gifted children.

This book develops mainstream educational ideas around curriculum and assessment by differentiating these for gifted children. Building on a solid base of knowledge ensures educational practices for gifted learners that are well connected to what teachers understand. Differentiating what we know about learners, how we teach, and outcomes for learners relies upon principles such as sophisticated and in-depth knowledge, practice-led inquiry, culturally responsive pedagogies, and real problems with real solutions—applied through the lens of giftedness.

Significantly, giftedness, as conceived by the authors, is inclusive of a wide range of abilities and qualities found across all cultures and amongst those with disabilities and other challenges, such as socio-economic and gender differences. How this broad concept is applied across different settings by different teachers for different children will vary, thus creating opportunities for critically analysing the text and evaluating effectiveness in relation to an array of cultures, practices and perspectives. I am pleased this book is not a prescription or recipe book, but rather an invitation—to explore, think, critique, trial, debate and get on with the education of our gifted children.

"We are all worms. But I do believe that I am a glow-worm."
—Winston Churchill[1]

I recently was on an adventure with a 3-year-old searching for glow-worms. As he dimmed his torch, they shone brightly. Then he looked up. He gasped a nearly breathless "wow" and quietly exclaimed, "Look at the glow-worms in the sky!" This little boy's sense of wonderment, as he translated what he knew about glow-worms to those stars, which he hadn't quite grasped, is something to be bottled up. He also had questions driven by his curiosity about why the glow-worms glimmer and sparkle in the night. They are tiny creatures that radiate their luminescent light into the darkness, like the stars.

The authors of this book are like those glow-worms on our land and in our night sky. This book provides a much needed and brightly glowing light across a vast landscape: practical knowledge and skills for identifying and providing for our young gifted learners across a range of settings. This book acts as a navigator, like the stars; the ideas will lead practice, underpin future research and guide advocacy. Readers will have their curiosity peaked as connections are made between that which we know and understand about early years education and gifted and talented education.

What *Giftedness in the Early Years: Informing, Learning and Teaching* creates for readers isn't simply a collection of current ideas based on theory, research and practice, but a seminal contribution to education in Aotearoa New Zealand. This book will no doubt influence the future with its originality and creativity, its pioneer-like leadership and forward thinking. It is one I will become reliant upon as I continue working with educators in our country.

As a teacher, I will continue learning more from my students. And so will you.

Associate Professor Tracy Riley
Massey University
January 2015

---

1 Violet Bonham Carter, *Winston Churchill as I Knew Him*, p. 16, remark made at a dinner given by Lady Mary Elcho.

Preface

Giftedness in the Early Years: Informing, Learning and Teaching is long awaited. While our Australian colleagues have produced books about giftedness in the early years since the nineties, an Aotearoa New Zealand book has been on the wish list for quite some time. We are proud and excited that this work has now come to fruition.

The book is edited and written by people who have a commitment to and passion for gifted education, and who have wide experience working in early years education. The authors are all passionate advocates for young gifted children: some have produced research theses explicitly on the early years, and some have early years teaching experience spanning decades.

The main audience for this book is teachers in the early years, but we believe that the content will also be informative and helpful to parents, managers, principals, policy makers and researchers. The book draws on a range of overseas and New Zealand research evidence and literature, shares our teaching experience and research findings, and suggests practical resources that have been found helpful for the early years educational context. Narratives, opinions, metaphors and experiences provide a framework through which early years teachers can consider giftedness in their own settings. These aspects all justify the keyword in our book subtitle: "informing." The other keywords "learning" and "teaching" acknowledge that we are all learners, and have much more to learn about giftedness. Our reference to "teaching" embraces all who support young children who are gifted: staff working in early childhood and school settings, parents and other family members, and other key individuals who make a difference in children's lives.

This book is important because the early years is a critical period in child development—the time when the young child forms their self-concept and makes decisions about their ability and worth. It is a time when the influence of the teacher, in noticing and recognising potential, can remove barriers to the child's learning and open windows of opportunity that best cater for the already confident and capable young child. Here the early years spans both early childhood (prior to school) settings and the first 3 years of school: in other words, children aged from birth to 8 years.

Giftedness is a phenomenon that requires understanding. Because it is so difficult to define, many within the field of education are unsure how to respond to it. But the ease and speed of learning these children display cannot be overlooked. This book is about changing perceptions, helping parents, early years teachers, and other key individuals to understand giftedness, and providing them with resources to help support identification and assessment for learning. It can be read cover to cover, or it can be read as parts or chapters that may be especially pertinent. The aim is to show what has been done effectively here in Aotearoa New Zealand, what can be expected, how to prepare for teaching, and how to differentiate curriculum so that young children in the early years who are gifted can reach their full potential.

The book is divided into four parts, each covering key aspects of gifted education in an early years context. The first part introduces and defines giftedness in the early years, providing essential information about definitions and the characteristics of giftedness, and giftedness through the lens of play. The second part examines assessment for learning, the types of tools that teachers can use to assess children, and examples of learning stories that illustrate gifted behaviour. The third part discusses practice issues. Quality teaching is essential to support all children, including the young and gifted. The chapters includes consideration of inclusive teaching, common myths, social and emotional issues, and approaches to curriculum differentiation, communication, collaboration and transition.

The final part of this publication acknowledges the support and inspiration that teachers and child advocates need, and we hope that the accompanying support materials support advocacy and practice. Brochures and learning stories are included as an important additional resource: they can be used as a quick reference to share with families and supporting professionals, or used to support teachers in their assessment and documentation (these can be downloaded from www.nzcer.org.nz/nzcerpress/giftedness). The inclusion of authentic learning stories provides a key point of difference between this book and others, building on the assessment approaches used by early childhood teachers in their daily work supporting all children.

Although the editors appreciate and accept the significant contribution of each chapter to the book as a whole, they also acknowledge that the chapter authors hold diverse perspectives, and the editors do not necessarily endorse all viewpoints taken by all authors.

Valerie Margrain, Caterina Murphy and Jo Dean

Acknowledgements

We wish to pay tribute to:

- all the contributing authors, consenting families and young children, without whom this book would not have eventuated—thank you to you all
- our husbands/partners and families, for supporting us as editors throughout long, concentrated periods of working on this book
- giftEDnz, for providing writing retreats that supported many of the authors to develop content.

Part 1: Key concepts of giftedness in the early years

Chapter 1: Introduction and definitions of giftedness in the early years

Caterina Murphy and Deborah Walker

Introduction

This book is about young children who are gifted—a group of unique individuals who, during active play and learning in early years environments, may struggle to have their giftedness noticed, recognised and responded to. There is no doubt that young children who are gifted exhibit an ease and speed of learning (Gagné, 2004) that is not often recognised as giftedness by early years teachers. This book has been written in the hope that it will support readers to become more confident in recognising the characteristics of giftedness, more competent in identifying children who are gifted in early years contexts, and more aware of the phenomenon of giftedness. Part of that professional growth will be a deeper understanding of the interests, successes, fears, frustrations and aspirations held by these children, their parents and family/whānau. But ultimately this book will be a resource that provokes reflection and responsiveness, and enhances learning for the youngest of learners, so that giftedness can be understood, discovered, developed and celebrated.

Terms

For the purposes of this publication the authors have chosen to use the phrase 'early years'. This definition encompasses the age span from birth to 8 years. By the end of this developmental phase children have already formed a conception of themselves as thinkers and language users and have made decisions about their abilities and their worth. It is a crucial time for all teachers in early years settings to be responsive to the advanced abilities of young children, and to support, accelerate and enrich their learning as they make the transition to primary school. Early identification and a supportive transition process are vital elements for teachers to engage with, because these children may be misunderstood in a teaching and learning context and left lacking the stimulation they deserve.

In New Zealand, the terms 'gifted' and 'talented' are often used to express the same concept (Ministry of Education, 2012), with gifted and talented education often being referred to as GATE. In this book the term 'gifted' is used to name a specific and unique group of learners who exhibit giftedness (which is defined later in this chapter) and who have the potential to excel in one or more areas of learning. The authors acknowledge that young children with advanced abilities may not yet have had the opportunity to develop their unique skills or advanced knowledge into a specific talent. However, in order to fulfil their potential and to have their passions, interests and strengths recognised and responded to, they must have a well-designed and supportive environment, which includes a differentiated curriculum. Relationships between teachers, children and their families/whānau are key (Ministry of Education, 1996) in order to engage in stimulating and enriching dialogue so that young children can gain authentic and meaningful understanding from within the context of their own social and cultural lives (Vygotsky, 1978).

Setting the scene

Gifted learners are found within every group in society, yet within the early years context there has been a reluctance to 'label by capacity', which creates further misunderstanding and delays in support (Porter, 2005). There is a long history of egalitarianism in Aotearoa New Zealand (Moltzen, 2011a), which this book hopes to challenge, from the viewpoint that we all come into this world differentiated. We are not all 'the same'. Teachers will most certainly have one, two or maybe more children in their setting each year who could benefit from changes in their curriculum and opportunities that best respond to their interests, specialised knowledge of certain topics and dispositional learning strengths. What's more, such curriculum changes enacted by teachers can benefit all children. Giftedness is a dynamic concept, and we all need to generate dynamic ideas about responsiveness. This will be discussed further in Chapter 8.

Specific learning interests and strengths that are advanced and unexpected at an early age (Murphy & Margrain, 2007) may not be catered for in educational contexts due to a lack of information and experience among early years teachers. Young children who are gifted have been shown, both nationally and internationally, to be under-identified (Clark, 2013), and a lack of identification leads to an absence of quality response, stimulation and enhancement of learning potential. Gifted children do not realise and reach their potential on their own (Moltzen, 2011b). These children need stimulating and enriched teaching and guiding, and access to an equitable education should not be a matter of chance.

In New Zealand the early years sector has a unique opportunity to identify giftedness in these children early and co-construct learning with children, utilising the principles of the curriculum documents (Ministry of Education, 1996, 2007) as holistic, responsive and inclusive guides. *Te Whāriki* (Ministry of Education, 1996) emphasises that "teachers should provide for children who require resources alternative or additional to those usually provided within an early childhood education setting" (p. 11).

It is also important for early years teachers to build effective relationships with one another, across both sectors, and we consider transition further in Chapter 9. Information needs to pass with the child as they transition to the primary school setting, where the National Education Guidelines (NEGs) and National Administration Guidelines (NAGs) require schools to assist all learners through appropriate teaching and learning strategies to reach their potential, including those identified as gifted and talented (Ministry of Education, 2012).

Defining giftedness

Although many theories of giftedness have been developed, there is no universally accepted definition (Ministry of Education, 2012). Broadly speaking, there have been three general approaches to defining giftedness (McAlpine, 2004):

- a conservative approach, which suggests a single criterion for giftedness (e.g., intelligence)
- a liberal approach, which uses a more broad-ranging and inclusive definition
- a multi-categorial approach, in terms of outstanding performance or potential in one or more areas (e.g., music, visual arts, leadership and other domains).

Two common views on the definition of giftedness currently favoured in New Zealand are those of Gagné (2009) and Renzulli and Reis (1986) (see Appendix A). Gagné is one of the few theorists to make a definitive distinction between the terms 'gifts' and 'talents', which he later renamed 'natural abilities' and 'competencies' respectively. His view allows for the acknowledgement of *potential* as well as performance, which is important because the concept of potential is crucial in the early years. As we have noted, this is the critical time when young children form lifelong conceptions of themselves.

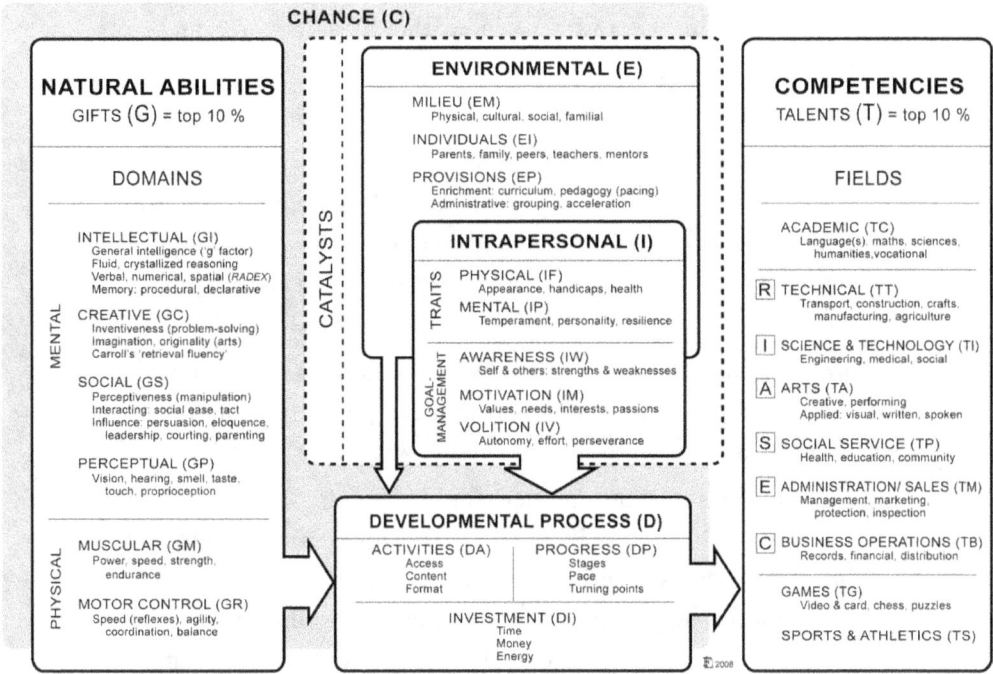

Figure 1.1. Gagné's Differentiated Model of Giftedness and Talent (DMGT)
Source: Gagné, 2014; downloaded, with permission from Gagné, from his website: http://www.gagnefrancoys.wix.com/dmgt-mddt

Children's gifts or natural abilities are more likely to be seen in the early years, whereas talents and competencies are age and training related. Margrain (2011) reminds us that it is in the application of specific natural abilities that young children who are gifted can be acknowledged, in areas such as memory, inventiveness, leadership, proprioception, endurance and agility. Gagné (2009) argues that talent or competency is demonstrated or more evident as time goes by, and this view promotes the early years as an optimal foundation time for gifted children. His model is encapsulated in Figure 1.1, which shows how the development of competencies is influenced by many factors—including natural ability, environment, intra-personal traits and developmental processes—but also acknowledges the role of chance. An overview of the DMGT, along with additional materials, is available at Gagné's website: http://www.gagnefrancoys.wix.com/dmgt-mddt

Renzulli and Reis (1986) argue that teachers should focus on traits demonstrated through observable behaviours rather than trying to define giftedness in the abstract sense. They discuss three areas of performance:

- *above average abilities* (e.g., recall, early language) or *specific abilities* (e.g., advanced drawing skills)
- *task commitment*, which comprises sustained motivation and attention in the development of ideas and products (e.g., the young child who stays at the carpentry table for long periods of time to complete a project)
- *creativity*, which involves problem solving, originality of thought, fluency, flexibility, and elaboration of ideas (e.g., the 18-month-old child who stacks chairs to see out a window).

Renzulli and Reis's (1986) model, the Three-Ring Conception of Giftedness, is illustrated in Figure 1.2. This conception presents the idea that giftedness is at the nexus of the three aforementioned essential elements: above-average ability, task commitment and creativity. As a result of these three elements interconnecting, giftedness is brought to bear on general performance areas (e.g., music, leadership or mathematics) and specific performance areas (e.g., film-making, electronics, whaikōrero/speech-making or sculpture).

Figure 1.2. Three-Ring Conception of Giftedness
Source: reproduced, with permission, from Renzulli and Reis, 1986

The models of giftedness from Gagné (Figure 1.1) and Renzulli and Reis (Figure 1.2) offer early years teachers an opportunity to consider the important role they have in supporting the development of potential in the early years (Margrain, 2011), although Renzulli and Reis's (1986) work may be more applicable in the early primary school environment.

Harrison (1999) defines giftedness in the early years in terms of a child

> who performs or has the ability to perform at a level significantly beyond his or her chronologically aged peers and whose unique abilities and characteristics require special provisions and social and emotional support from the family, community and educational context. (p. 20)

Her work will be further discussed within this book, and the definition is particularly useful for the early childhood education sector.

An additional consideration for the Aotearoa New Zealand context is a Māori perspective of giftedness. Bevan-Brown's (1993) research suggests that how we define giftedness in early childhood in New Zealand needs to be broadened to encompass both the commitments we have made to *Te Tiriti o Waitangi* (the *Treaty of Waitangi*) and the multicultural society in which we now live. Aspects of Māori culture and customs that are valued by Māori can be incorporated into our national concept of giftedness, and teachers need to receive professional development in order to recognise giftedness from a Māori perspective. Māori concepts of giftedness should be viewed holistically, reflecting the customs, beliefs, values and attitudes of Māori people (Ministry of Education, 2000). Bevan-Brown's work will also be further considered in later chapters.

Aotearoa New Zealand policy makers and researchers have shared their criteria of how giftedness is defined via the Working Party on Gifted Education (2001); Riley, Bevan-Brown, Bicknell, Carroll-Lind and Kearney (2004); and the Ministry of Education's Gifted and Talented Advisory Group. These criteria, further promoted in *Gifted and Talented Students: Meeting Their Needs in New Zealand Schools* (Ministry of Education, 2012), remind us that a definition needs to:

- be multi-categorical
- reflect bicultural approaches

- recognise multicultural values, beliefs, customs and attitudes
- acknowledge that gifted children demonstrate exceptionality in relation to their same-age peers
- reflect the context and values of the community
- acknowledge that giftedness is evidenced in all societal groups
- recognise that a child may be gifted in one or more areas
- recognise that human development will differ for all individuals
- recognise that gifts may emerge in circumstances that are unique to that child.

The same Working Party also included the place of the early years in gifted education by identifying core principles to support the well-being of the very young. Some of these core principles, acknowledged by the Minister of Education (2002), were as follows.

- Gifted and talented learners are found in every group within society.
- The early years environment is a powerful catalyst for the demonstration and development of talent.
- Māori perspectives and values must be embodied in all aspects of the definition of, identification of and provision for gifted and talented learners.
- Early years settings should provide opportunities for parents, caregivers and whānau to be involved in the decision making that affects the learning of individual students.
- Early years settings should aim to meet the specific social and emotional needs of gifted and talented learners.
- Programmes for gifted and talented children should be based on sound practice, take account of the research and literature in this field, and be regularly evaluated.

These guidelines and core principles allow educational settings to set their own definition of giftedness, to develop procedures and practices in context, and to support their gifted learners. However, it is not enough for teachers to abdicate this responsibility to their workplace environment. Teachers need to have rigorous discussion and debate to ensure their own philosophy allows for the acceptance of this diverse group, as well as room to grow their understanding.

The historical perspective of gifted education (both nationally and internationally) has been that defining giftedness is not an easy task. Contemporary research (Ministry of Education, 2012) provides evidence that giftedness is valued according to the communities, cultures, religions and societies in which gifted individuals emerge. In other words, giftedness would be viewed quite differently by a remote farming community in New Zealand in comparison to a multicultural suburb of a regional township, or a community of university graduates in Wellington. A final decision on a single definition of giftedness will probably never happen: the sentence 'Gifted is …' will never be definitive. Nor should it be.

Current trends over the last two decades emphasise a move away from defining giftedness in terms of only one factor, such as IQ. Nutall, Romero and Kalesnik (1992) argue that the concept of giftedness should expand beyond the traditional emphasis of general academic prowess. In recognising this, these researchers propose that young children who are gifted show sustained evidence of advanced capability relative to their peers. This could be in general academic skills and/or in more specific domains such as music, art or leadership, to the extent that they need differentiated educational programmes A wide-ranging and diverse 'menu' of abilities and qualities that reflect the diversity of the multicultural nature of our country is now recognised as contributing to the concept of giftedness.

In the early years we cannot afford to underestimate the importance of the responsive learning environment, because it gives teachers the opportunity to recognise the potential—as well as the performance—of these children, and it helps to bring the advanced abilities of early years children with giftedness to the fore. Riley (2015) argues that it is vital to step back and assess the effectiveness of any learning environment for gifted and talented learners. She maintains that these learners already enter their places of learning with individual strengths, abilities, passions and needs, and she challenges educators to respond supportively to these individual factors.

A teacher's responsibility

Few would disagree that a child's educational environment plays a key role in influencing their development. The environment influences the progression from potential to performance, from ability to achievement. Every teacher in New Zealand has a legal and moral right to develop the potential of all children, regardless of their abilities. Acknowledging the learning requirements of young children who are gifted is one of the many roles and responsibilities of a teacher.

Young children who are gifted enjoy development that is dynamic and personalised, and our teachers are in a prime position to observe the manifestation of clusters of traits that may indicate outstanding potential or development. It is critical in these formative learning years that positive dispositions are nurtured, and that secure, safe and stimulating environments allow for all levels of learning. These early years provide the foundation for learning and child–teacher relationships. Personalising the curriculum for gifted learners can change the dynamics of the relationship, because the child's attitude and enthusiasm for learning are lifted, thereby strengthening the classroom community (Heacox, 2002; Tomlinson, 2001).

An underestimation of giftedness increases the risk that the child may not receive best-fit learning experiences (Hodge & Kemp, 2006). The regular curriculum, unadapted, is unlikely to effectively stimulate and enrich the gifted child, and so timely identification is essential in order to understand the curriculum modifications needed. Early years teachers not only have the opportunity but also the privilege of being alongside a child's learning journey. They also have the responsibility to partner with the child in the most favourable way to ensure rich conversations and interactions. New Zealand early years researchers (Dean, 2011; Gallagher, 2008; Margrain & Farquhar, 2012; Murphy, 2004a, 2004b, 2006; Murphy & Margrain, 2007; Radue, 2009) have suggested that in New Zealand, young children who are gifted are an overlooked group of learners, and they challenge teachers to notice, recognise and respond in order to provide a differentiated curriculum.

Conclusion

Defining giftedness is a complex issue because there are many perspectives to consider. This fact should not, however, cause a barrier to identification and provision. It is too easy for teachers to put 'gifted' into the too-hard basket, which means another generation of gifted learners fail to have a stimulating environment. So while rigorous discussion should be engaged in, early years teachers need to focus on exhibited characteristics and early identification rather than on definition. It is the responsibility of all early years teachers to engage with giftedness. The various chapters in this book will support this idea.

References

Bevan-Brown, J. (1993). *Special abilities: A Māori perspective.* Unpublished master's thesis, Massey University.

Clark, B. (2013). *Growing up gifted: Developing the potential of children at home and at school* (8th ed.). Upper Saddle River, NJ: Pearson.

Gagné, F. (2004, April). *A differentiated model of giftedness and talent.* Keynote address presented at the Gifted Children: Getting it Right: Meeting the Challenge of Teaching the Gifted conference, Auckland.

Gagné, F. (2009). Building gifted into talents: Detailed overview of the DMGT 2.0. In B. MacFarlane & T. Stambaugh (Eds.), *Leading change in education: The festschrift of Dr Joyce Van Tassel-Baska* (pp. 61–80). Waco, TX: Prufrock Press.

Gagné, F. (2014). *Differentiated model of giftedness and talent* (DMGT). Retrieved from http//www.gagnefrancoys.wix.com/dmgt-mddt

Gallagher, G. (2008). *Gifted and talented children in transition to school: What do we need to know and do? To whose voices do we need to listen?* Paper presented at the New Zealand Association for the Gifted Child conference, Auckland.

Harrison, C. (1999). *Giftedness in early childhood.* Sydney, NSW: GERRIC.

Heacox, D. (2002). *Differentiating instruction in the regular classroom: How to reach and teach all learners, grades 3–12.* Minneapolis, MN: Free Spirit Publishing.

Hodge, K., & Kemp, C. (2006). Recognition of giftedness in the early years of school: Perspectives of teachers, parents, and children. *Journal for the Education of the Gifted, 30,* 164–204.

Margrain, V. (2011). Assessment for learning with young gifted children. *Apex: The New Zealand Journal of Gifted Education, 16*(1). Retrieved from http://www.giftedchildren.org.nz/apex/v16art04.php

Margrain, V., & Farquhar, S. (2012). The education of gifted children in the early years: A first survey of views, teaching practices, resourcing and administration issues. *Apex: The New Zealand Journal of Gifted Education, 17*(1). Retrieved from http//www.giftedchildren.org.nz/apex

McAlpine, D. (2004). What do we mean by gifted and talented?: Concepts and definitions. In D. McAlpine & R. Moltzen (Eds.), *Gifted and talented: New Zealand perspectives* (2nd ed.). Palmerston North: Kanuka Grove Press.

Minister of Education. (2002). *Initiatives for gifted and talented learners.* Wellington: Ministry of Education.

Ministry of Education. (1996). *Te whāriki: He whāriki matauranga mō ngā mokopuna ō Aotearoa.* Wellington: Learning Media.

Ministry of Education. (2000). *Gifted and talented students: Meeting their needs in New Zealand schools.* Wellington: Learning Media.

Ministry of Education. (2007). The New Zealand curriculum. Wellington: Learning Media.

Ministry of Education. (2012). *Gifted and talented students: Meeting their needs in New Zealand schools.* Wellington: Learning Media.

Moltzen, R.. (2011a). Historical perspectives, In R. Moltzen (Ed.), *Gifted and talented: New Zealand perspectives* (3rd ed., pp. 1–30). Auckland: Pearson.

Moltzen, R. (2011b). Underachievement. In R. Moltzen (Ed.), *Gifted and talented: New Zealand perspectives* (3rd ed., pp. 404–433). Palmerston North: Kanuka Grove Press.

Murphy, C. (2004a). Out and about: Education for the gifted. *Early Education, 36,* 33–37.

Murphy, C. (2004b). Teachers' perceptions of the play patterns and behaviours of young children who are gifted, in an early childhood setting. *New Zealand Research in Early Childhood Education, 7,* 57–72.

Murphy, C. (2006). Giftedness in the early years: Support for teachers and parents. *The Space, 6,* 12–13.

Murphy, C., & Margrain, V. (2007). Do roosters have chins? Insights into parenting a gifted child. *The First Years Ngā Tau Tuatahi: New Zealand Journal of Infant and Toddler Education, 9*(1), 16–20.

Nutall, E. V., Romero, I., & Kalesnik, J. (1992). *Assessing and screening preschoolers: Psychological and educational dimensions.* Needham Heights, MA: Allyn and Bacon.

Porter, L. (2005). *Gifted young children: A guide for teachers and parents* (2nd ed.). Sydney, NSW: Allen & Unwin.

Radue, L. (2009). The forgotten children. *Apex: New Zealand Journal of Gifted Education, 15*(4), 45–55.

Renzulli, J. S., & Reis, S. M. (1986). The three-ring conception of giftedness: A developmental model for creative productivity. In R. J. Sternberg & J. E. Davidson (Eds.), *Conceptions of giftedness* (pp. 53–92). New York, NY: Cambridge University Press.

Riley, T. L. (2015). Differentiating the learning environment. In F. Karnes & S. Bean (Eds.), *Methods and materials for teaching the gifted* (4th ed., pp. 201–221). Waco, TX: Prufrock Press.

Riley, T., Bevan-Brown, J., Bicknell, B., Carroll-Lind, J., & Kearney, A. (2004). *The extent, nature and effectiveness of planned approaches in New Zealand schools for identifying and providing for gifted and talented students*. Wellington: Ministry of Education.

Tomlinson, C. A. (2001). *How to differentiate instruction in mixed ability classrooms* (2nd ed.). Alexandria, VA: Association for Supervision and Curriculum Development.

Vygotsky, L. S. (1978). *Mind in society: The development of higher mental processes*. Cambridge, MA: Harvard University Press.

Working Party on Gifted Education. (2001). *Report to the Minister of Education*. Wellington: Author.

Chapter 2: Identifying characteristics of giftedness in the early years

Caterina Murphy and Sue Breen

Introduction

Young children who are gifted are capable of producing mature expressions of their learning (Murphy, 2005). However, they are more likely to fulfil their potential when their environment has many positive, rich influences and experiences. This includes having teachers who can identify the characteristics of giftedness and understand the phenomenon, which is one of the key reasons for writing this book.

This chapter considers the characteristics of giftedness in babies and young children from multiple perspectives. It also looks at how early years teachers can begin to identify these children in their early years settings. Murphy (2005) emphasises the importance of relationships in the early years, such as where there is a special teacher–child relationship. Early years teachers need an understanding of the characteristics that distinguish such children from their peers and ways to differentiate the curriculum in order to respond effectively.

Clark (1997) suggests that how giftedness is expressed depends on two things: the genetic patterns and anatomical structure of each individual brain, and the support and opportunities provided by the individual's environment. Those teaching in early years settings should be mindful that many children may not have had educational support of any quantity or quality before coming to the setting. Some children will not have been a participant of as vast an array of experiences as other children, and so it is crucial that such children do not go unrecognised or that only privileged children are recognised. The first half of this chapter focuses on describing characteristics, and the second half looks at a range of approaches to identification. One of the most important issues concerning identification is not merely who we identify, but who we might miss. We hope that this content helps in the recognition of young gifted children to minimise the issue that Radue (2009) highlights, which is that gifted children are often the "forgotten children" in early childhood.

Characteristics of giftedness

There will be children in early years settings who do exceptionally well and appear advanced in one or more areas of development. Young children who are gifted tend to demonstrate advanced knowledge or skill far beyond what would be expected for their age. These children are precocious in that they may be unusually verbal or advanced in one or more domains of intelligence. Some of them may stand out from others. However, no single list applies to all gifted children. Many will be verbally precocious, but not all will be. Some may learn to read early, but not all will.

There are always differences among children (Barbour, 1992), so teachers do need to be mindful that not all early years children who are gifted will show all of the characteristics we are aware of. It is also important to note that characteristics of giftedness may be observed in many children to some degree. However, when high levels of a number of these characteristics are combined and evident, an indication of giftedness is strongly indicated. All children are unique, all children have their own particular strengths, but only some children are gifted: they demonstrate characteristics that should alert us to the need for a different level of support and response.

In this section we begin by considering various perspectives of giftedness in young children and then detail the specific characteristics of young gifted children. We also consider particular issues relating to infants, peer relationships, uneven development, Māori children, and play as a context for observing these characteristics.

Multiple and diverse perspectives
All children arrive in this world with their own unique characteristics, history, identity and wisdom. They develop at their own rate from the time they are conceived. They have diverse behaviours, unique developmental rates, and display potential and performance in varied ways. All of these elements are influenced by the learning environment, the cultural contexts in which the child lives, and the child's genetic foundation, or 'hard wiring' (Clark, 1997).

Identifying the characteristics of giftedness requires teacher patience and a broad holistic approach, focusing on learning dispositions, behaviours, cultural nuances and characteristics, rather than looking just for specific areas of strength or outstanding performance. It involves careful, focused observation and a keen listening ear. Teachers need to "listen to children's thinking, not just what they think, but how they think" (Murphy, 2007, p.13), because it is within intersubjective dialogue that the characteristics of giftedness often become evident.

Many researchers have said that young children who are gifted have the ability to think and synthesise abstractly, and have a sensitivity to learning and the ability to generate original ideas and solutions (Hollinger & Kosak, 1985; Lewis & Louis, 1991; Lewis & Michaelson, 1985; Parke & Ness, 1988; Roedell, Jackson, & Robinson, 1980; Van Tassel-Baska, 1988). Readers may already be thinking of a specific child as they read this chapter.

A high level of language development and an accelerated pace of thought may be evident. So might long concentration spans on subjects of interest to them, or the development of 'passion' areas in which they are intensely interested. Because in Aotearoa New Zealand we take a broad sociocultural view of the holistic child, we need to consider Māori perspectives of giftedness, sociocultural perspectives on learning and teaching, and the value teachers place on group collaboration within a community of learners. These contextualised nuances have an impact on how we view giftedness.

Often these comments are heard: "There is no such thing as a gifted child!" or "All children are gifted!" These very real-world views can often produce barriers to teacher responsiveness, even for the most experienced teacher, and they are simply not true. What we do know is that there are young children who are gifted in every ethnic group and at all socioeconomic levels (Ministry of Education, 2002). However, in a survey of 125 people involved with the provision of early years education services, just under one-quarter (21.5 percent) stated that they believed all children are gifted: in other words, every child is special or has something special about him or her and none should be singled out as being gifted (Margrain & Farquhar, 2012). A further 8 percent of the survey respondents thought it possible for there to be no gifted children in any one early childhood or junior school class. These findings reflect that societal beliefs about giftedness range from the idea that giftedness is inherent in everyone to the assertion that it does not exist at all. This diversity of beliefs compounds the complexity of definition, identification and provisions.

It is important to assert early in this chapter that when observing for giftedness, children with disabilities should not be overlooked, nor should children from low-income backgrounds (Karnes & Johnson, 1989). It is imperative that teachers not look for giftedness in ways that merely reflect the values, attitudes and beliefs of the majority, and that they approach identification with humility, because there will always be children we might miss during the process.

Harrison (1999) holds the view that careful and systematic observation of children who are gifted provides a fundamental guide to provision and responsiveness. Teachers in the early years teach with the guidance of *Te Whāriki* (Ministry of Education, 1996) and *The New Zealand Curriculum* (Ministry of Education, 2007). Assessment for learning needs to be in tune with the child's knowledge, skills, abilities and interests (Murphy, 2005), while recognising that what a child brings to the context is highly valued; for example, their traditions and histories, their mana (prestige), and their whakapapa (genealogy) (Ministry of Education, 2009). Taking a holistic view of the child ensures that teachers are best equipped to be responsive to children's learning and the aspirations children and their family/whānau have. In Chapter 4 we explicitly discuss assessment for learning; in the present chapter the focus is on identification as a diagnostic approach. Teachers need to do more than observe: they need to have sufficient knowledge to understand what they are seeing, and therefore be able to notice, recognise and respond to giftedness.

Specific characteristics of giftedness in young children

Some children hide their abilities, but the behaviour of many young children who are gifted is noticeably different to that of other children. Parents often get used to the "Wow isn't she clever" comments from friends, family, colleagues and even strangers at the supermarket. People notice and comment on advancement and exceptionality—though not always constructively.

Young children who are gifted often 'identify' themselves through behaviours such as the examples given below.

- A child has a noticeably much larger vocabulary at 2 years old.
- A child is comfortable with our 'counting system' and is able to count forwards and backwards, and count in twos or fours, before they turn 3.
- A young child is playing chess with another 4-year-old and they are heard explaining to each other why 'this move' is better than 'that move', which will lead to checkmate in a few moves. Neither is concerned about who wins.
- A very young child has very good fine motor skills and is drawing recognisable objects. (Dinosaurs, insects, planets, vehicles or animals are often passions for these children.)
- A child is the recognised 'expert' on one or more topics.
- A child is an early reader and writer.

The following helpful lists of characteristics have been provided, with permission, by the New Zealand Centre for Gifted Education (see Appendix B). They indicate the most highly indicated characteristics in the first instance and following those, other characteristics often exhibited.

The gifted child:

- needs very little sleep
- began to talk very early or was very late in talking but then learned fast
- has a large vocabulary; uses unusual or 'big' words
- talks very fluently; uses language easily and correctly
- generally reached physical milestones earlier than most

- demands attention constantly; is persistent
- is intensely curious; is always asking "Why?"; really wants to know the answer
- is very observant of detail
- has an excellent memory
- is very independent; insists on doing things for him/herself
- loves being read to; follows story closely
- is beginning to read / is reading / has asked to be taught to read
- is quickly bored with simple or repetitive games and toys
- shows impatience with tasks that seem meaningless
- can concentrate for long periods when interested
- creates make-believe playmates, invents games, makes up lots of stories (often complicated)
- can not only count but also is beginning to grasp maths concepts
- arranges toys and other items, putting the same kinds of things together
- has a highly developed, quite sophisticated sense of humour
- learns easily—only needs to be told things once or twice
- is very sensitive, and is distressed by hurts experienced by other people or creatures
- is generally the leader in any group of children
- seems to prefer the company of older children or adults
- doesn't seem to fit in with other children
- can be impatient with others who don't think as fast or do things as well as s/he does
- often seems frustrated when ideas outreach ability to perform.

A gifted child often:
- achieves milestones much earlier
- has heightened sensitivity
- has a good sense of humour
- has a high degree of creativity
- has a high degree of energy

- has a long attention span
- has a preference for older friends or adults
- has a sense of justice and moral sensitivity
- has a variety of interests
- has a vivid imagination
- has above average ability with numbers
- has above average language development
- has an advanced vocabulary
- has an excellent memory
- has apparent maturity in judgement
- has keen powers of observation
- has good problem-solving and reasoning abilities
- has leadership qualities
- has non-conformist behaviour
- has unusual curiosity
- has unusual emotional depth and intensity
- is a rapid learner
- is able to master more complex jigsaw puzzles
- is an early and avid reader
- is persistent
- is very alert
- is very curious
- is very observant
- shows perfectionism traits.

During infancy

Signs of giftedness can be observed in young infants (Gottfried, Gottfried, Bathurst, & Guerin, 1994; Harrison, 2005; Roedell et al., 1980), and parents and whānau are often the first to notice how alert their children are. Listening to parents is an important aspect of teacher professional practice. Parents are experts on their child, especially when there is evidence of different, advanced or exceptional behaviours from babyhood (Murphy, 2007). The common need for little sleep, high levels of alertness, and intense and complex questions at a very early age are signals parents may mention to teachers. Typical characteristics (Bainbridge, 2013, 2014; Harrison, 2005; Moltzen, 2011; Parke & Ness, 1988) of babies who are gifted include:

- being extremely alert—always looking around
- needing almost constant stimulation when awake
- needing less sleep than most other babies[1]
- being able to mimic sounds earlier than other babies
- being exceptionally sensitive to tastes, smells, sounds and textures
- walking at, or before, 9 months old
- stringing words together in 'sentences' before they are a year old.

Māori perspectives

A Māori perspective on giftedness is an opportunity for teachers to view giftedness through an indigenous cultural lens—one that is important to Aotearoa New Zealand. The Ministry of Education (2009) recognises that "children emerge from rich traditions, surrounded by whānau, both visible and invisible, living and dead" (p. 49). Māori children are seen to be an iwi's greatest asset (Hemara, 2000)—powerful, emotional, spiritual, and an active force of life (Ministry of Education, 2009).

Bevan-Brown (1993) has suggested that teachers need to receive professional development in order to recognise giftedness from a Māori perspective, because giftedness needs to be viewed holistically, reflecting the customs, beliefs, values and attitudes of Māori people (Ministry of Education, 2000). Bicultural competence is a critical competency of early years teaching, demonstrating commitment to *Te Tiriti o Waitangi* (the *Treaty of Waitangi*).

Bevan-Brown (1993) stresses the importance of both qualities and abilities. She argues that giftedness from a Māori perspective is grounded firmly in kaupapa Māori (Māori principles and purposes), is holistic, and honouring of mana whenua (tribal people who uphold the prestige of power from the land). Spirituality, mana, the transmission of traditional knowledge, and caring for and service to others were some of the characteristics of giftedness identified by Bevan-Brown

---

1 If a baby sleeps well, that doesn't mean she or he is not gifted.

(1993). We further connect to Bevan-Brown's work in Chapters 4, 5 and 8 of this book.

Characteristics of giftedness evident in play

Characteristics of giftedness evident during play in Murphy's (2005) Aotearoa New Zealand study were observed in young children who were 3 and 4 years old. It was found that these children exhibited:

- advanced language and knowledge
- perfectionism/frustration
- highly imaginative, abstract, conceptual thinking
- heightened interpersonal awareness
- ambidexterity
- an advanced sense of humour
- boredom
- a love of learning
- high levels of curiosity.

Further discussion of the play patterns and behaviours of young children who are gifted is provided in Chapter 3.

Like-minded peers

Everyone needs at least one close friend. Often the young child who is gifted has no-one in their learning environment (except possibly an adult or two) with whom they can discuss their latest 'findings'. Their peers may not be found within their own age group. Their age peers may not even be talking yet, and their intellectual peers may be much older (Murphy & Margrain, 2007). This becomes more obvious when a child is aged 4 or 5 and is accepted by and mixes confidently with older children and adults.

Young children who are gifted need to be able to mix with like minds: children who need to discuss their passions or who want to play board games with their friends. Together they can construct unusual creations or experiment with mixtures and solutions. You may like to consider whether there is the flexibility in your early years environment for a younger child to work with older children for all, or part, of the session. Imagine how frustrating it will be for a young child who is speaking in complicated sentences and asking sophisticated questions to spend hours with children who are not. Is it difficult to organise for a 3-year-old who is capable and ready for the experience to learn and play with older 4- or 5-year-olds?

In Aotearoa New Zealand a child doesn't have to start school until 6 if they are not ready for the transition, but a child cannot start before 5 even if they are more than ready. This is one of those inequities that, while politically understandable, is frustrating for children and parents alike.

Uneven, rapid and spontaneous development
Uneven, or asynchronous, development is frequently evident in gifted individuals. When it comes to the relationship between intellectual development and the development of physical skills, this uneven development can be very obvious. It can also be very frustrating for the child who knows exactly what he or she wants the finished product to look like. Having the ability to talk intelligently about gravity and density while not yet being able to hold a pencil correctly or manage scissors is quite common. Interestingly, Murphy (2004) noticed asynchrony while working with a group of kindergarteners in Sydney in a school holiday programme for young children who were gifted. She observed a young child whose brain could process numbers in ways she could never have imagined, yet a mouth and tongue that could not achieve control and normal function.

Many researchers have noticed discrepancies between physical and intellectual development (e.g., Roedell, 1990; Webb, 1994; Webb & Kline, 1993). For example, often fine motor skills lag behind cognitive and conceptual abilities, and so young children may visualise in their minds what they want to draw/create but may not have developed the motor skills to allow them to achieve the task. Teachers need to give consideration to this across all areas of development. In the emotional affective development of young children who are gifted, their mature vocabularies and frequently uneven development make them vulnerable to social isolation if they lack interaction with children of similar abilities.

In some cases the child's abilities develop in rapid spurts, depending on their interests. One example is that early reading ability might appear to develop almost overnight, with the children seemingly having taught themselves to read. Children who know all their letters and letter sounds at age 2 may remain at that level until age 4, and then shortly afterwards can be reading fluently at an 8- to 15-year-old level, or higher. Margrain (2005) studied 11 early (precocious) readers, none of whom had been formally taught. Parents repeatedly used the words "spontaneous" to describe the children's learning, saying that the ability appeared to "come from nowhere". Similar patterns of unexpected, unexplained and rapid learning can happen in any domain of learning.

Identification of giftedness in the early years

Despite evidence that early intervention is critical to support children's cognitive and affective growth, young children who are gifted still fail to be recognised in educational settings. Under-identifying leads to lack of appropriate provision. Because there is no such thing as a 'typical' gifted child, identification is not an easy process. However, the past 25 or so years have seen a paradigm shift in the field of education, from a conservative focus on identifying gifted children for their observed intelligence alone, to a more liberal perception of one size does not fit all, especially in the area of gifted education (Matthews & Foster, 2005). This is a movement from "intelligence as giftedness" to "giftedness beyond intelligence". Through identifying the common characteristics of giftedness early, teachers are better able to recognise a young child who will need their curriculum differentiated.

The importance of identifying giftedness at an early age cannot be overestimated. We know children's learning capacity is powerfully affected by the beliefs they hold about themselves, and as teachers we provide some of these messages—directly and indirectly. Dweck (2006) has suggested that we make 'mind-set' judgements about ourselves as learners, and these mind sets can enhance or inhibit our future development. She found that learners who believe abilities can be developed through persistence and effort ultimately develop positive learning dispositions. This is important, because teachers advocate the need for young children to have a strong view of self and to be able to enjoy positive relationships with others.

The main purposes of identification are for development, stimulation and support (Silverman, 1981). The greatest requirement is to follow the child closely with observation and careful, regular record keeping. This will assist and affirm the process for the teacher and the teachers that follow. These records are extremely valuable, and may cover a range of sources and be collated in equally diverse ways. Gallagher (1979) reminded us over 30 years ago not to provide personalised opportunities solely for children who demonstrate early signs of ability or productivity, because potential can be missed. Opportunities for identification and growth need to be ongoing and continuous, to match the evolving nature of talent development.

The activities teachers provide, the language they use and the questions they ask are important tools to identify the children that could be missed. Some very quiet, shy children may be taking everything in but not taking part in discussions. Teachers need to watch body language and facial cues, such as a child who smiles at a joke that other children missed completely, or a shake of the head when someone else answers incorrectly. In addition, watch for the child who is always on the fringe of any activity. It may be that they need personal space, are very sensitive to noise, or are uncomfortable in 'crowds'. Teachers can be on the alert for the child who answers questions with ease or who asks sophisticated questions, even though they are outside the group they are working with.

Core principles of identification

Any identification procedures undertaken need to abide by the core principles of identification, as outlined by the Ministry of Education (2000), to ensure that all children, regardless of age, gender, culture, race and socioeconomic status, have an equal chance of being identified. It is important that restricted learning opportunities and socially biased identification procedures do not occur and thereby disadvantage the many potentially gifted children from cultural minorities and low-income families.

The following eight principles provide critical guidance for anyone working in the early years area. Identification is the responsibility of all who work with children. These principles promote a categorical, dynamic and responsive approach (Ministry of Education, 2000).

1. Identification should begin early
Because of the nature of young children's abilities and interests, teachers need to be cautious about 'labelling' children, but intent on offering a responsive learning environment to serve their needs.

2. There should be open communication.

In the early years we value our partnership with parents and family/whānau. Communication throughout the identification process needs to be sensitive to the values and beliefs of whānau and should recognise that parents are experts when it comes to their children. Listen to parents! Gifts valued by Māori need to be identified by parents and whānau and then those gifts looked for in their children. There needs to be greater consultation with Māori, including a strong whānau–school network (Bevan-Brown, 2012). Often parents are the first to notice that their child is developing at a faster rate than others are, and their contributions to the process of identification should never be overlooked.

3. Identification should be a continuous and dynamic process.

Young children are constantly changing, and their emerging abilities and developing language are constantly coming to the fore. Children exhibiting giftedness develop quickly, and because milestones occur so intensely at this time of child development we need to be on the lookout each and every day. A danger with IQ is that people focus on the number rather than the person and assume no other assessment is required. An IQ test does not define a person: it is merely a measurement, like shoe size, height or weight (Beresford, 2008). This view is not exclusive to psychometric assessment—the benefits of the assessment are more important than the measurement.

4. Identification should be a means to an end, not an end in itself

Teachers need to spend time recognising giftedness so that they can focus on how best they are going to respond to and support children's learning. This point is elaborated on in Chapter 4 on assessment for learning, and in Chapter 8 on curriculum differentiation.

5. Identification should be unobtrusive

This can perhaps happen more easily in early childhood settings where there is more than one teacher in any immediate environment. Classroom teachers might want to think through various strategies to make this happen; for example, team teaching opportunities, when teacher aides or parents are present, or during Discovery Time (Fisher & Martin, 2006).

6. A team approach is required
A number of teachers should be involved in the process to avoid bias. Parents and whānau are valuable sources of information about their child. Other children are very observant, too, as discussed later in the peer nomination section of this chapter.

7. Be alert to all children
This includes minority groups; those of differing ethnicity; those with physical, learning or sensory disabilities; quiet children; children who appear bored; children who have a solid general knowledge; those with challenging behaviours; and those from lower socioeconomic groups.

8. Use a multi-method approach
Identification should not depend on one method alone. Some common methods are: anecdotal observations, checklists, learning stories, narratives, curriculum linking sheets, child profiles, photographs, art samples and parent interviews.

It is important that teachers use identification procedures that are culturally responsive (Bevan-Brown, 2012). The early childhood strategic plan (as one example) emphasised a greater requirement on early childhood settings to be responsive to the care and educational needs of Māori children (Ministry of Education 2002). Māori children are likely to show a greater ability in areas valued by their culture, which can include: sporting prowess, service to Māoridom, whakapapa (genealogy), waiata (singing), carving, weaving, mana (prestige), and leadership ability. It is important, however, to always be wary of stereotyping any cultural group.

Methods of identification
The methods described here are those that are accessible to teachers as part of the regular everyday assessment work teachers do for all children. The focus of assessment for learning is discussed further in Chapter 4; here we concentrate on opportunities that assessment offers teachers to contribute to the identification of giftedness. The characteristics of giftedness noted earlier in this chapter need to be to the fore of teachers' minds as they engage with these identification methods.

Parent and whānau nomination
Parents are the experts when it comes to their own children. Each and

every day parents and whānau drop their children off at school or early childhood services, totally entrusting teachers with the care of their children. It is important that teachers not underestimate the value of the knowledge provided by parents about experiences that occur at home or in the community. Often parents are the first to notice that their child is developing at a faster rate than others, or that their child has an unusual talent. Research suggests that parents are in fact more accurate at identifying giftedness than teachers (Hodge & Kemp, 2006). Giving parents the opportunity to share their experiences enables us to get a fuller picture of the child. Lots of opportunities need to be created for teachers to engage in dialogue with parents. Some services and schools use parent nomination forms, but be aware that there may be cultural limitations to the participation of parents with regard to nomination forms.

Teacher nomination
Teacher nomination is one of the most commonly used methods of identification. Take time at each of your team meetings to discuss children you may be observing or are concerned about. Teachers are there, working hands-on with children, and are well equipped to notice signs of boredom, extreme curiosity, unusual behaviour, etc.

Peer nomination
Although peer nomination is a technique normally associated with older, school-age children, it also has a place within early childhood settings. The first author of this chapter (Murphy) successfully developed and utilised peer nomination with 3- and 4-year-olds, and the peer nomination form she developed is provided in Appendix C of this book. Peer nomination can take place during one-to-one child interviews or through quiet conversations.

Self nomination
Self-identification can also occur. Young children may at times share the view that they are best at a certain skill or knowledge set within their own peer group. When the first author (Murphy) utilised a peer nominations system, on occasion a child would self-nominate, for example, "I think I would have to say me because I make the most interesting flags" (a 3-year-old at an early childhood centre).

Narrative assessment

Whether and how child profiles or e-profiles are compiled varies in early years settings in Aotearoa New Zealand. Whether or not teachers utilise stories of learning, portfolios, displays, photographs, diaries or journals, they are a rich and valuable resource for identification. In Part 2 of this book the specific use of learning stories illustrates the opportunity for connecting teaching and learning in assessment for learning. Authentic learning stories of young children who are gifted are available to download at www.nzcer.org.nz/nzcerpress/giftedness.

Observation scales

Allan (1999) developed an Aotearoa New Zealand diagnostic tool called the *Giftedness in Early Childhood Scale*, subsequently published as part of *Identifying and Providing for Giftedness in the Early Years* (Allan, 2002), to support early years teachers to identify behavioural characteristics of giftedness. The scale has proven to be a valuable identification and assessment tool as part of the *Identifying and Providing for Giftedness in the Early Years* resource. The scale is based on a range of "research-based indicators of giftedness for children 3 to 5 years" (Allan, 2002, p. 5), which were sensitively crafted to include Māori concepts of giftedness.

Allan suggests that both teachers and parents contribute to completing the scale, because often traits and behaviours are more likely to occur at home than within the early years setting, and vice versa. Multiple teachers within the teaching team should also complete the scale to ensure there are no biases in opinions. To be effective, the application of this scale needs to be carried out over 2 to 3 months. The scale focus on indicators grouped into four key areas: a child's approach to learning, cognition and language, creativity, and social competence. A valuable teaching resource, the scale is downloadable for personal use from the gifted and talented online community at the Ministry of Education Te Kete Ipurangi website (see http://gifted.tki.org.nz/Early-Childhood-Education-ECE/Identification).

Allan's (2002) diagnostic tool was used effectively by this chapter's first author (Murphy) over a period of 4 years in an early childhood centre to recognise giftedness.

Margrain (2005) used a diagnostic tool for older children developed by McAlpine and Reid (1996), the *Teacher Observation Scales for Identifying Children with Special Abilities.* Teachers in primary schools may find it useful to examine each of these tools and determine which is most useful to their context. We encourage the wide use of a range of tools for both identification and observation. Professional awareness and growth will occur during the process of identification (Allan, 2006), and an understanding of giftedness will develop as teachers observe and provide for those children needing accelerated, extended and/or enriched learning.

Overall, key recommendations for identifying in the early years are:

- develop a centre/school policy
- begin identification early
- ensure open communication between all stakeholders
- ensure identification processes are ongoing
- use unobtrusive methods to respect the child and the early years environment
- take a teaching team approach to avoid bias
- reflect on who you might have missed!
- use a range of tools—there is no one correct tool.

Supporting parental input into identification

Parents are often unsure why their child is so advanced, appears different or wants to play with adults or older children. Parents also feel frustration, and can be unsure about how to advocate for their child and what to say to education professionals. The following parent reflection statements (provided by the second author, Breen, see Appendix D) can be given to parents to gain further information and knowledge, and to strengthen the partnerships teachers have with parents and whānau, and, of course, with their child. Some parents may feel more comfortable writing about their child rather than having to explain.

- To bring out the best in my child ……….
- The ways my child shows values and emotions are ……….
- My child struggles with ……….
- Evidence of my child's abilities ……….
- Something amazing my child did was ……….

- If only ……......
- People don't realise ……...... about my child.
- The balancing act in parenting my child is ………...
- Something I don't understand about my child is ……..…
- Other people have told me my child is absolutely passionate about ……..…
- I worry about my child because ……….
- My child combines ……….
- My child 'comes alive' when ……….

Formal testing

Whether or not to seek psychometric IQ testing is an issue often considered by parents of children who have started school. It is less likely to be a topic of discussion in early childhood centres and services, where assessment for learning includes a collaborative process (child, parents, whānau and teachers) in order to understand a child's learning better, and to strengthen the identity of the child and their sense of place in the world (Ministry of Education, 1996, 2009).

A formal assessment can be very useful when advocating for extension and enrichment opportunities, when seeking access to particular programmes, or to support transition, and it is critical when considering acceleration. Formal testing may be useful if parents need to prove to the school that their child needs something more or something different for their educational experience, or when an assessment is needed to gain entry into a particular programme.

The view could be taken that if parents already know their child is advanced, and they are already able to provide a rich environment, then a test result isn't necessary. However, if a young child who is gifted is not making the progress expected because of other factors, formal testing might be useful, especially if there is advancement in one area and severe lag in another (the asynchronous or uneven development discussed earlier in this chapter). Possible scenarios might include:

- a child with very poor fine motor skills who can discuss his/her current passion with adults—for hours!
- a child who is unhappy or frustrated with his/her own achievements because they are having difficulty expressing themselves, except inside their own head.

A variety of assessment tools are available. The reason for needing or wanting an assessment will have a bearing on what type of test is used. Some factors to take into account include: the cost of the testing, the time the test involves, the age of the child, how accepted the particular test is, and in what form the data collected will be presented. It is most likely that the parents will have to pay a substantial cost for a psychologist to complete an assessment and prepare a report, and so it is important to think carefully about the value and purpose of any assessment.

Beresford (2008) has noted that in New Zealand the most widely used, reliable and valid IQ testing tools are the following, which are "all helpful in different ways" (p. 2):

- Stanford-Binet
- Weschler Pre-School and Primary Scale of Intelligence
- Weschler Intelligence Scale for Children
- Woodcock-Johnson.

A case study of dynamic assessment: Small Poppies and Poppy Peeks

The New Zealand Centre for Gifted Education runs an early years programme called Small Poppies, which is designed specifically to meet the needs of young gifted children and their parents. It provides an enrichment and extension programme that allows young gifted children to work at their own pace and level with children of similar abilities and similar interests. It also provides an opportunity for parents to meet others facing similar parenting challenges.

Small Poppies is a child-centred programme in which a range of challenging learning experiences are offered. Emphasis is placed on stimulating the child's learning process rather than on achieving any specific end result or product. Entry into the programme is through a Poppy Peek. A Poppy Peek is a 2-hour, hands-on dynamic assessment session based on the Small Poppies programme. It provides a chance for the parents to have a 'peek' at the programme and for the teacher to have a 'peek' at the child. In this safe environment parents are able to celebrate their child's strengths and achievements as well as commiserate with each other about the challenges. Small Poppies teachers consider the following evidence during a Poppy Peek:

- commitment to the task
- concentration span
- language usage—listening to discussions with parents
- language usage—in discussions with the teacher
- fine motor skills
- independence
- language
- logical thinking
- mathematical ability
- measuring and estimating
- ability to predict
- sorting
- spatial awareness
- creative thinking
- creativity in action (e.g., in drawing or when using 'building' materials).

In 2012 the second author of this chapter (Breen) asked 'Small Poppies' parents to fill out 'parent reflective statements' (which are provided in Appendix D for your own adaptation and usage). The idea was to consider the young child who is gifted and share strengths, challenges and concerns. Teachers might like to develop a similar dynamic and partnership-based assessment approach for their own early years settings.

Conclusion: Making a positive difference

Every child needs interaction with and responsiveness from a large pool of people in order to grow into a happy, healthy, well-adjusted, valued and valuable member of society. Every young gifted child needs to mix with other like-minded children and with others who share their interests and passions. Supportive interventions (programmes and/or people) are needed to ensure that young children who are gifted are identified and their unique characteristics acknowledged. All children deserve to be learning at the pace they need, to have their interests noticed, recognised and responded to, and to have a sense of well-being and belonging (Minister of Education, 2002; Ministry of Education, 1996).

Teachers can make a critical positive difference by:
- offering activities, equipment, ideas and enthusiasm
- giving the children a positive, caring environment
- encouraging friendship
- listening and observing
- ensuring that each child has 'peers'—children who think, act, talk, reason, read at a similar level and/or in a similar way (these peers need not necessarily be the same age)
- liaising with parents, psychologists, gifted education specialists and others who can provide advice.

Young children who are gifted need the opportunity to realise that there are other children like them, with similar interests, needs and aspirations. They also need to feel that teachers 'know' them well.

References

Allan, B. (1999). *Identifying giftedness in early childhood centres.* Unpublished master's thesis, Massey University.

Allan, B. (2002). *Identifying and providing for giftedness in the early years: The early years research and practice series (1).* Palmerston North: Kanuka Grove Press. Retrieved from: http://gifted.tki.org.nz/Early-Childhood-Education-ECE/Identification

Allan, B. (2006, August). *Giftedness in NZ early childhood centres.* A presentation at the Rising Tides: Nurturing Our Culture, National Gifted and Talented conference, Auckland.

Bainbridge, C. (2013). *Dabrowski's overexcitabilities or supersensitivities in gifted children.* Retrieved from http://giftedkids.about.com/bio/Carol-Bainbridge-19284.htm

Bainbridge, C. (2014). *Signs of giftedness in infants.* Retrieved from http://giftedkids.about.com/od/younggiftedchildren/qt/infant_signs.htm

Barbour, N. B. (1992). Early childhood gifted education: A collaborative perspective. *Journal for the Education of the Gifted, 15*(2), 145–162.

Beresford, L. (2008). *The need for recognition of gifted new entrants.* Paper presented The Early Years (0–8 Years): Building a Solid Foundation for Our Tall Poppies to Grow. Retrieved from http://www.giftedchildren.org.nz/agm08/lynntxt.pdf

Bevan-Brown, J. (1993). *Special abilities: A Māori perspective.* Unpublished master's thesis, Massey University.

Bevan-Brown, J. (2011). Gifted and talented Māori learners. In R. Moltzen (Ed.), *Gifted and talented: New Zealand perspectives* (pp. 82–110). Auckland: Pearson.

Clark, B. (1997). *Growing up gifted.* Upper Saddle River, NJ: Prentice-Hall.

Dweck, C. S. (2006). *Mindset.* New York, NY: Random House.

Fisher, R., & Martin, B. (2006). An evaluation of the discovery time programme. *Kairaranga, 7*(2), 31–35.

Gallagher, J, J. (1979). Issues in education for the gifted. In A. H. Passow (Ed.), *The gifted and talented: Their education and development* (pp. 22–44). Chicago, IL: University of Chicago Press.

Gottfried, A. W., Gottfried, A. E., Bathurst, K., & Guerin, D. W. (1994). *Gifted IQ: Early developmental aspects: The Fullerton longitudinal study.* New York, NY: Plenum Press.

Harrison, C. (1999). *Giftedness in early childhood.* Kensington, NSW: GERRIC.

Harrison, C. (2005). *Young gifted children: Their search for complexity and connection.* Exeter, NSW: Inscript Publishing.

Hemara, W. (2000). *Māori pedagogies. A review from the literature.* Wellington: New Zealand Council for Educational Research.

Hodge, K. A., & Kemp, C. R. (2006). Recognition of giftedness in the early years of school: Perspectives of teachers, parents and children. *Journal for the Education of the Gifted, 30,* 164–204.

Hollinger, C., & Kosak, S. (1985). Early identification of the gifted and talented. *Gifted Child Quarterly, 29*(4), 168–171.

Karnes, M. B., & Johnson, L. J. (1989). Training for staff, parents, and volunteers working with gifted young children, especially those with disabilities and low-income homes. *Young Children, 44*(3), 49–56.

Lewis, M., & Louis, B. (1991). Young gifted children. In N. Colangelo & G. Davis (Eds.), *Handbook of gifted education* (pp. 365–381). Needham Heights, MA: Allyn and Bacon.

Lewis, M., & Michaelson, L. (1985). The gifted infant. In J. Freeman (Ed.), *The psychology of gifted children: Perspectives on development and education.* Chichester, West Sussex, UK; New York, NY: Wiley.

Margrain, V. G. (2005). *Precocious readers: Case studies of social support, self-regulation and spontaneous learning in the early years*. Unpublished doctoral thesis, Victoria University of Wellington.

Margrain, V., & Farquhar, S. (2012). The education of gifted children in the early years: A first survey of views, teaching practices, resourcing and administration issues. *Apex: The New Zealand Journal of Gifted Education, 17*(1). Retrieved from http://www.giftedchildren.org.nz/apex

Matthews, D. J., & Foster, J. F. (2005). Mystery to mastery: Shifting paradigms in gifted education. *Roeper Review, 28*(2), 64–69.

McAlpine, D., & Reid, N. (1996). *Teacher observation scales for children with special abilities*. Wellington: NZCER and Massey University ERDC Press.

Minister of Education. (2002). *Initiatives for gifted and talented learners*. Wellington: Ministry of Education.

Ministry of Education. (1996). *Te whāriki: He whāriki mātauranga mō ngā mokopuna o Aotearoa: Early childhood curriculum*. Wellington: Learning Media.

Ministry of Education. (2000). *Gifted and talented students: Meeting their needs in New Zealand schools*. Wellington: Learning Media.

Ministry of Education. (2002). *Initiatives in gifted and talented education*. Wellington: Ministry of Education.

Ministry of Education. (2007). *The New Zealand curriculum*. Wellington: Learning Media.

Ministry of Education. (2009). *Te whatu pōkeka: Kaupapa Māori assessment for learning: Early childhood exemplars*. Wellington: Learning Media.

Moltzen, R. (2011). Characteristics of gifted children. In R. Moltzen (Ed.), *Gifted and talented: New Zealand perspectives* (3rd ed., pp. 54–81). Auckland: Pearson.

Murphy, C. (2004). Out and about: Education for the gifted. *Early Education, 36*, 33–37.

Murphy, C. (2005). *Play patterns and behaviours of young children who are gifted in an early childhood setting*. Unpublished master's thesis, Massey University.

Murphy, C. (2007). How do young children who are gifted play in an early childhood setting? *New Zealand Research in Early Childhood Education, 10*, 191–198.

Murphy, C., & Margrain, V. (2007). Do roosters have chins? Insights into parenting a gifted child. *The First Years Ngā Tau Tuatahi. New Zealand Journal of Infant and Toddler Education, 9*(1), 16–20.

Parke, B. N., & Ness, P. S. (1988). Curricular decision-making for the education of young gifted children. *Gifted Child Quarterly, 32*(1), 196–199.

Radue, L. (2009). The forgotten children. *Apex: The New Zealand Journal of Gifted Education, 15*(4), 45–55.

Roedell, W. C. (1990). *Nurturing giftedness in young children.* Report No. EDO-EC-90. Reston, VA: Council for Exceptional Children.

Roedell, W. C., Jackson, N. E., & Robinson, H. B. (1980). *Gifted young children.* New York, NY: Teachers College, Columbia University.

Silverman, L. K. (1981). *Early indications of superior ability as reported by 40 parents: Unpublished raw data.* Denver, CO: Gifted Child Development Center.

Van Tassel-Baska, J. (1988). Curriculum for the gifted: Theory, research and practice. In J. Van Tassel-Baska, J. Feldhusen, K. Seeley, G. Wheateley, L. Silverman, & W. Foster, *Comprehensive curriculum for gifted learners* (pp. 1–17). Needham Heights, MA: Allyn and Bacon.

Walker, B., Hefenstein, N. L., Crow-Enslow, L. (1999). Meeting the needs of gifted learners in the early childhood classroom. *Young Children, 54*(1), 32–36.

Webb, J. T. (1994). *Nurturing social-emotional development of gifted children.* Report No. EDO-EC-93-10. Reston, VA: Council for Exceptional Children.

Webb, J. T., & Kline, P. A. (1993). Assessing gifted and talented children. In J. Culbertson, & D. Willis (Eds.), *Testing young children* (pp. 383–407). Austin, TX: ProEd.

Chapter 3: Through the lens of play: Complexities of giftedness

Caterina Murphy

Introduction

In Aotearoa New Zealand, early years teachers acknowledge the value of play as an active, child-initiated learning mechanism. Play enables empowering learning experiences for the child, is naturally designed and enhances the child's autonomous learning (Dockett & Fleer, 1999). Play is an important vehicle through which knowledge can be co-constructed and social competence developed (Coolahan & Mendez, 2000; Fisher, 2002). Play is relatively free of constraints and allows a child to release the energies from within their own intrinsic motivation. According to Fisher (2002), it

> is the natural way in which children go about the business of learning. It enables them to integrate and consolidate a wealth of experiences that enhance their cognitive, physical, social and emotional development. (p. 128)

Child-directed play experiences enable children to control their own development, holistically and with meaning, and this is possibly why open-ended play is often favoured by young children who are gifted. Ordinary objects such as cardboard tubes, balls, pieces of fabric, blocks, water and sand—these open-ended materials are building blocks of a powerful learning experience called *open-ended play*. They are objects which house multiple uses and offer infinite possibilities. There is no pressure to produce a finished product, no rules as to how to use the resources; they can be used in a solitary way and it's all about free play and discovery. Fisher and Martin (2006) emphasise that opportunities to play in this way are often reduced when children begin school. This is a concern because child-initiated and open-ended play encourages young children to become active agents in the thinking processes that such play can offer.

Discovery Time, "a ninety minute, action packed, activity based programme designed for schools", as one example, has been noted by classroom teachers as putting "balance back into the curriculum" (Discovery Time, 2012, p. 1). Hands-on activity enables early years teachers to further understand a child's capacity to learn by noticing the abstract and conceptual themes that emerge, especially the more detailed and complex play arrangements exhibited by young children who are gifted.

There are also cultural considerations in the context of a child's play. Content that is relevant and valuable to Māori may come to the fore during play episodes, and early years teachers must ensure that play opportunities for Māori children enhance self-worth and personal competence during play so that increased displays of further cultural talent can be recognised.

Play opportunities in the early years are important because informal learning takes place. The vehicle of play offers opportunities for the young child to further develop abstract thought, construct new knowledge, socially interact, and develop and strengthen their interests. In addition, a sense of their own ability and competence emerges and is an important factor in how motivated a young child is (and becomes) to participate fully and achieve in the school environment (Lillemyr, Søbstad, Marder, & Flowerday, 2011). Dispositions such as confidence and competitiveness become apparent as a child's play matures and further develops. Whether play occurs in the school playground, in the family play area, in the sandpit or while climbing a tree, play is the vehicle through which the characteristics of giftedness can be observed most freely.

This chapter draws heavily on my own research into the play patterns and behaviours of young children who are gifted, shares with you the voices of various young gifted children and their teachers (Murphy 2004, 2005), and offers early years teachers questions to reflect on concerning play. I hope this chapter will help teachers to notice, recognise and respond to giftedness through the lens of play. *Te Whāriki* guides early years teachers to "listen to children attentively" (Ministry of Education, 1996, p. 73), and the first observation below sets the tone for what I want to share about the important relationship between a child and teacher, and the need to *listen* to children's advanced abstract thinking (Murphy, 2005) during play.

MJ (4 years) is sitting alone on a piece of carpet outside. He is making loud noises and waving his arms around in the air.

Cat: What are you doing? Looks exciting!

MJ: I'm flying to the moon on my flying carpet.

Cat: I wonder if I could come too.

MJ: No you can't. The carpet is only big enough for one of us and it won't take the heaviness of more than one person, even though it's magic.

Cat: OK. I'll watch you on your journey then.

MJ: You can't watch me. You won't see me. I'll be flying far too fast [looks irritated].

Cat: How fast do you think you'll be going?

MJ: [Looking exasperated] Don't you know how far the moon is away? I have to work everything out.

Cat: Why? Is there a problem?

MJ: Yes there's a problem. I've got to, got to um, think of two things. I've got to imagine all the things I'm going to see along the way and … and … and … I've got to work out how far I have to go and at what speed.

Cat: Gosh! You've got a lot to think about then.

MJ: Three things actually. I wish SJH could help me [his teacher].

Cat: I could help you if you like?

MJ: You can't help me.

Cat: Maybe one of the other children could help you?

MJ: Nah. They don't understand my adventures. I need SJH to help me.

Teacher perceptions of play patterns and behaviours

Characteristics of play among young gifted children

In 2003 I conducted a small research investigation with four early childhood teachers (Murphy, 2004), who were interviewed about their perceptions of giftedness and the characteristics they noticed through the lens of play. Teachers perceived that young children who are gifted:

- enjoy one-to-one attention with the teacher, often choosing the teacher as a play partner over other children
- are selective about friendships and will exclude children from their play, preferring instead to befriend those who have a similar approach to thinking and solving problems
- have a love of learning and ask detailed questions to advance their own knowledge— simplistic versions of an answer are brushed aside by the child
- cannot be rushed through routines, and show perfectionism in their play
- like to take the lead and control their play, and are much more likely to initiate or develop a new game rather than join one that has already started
- think laterally, divergently and creatively, incorporating aspects into play which teachers do not think of themselves, especially in fantasy games
- play longer when topics of learning are of interest to them, and can present as bored with the curriculum.

Play patterns

In 2005 I examined the play patterns and behaviours of young children who were gifted (MJ, 4 years old; MC, 3 years old), who were identified as gifted by the teaching staff. Key findings were that these children have certain play preferences, and that during play, elements such as rhythmical language, expressions of their self-concept and depth of imagination come to the fore. The results showed five different types of play preference: open-ended play, solitary play, pretend play, undisrupted play, and rule-oriented play.

Open-ended play

MJ spent considerable time alone playing with balls across a range of surfaces, particularly bouncing them on grass, concrete and sand. In my role as researcher I contemplated how he would transition to a school playground if no balls were available.

> MJ: Balls are a favourite thing.
>
> Cat: Why are balls a favourite thing?
>
> MJ: Then I can chase after them and get them. I don't know which way it will go. It surprises me.
>
> Cat: What are you looking forward to at school?
>
> MJ: Playing in the playground with bigger balls and bigger maps and hidden caves and exciting stories.
>
> Cat: School sounds exciting.
>
> MJ: I'm not sure if it is yet. I'm making all these pictures in my head about all the new things I'm going to be doing.

Solitary play

MC displayed solitary play and also persistence by repeatedly climbing up a tree at his centre and hanging from it as long as he could before dropping down. He repeated this sequence 17 times: "I like hanging down off the tree and pretending to fly" (MC). Another child in the study, MJ, also exhibited solitary play. One of his teachers commented:

> People think he's a social buzzy bee but if you look closely, he's not. He [MJ] is playing in a group but playing on his own most of the time. He is making his own games and will play alone if the others don't follow his rules. He's in his own little imaginary world. He reads to himself, sings to himself and plays by himself. (Teacher B).

Pretend play

MJ is in pretend play with another child. He points to an open space and says that this can be their home.

> Child: How will we get down?
>
> MJ: I'll show you. It's easy. Use the chimney.
>
> Child: You can't go through a chimney.
>
> MJ: Yes you can, silly. Use your imagination and you will see.
>
> Child: Where is an imagination? Is it inside the house?
>
> MJ: It's in your head. Silly, silly, silly billy it's so chilly. It's pictures, pictures, in your head.

Undisrupted play

I found many instances where the two children who were the focus of the research did not like being disrupted in their play.

> And they don't like to be disturbed to come for lunch or something. If they're doing an activity, they definitely don't want to come for a meal or lunch or to have a nappy done or things like that. MC gets very frustrated when others disrupt him. They like structure to a certain degree as long as they're given the opportunity to go back to what they are doing. Sometimes I feel we disrupt them too much and this leads to frustration. Gifted children need to have quiet time on their own and not to be disturbed. (Teacher A)

> When they're in the middle of creating a castle or a farm or they want to get to the end product and they find it challenging when people come in and disrupt them. We actually tried, when we created the gifted programme at my previous centre, we did a rolling morning tea, but then found these particular children can go for three hours, four hours … so you have to remind them and prompt them to eat because they just remain on task. (Teacher B)

The teacher calls everyone to tidy up for afternoon tea. MC has spent 2 hours alone in the block corner building a massive and intricate construction: "I don't want to. I want to line up my cars. We're going on a trip and the driver's not in yet" (MC).

Rule-oriented play

The two children in the study did not like rules to be broken and this was exhibited during many instances involving other children or at mat times with the teacher.

> I have seen gifted children add on at the end of another game, but they change the game, reorganising the rules first, then often the peers cannot keep up. (Teacher A).

> Child: Let's sing row row row.

> MJ: No not yet. I've told you to wait. First we have to sing row row in full then we get to the screaming bit. When we get to that bit you can eat me. Right, let's sing!

Interactions during play

As part of my research, I examined interactions during play, and found that there was a preference for seeking play with the teacher and many incidences of either repelling or ignoring their age peers.

> Cat: Do you like playing with your friends more or with SJH [teacher] more?

> MJ: I like playing with SJH more.

> Cat: Why do you like SJH so much?

> MJ: Because she's my favourite teacher

> Cat: She's a nice teacher isn't she?

> MJ: Yeah, but when I do bad things that SJH don't like she tells me off, but I, I still love her when she does that.

> At mat time MC pushes to the front and places his hands on the teacher's knees. She starts a song, "Open, Shut Them, Open, Shut Them", and MC participates. He stays seated at the front through the song and has his hands on his lips ready to "blow a little kiss" (how the song finishes). When the teacher asks what song to sing next, MC chooses "Baa Baa Black Sheep". He pushes a child away who sits too close to him. As the mat time gets noisy, MC covers his ears. He responds to all of the teacher's questions.[1]

---

[1] Observed from video footage.

In addition, there was ample evidence of gifted children dominating and leading their peers during play:

> MJ: I'm telling you. You are a fish and I'm going to eat you. That's the game because I'm the Daddy crocodile.

> MJ: This is the king's ladder and I am the king. If you want to play, you will have to be the queen.

> He [MJ] generally starts the play, but not always. Sometimes other children have started it and then he will go in on it and will often try to take over. You can tell that he's going to control the play before long. He will be telling the other children, you be the dog … and next thing you know he's got all these children controlled and they're all dogs barking around. (Teacher B)

Interestingly, the young gifted children held a self-perception as teacher's peer, equal and helper, and there was a preference for interacting with the teacher.

> MJ likes 'one to one'. He does like that, if I spend time with him. If I'm not, if I'm spending time with other children, he will come and stand over me, to ask when it's his turn. I suppose he just likes that older person. (Teacher B)

> At the clay table with 12 other children *his own age*, MJ [4 years] continues to interact with the teacher. His body is turned to where the teacher is sitting. He moves behind the child next to him to be right next to her [the teacher]. He whispers in her ear, 'One of the babies is making a mess. He's got clay on him like a mask.' (Murphy)

Complexities of play

There has been much written globally about the play of young children who are gifted, particularly in the last 30 years. What is clear is that these children have advanced play behaviours and interests (Robinson, 1993), and they often master games with rules earlier than other children (Mares, 1991). Despite the usual teacher expectations of children in the early years, more sophisticated levels of play skills and patterns may emerge. Exposure to more abstract concepts in comparison to their peers is enjoyed (Clark, 1997), as is play experiences focused on fantasy and pretend play, or intellectual board games (Gross, 2004).

Young children who are gifted have a deep enjoyment of complex and detailed fantasy or pretend play (Gross, 2004; Murphy, 2004, 2005).

It must be noted that these children prefer to seek out like-minded playmates who are cognitively stimulating for them (Harrison, 1999). My own research has shown that these children seek out those who are like themselves and are fussy when choosing playmates (Murphy, 2004, 2005). Almost a century ago Hubbard (1929) observed a group of children aged 3 years old in a nursery school and generated data on the number of times they chose each other as playmates and the length of time they spent playing as a group (cited in Gross, 2004, p. 134). The findings clearly demonstrated that playing together for longer periods occurred when there was a greater match in mental age.

Because their play is more sophisticated and they exhibit a love of rules such as at mat times and when interacting with peers, and changing the rules during play with others—social frustrations and rejections can be experienced by young gifted children (Gross, 2004). Arguments during play may erupt due to the acceptance or non-acceptance of play and game rules. Gross (2004) suggests that conflict can arise when the highly gifted child seeks to overturn the rules "either to improve the game or simply for the intellectual stimulation of the ensuing argument" (p. 132).

> With one child he would initiate a game that was all organised in his head and then would be stressed out if it didn't turn out like he visualised. (Teacher C)

Gross (2004) reflects on whether it is commonplace for young children who are exceptionally gifted to invent games of "considerable structural complexity" (p. 132). A very early study by Hollingworth (1931) suggested that in the early years, exceptionally gifted children have conspicuous challenges with play. That researcher argued that

> these children were unpopular with their age-peers because they always wanted to organise the play into some complicated pattern with some remote and definite climax as the goal. (Gross, 2004, p. 132)

Gross (2004) suggests that resentment may develop in other children in response to attempts to reorganise play. Restructuring the conditions of both play and the rules may cause frustration. Gross argues that the vision of the average ability child is narrower, and that altering new rules during play may destroy the very fabric of it, whereas the gifted child may perceive change to be one way of making the experience more challenging. Similar findings arose from my own study (Murphy, 2004), where teachers confirmed that young children who are gifted like to make the rules, and get frustrated when play does not evolve as expected.

Having the opportunity to experience story sequence and characterisation (drama) enhances opportunities for critical thinking, abstract thought and language. O'Day (1996) suggested that young children who are gifted "appreciate the silly and the absurd" (p. 16). Grant (2002) reported that in dramatic play situations there was the need to dominate play, which meant the success of social interaction was reduced at times but could be sustained through the inclusion of some "teacher direction". Socially, the cohort in that study appeared to prefer to play on their own or to interact socially with adults. "Socialising with other children was most successful only when it was mediated by an adult" (Grant, 2002, p. 7). Similar findings were made in my own research (Murphy, 2004), in that teachers perceived young gifted children as being much more likely to start a new game of their own rather than join in an existing game successfully, and that there is a high need to dominate play.

Children between the ages of 4 and 6 years both respond to and enjoy riddles and "silly rhyming slapstick" (O'Day, 1996, p. 16). The creation of rhymes and stories that Harrison (1999) writes about can be evident during solitary or group play episodes:

> MJ: I like games but I only like them if I can be the winner. I'm really good at tumbling monkeys. I always win. I want to win win win, what a spin, that's what I want to do.

Intellectual pursuits, such as playing with words, puzzles, concepts such as time, death and distance, and board games rank highly on the list of play interests for children who are gifted (Harrison, 1999; Hollingworth, 1942; Silverman, 1989).

> Today, tomorrow, yesterday. Things like that gifted kids are the ones that pick it up. Like the concept of time. They seem to pick this up early. Other children have some realisation and understanding, but

they question concepts of time much earlier than other children. They think about these concepts in their play and ask lots of questions about them. Yes, these children nut them out very quickly. They're interesting to them. (Teacher D).

He [MJ] likes the abstract. He's fascinated with maps and travel and how long it takes to get somewhere or do something. Even posting letters. (Teacher A).

He [MJ] likes mathematical concepts like time, speed, distance. He was very interested in death the other day, much more than the others. (Teacher D).

MC (2 years) displayed similar interests:

Imagine how far the bird can fly while I am walking? (MC)

MC was in the family play area:

MC: I'm not just an ordinary crocodile you know.

Cat: I can see how big you are!

MC: Yes, but it's not really about how big I am, it's about how old I am. I am so old I was here before McDonalds!

Nelson (1979) sees the virtues of learning games and simulations as being a "powerful means of tapping and releasing the potential in gifted children" (p. 348). Nelson suggests that these types of play activities accommodate and utilise the gifted child's "superior creativity, imagination, wide-ranging interests and abilities and limitless energy" (p. 348). Because young children who are gifted thrive on discovery and enjoy playing around with ideas, these types of open-ended play activities are ideally suited to them. Role-playing experiences, in particular, may allow young children who are gifted to expose their sense of humour, creativity and individuality. In particular, exaggeration, chance, humour and competition are elements in play that are responded to with some enthusiasm. However, according to Nelson (1979), making connections with reality in simulated play is recommended.

Curriculum documents relating to the early years (Ministry of Education, 1996, 2007) suggest that teachers should identify strategies and techniques that encourage social integration. However, early years teachers must consider the level of a child's giftedness, because research indicates that the higher the IQ, the more solitary the play becomes. Hollingworth (1936) illuminated the social difficulties of finding suitable playmates "who are appropriate in size and congenial in mentality" (as cited in Gross, 2004, p. 134). Similarities in mental age rather than chronological age are a high priority when choosing playmates, and this is something for early years teachers to take into consideration when encouraging friendships.

The role of the teacher

In the discussion below suggestions for teachers are shared, but it is acknowledged that teachers are not the only educators in a young child's life. The strategies and suggestions are relevant for all supporting adults, including parents who are first to support their children.

A teacher's role in supporting play

Teachers of young children who are gifted play an important role in facilitating learning, allowing children autonomy with their own play experiences and development. Teachers can place themselves in a position where they can listen, notice, recognise, respond, document and reflect; then challenge, stimulate and facilitate the learning in order to enrich it. One suggestion is to respond more directly to the child during play, acting as a cognitive match, understanding play partner and mediator (Murphy, 2005).

The teacher plays a crucial role in promoting group collaboration and the development of friendships. Your response needs to be one of quality engagement and interaction, whereby you utilise your own critical thinking skills to transfer open-ended enquiry and growth of understanding in these children. According to Meade (2000), this view supports theories of Vygotsky (1978), who viewed such 'conveyance' as central to children's thinking.

Strategies for supporting the play of gifted children

As every early years setting can potentially have a gifted child (Minister of Education, 2002), all teachers should be prepared to consider teaching strategies that are responsive to giftedness, and exercise willingness to develop special relationships with young children who are gifted, Meade (2000) comments on the need for early years teachers to engage, to offer guided participation, and to offer joint attention, and these insights are most thought provoking for teachers of children who are gifted. Teachers need to be particularly attuned to the intellectual capacity of these children so that play is stimulating, is thought provoking, and contains elements of *divergent thinking*. My own experiences have taught me that often children (as young as 2 years) know more about certain topics than I do!

It is important to be aware of the differences between *convergent* and *divergent* thinking. In convergent thinking, the right or best answer is attempted by an individual, whereas in divergent thinking, many varied and unique possibilities or answers are generated by the individual (Maker & King, 1996; Maker & Nielson, 1996). The abstract conceptualisations that can occur during divergent dialogue with a teacher, for example, can, in my experience, be very stimulating for these children. Both types of thinking have an important place in play. Open-endedness, however, implies a difference in teacher attitude. Maker and Nielson (1996) and Maker and King (1996) argue that this is reflected in the content of questions and the actual questioning techniques, in the design of materials and learning experiences, and in the willingness to critically analyse and reflect on children's responses to questions.

Open-ended questions during play encourage children to give a response. They also encourage group interaction rather than teacher–child interaction. They elicit more complete and more complex responses, allowing children to give knowledgeable answers and encouraging children to question themselves (Maker & Nielson, 1996). In other words, open-ended discussion stimulates further thought, learning and exploration. For example, a strategy I find useful when engaging with these children during play is to start sentences with "I wonder how …" or "I wonder why…" These are key elements of critical thinking which encourage taking joy in the unknown and the surprising, allowing the child to make discoveries. A teacher who always provides answers or asks closed questions during play experiences is not responding to the potential of the young child.

Pausing after open-ended questioning is even more crucial when engaging in critical thinking dialogue with young children who are gifted. Open-endedness implies that it is acceptable for a child to know more about a certain topic than the teacher. If creativity involves fluency, flexibility and originality of thought (Renzulli & Reis, 1986), then open-ended discussions stimulate the 'creative juices' of a child, encourage playfulness, allow full use of the imagination during play, and promote openness to new, more advanced and complex play experiences. These skills are important for teachers to develop in all children, but young children who are gifted may have advanced knowledge compared to the teacher, or advanced development, such as interpersonal awareness, and so sensitivity and avoiding making assumptions during play are required.

Melodrama, a type of dramatic play with exaggerated characters and exciting pivotal moments, combines humour (which young children who are gifted may often demonstrate) and drama, in order to engage the imaginations and appeal to the emotions of these children. Teachers can encourage and support this type of dramatic play as not only does melodrama help children to learn about plot and characterisation, but there is also the opportunity for these children to draw on prior knowledge during dramatic play episodes.

Conclusion

Young children who are gifted need the opportunity for self-directed and discovery learning (Harrison, 1999). This freedom to self-select allows the child to act on their own intrinsic motivation and can be achieved through long periods of uninterrupted play, flexibility in centre and classroom routines, accessible resources, and the self-selection of activities. In other words, by 'removing ceilings' and maintaining a flexible attitude, teachers can leave the world wide open for these children to use the higher-order thinking skills of analysis, synthesis and evaluation in their play.

Reflective questions (see Appendix E)

The following questions have been adapted from my earlier interview questions with teachers (Murphy, 2004). They generated so much discussion at the time of that research I think they will continue to be of value. I suggest taking a team approach: arrange for a group of teachers to consider these questions individually, thinking of a specific child they have noticed who plays differently to other children, then discuss the answers as a team and consider how best to respond in order to enrich the child's learning.

1. What specific aspects come to mind when you think of the play you have observed this child engaging in?
2. Have you observed this child utilising resources in ways that differ from their peers?
3. Have you observed this child seeking out or repelling adults during their play?
4. Have you observed this child seeking out or repelling peers during their play?
5. Are requests for help during play similar to those of their peers, or does this child demonstrate a need for more or less assistance?
6. When you observe this child playing in a specific learning area (e.g., dramatic/fantasy play), do you find the games created by him or her to be more imaginative, less imaginative or similar to those of their peers?
7. Have you observed this child engaged in play for longer periods than their peers, despite distractions? If so, what do you think determines this?
8. Which areas of play or aspects of learning appear to be of most interest to this child?
9. Have you found that questions generated from play and during play are different to those of their peers? If yes, then in what way?
10. Have you observed any direct links between the types of learning experiences this child chooses to engage in and the types of thinking these learning experiences generate?
11. In your experience, what types of play experiences does this child most often engage in?
12. Do you think this child chooses these experiences for particular reasons; for example, the people participating with them, the challenge of resources?
13. What sort of games do you see this child generating?
14. Why do you think he/she engages in these experiences more so than others?

References

Clark, B. (1997). *Growing up gifted*. Upper Saddle River, NJ: Prentice-Hall.

Coolahan, K., & Mendez, J. (2000). Preschool peer interactions and readiness to learn: Relationships between classroom peer play and learning behaviours and conduct. *Journal of Educational Psychology, 92*(3), 458–465.

Discovery Time. (2012). *What teachers are saying*. Retrieved from http://www.discoverytime.co.nz/

Dockett, S., & Fleer, M. (1999). *Play and pedagogy in early childhood: Bending the rules*. Sydney, NSW: Harcourt Brace.

Fisher, J. (2002). *Starting from the child: Teaching and learning from 3 to 8* (2nd ed.). Philadelphia, PA: Open University Press.

Fisher, R., & Martin, B. (2006). An evaluation of the Discovery Time programme. *Kairaranga, 7*(2), 31–35.

Grant, A. (2002, October). *Gifted children at preschool: A report on an early childhood program for gifted preschoolers*. Paper presented at the 9th national conference of the Australian Association for the Education of the Gifted and Talented, Sydney, NSW.

Gross, M. U. M. (2004). *Exceptionally gifted children* (2nd ed.) London, UK: Routledge.

Harrison, C. (1999). *Giftedness in early childhood*. Sydney, NSW: GERRIC.

Hollingworth, L. S. (1931). The child of very superior intelligence as a special problem in social adjustment. *Mental Hygiene, 15*(1), 3–16.

Hollingworth, L. S. (1936). The development of personality in highly intelligent children. *National Elementary Principal, 15*, 272–281.

Hollingworth, L. S. (1942). *Children above IQ 180*. New York, NY: World Books.

Lillemyr, O. F., Søbstad, F., Marder, K., & Flowerday, T. (2011). A multicultural perspective on play and learning in primary school. *International Journal of Early Childhood, 43*(1), 43–65.

Maker, C. J., & King, M. A. (1996). *Nurturing giftedness in young children*. Reston, VA: Council for Exceptional Children.

Maker, C. J., & Nielson, A. B. (1996). *Curriculum development and teaching strategies for gifted learners*. Austin, TX: PRO-ED Inc.

Mares, L. (1991). *Young gifted children*. Melbourne, VIC: Hawker Brownlow Education.

Meade. A. (2000). If you say it three times, is it true? Critical use of research in early childhood education. *Journal of Early Years Education, 8*(1), 15–26.

Minister of Education. (2002). *Initiatives for gifted and talented learners.* Wellington: Ministry of Education.

Ministry of Education. (1996). *Te whāriki: He whāriki mātauranga mō ngā mokopuna o Aotearoa: Early childhood curriculum.* Wellington: Learning Media.

Ministry of Education. (2007). *The New Zealand curriculum.* Wellington: Learning Media.

Murphy, C. L. (2004). Teachers' perceptions of the play patterns and behaviours of young children who are gifted, in an early childhood setting. *New Zealand Research in Early Childhood Education, 7,* 57–72.

Murphy, C. L. (2005). *Play patterns and behaviours of young children who are gifted in an early childhood setting.* Unpublished master's thesis, Massey University.

Nelson, R. L. (1979). Injecting play and reality into education of the gifted. *Gifted Child Quarterly, 23*(2), 346–350.

O'Day, S. (1996). Creative drama engages children's imaginations. *Gifted Child Today Magazine, 19*(5), 16.

Renzulli, J. S., & Reis, S. M. (1986). The enrichment triad/revolving door model: A schoolwide plan for the development of creative productivity. In J. S. Renzulli (Ed.), *Systems and models for developing programs for the gifted and talented* (pp. 216–305). Mansfield Center, CT: Creative Learning Press Inc.

Robinson, N. M. (1993). Identifying and nurturing gifted, very young children. In K. A. Heller, F. J. Monks, & A. H. Passow (Eds.), *International handbook of research and development of giftedness and talent* (pp. 507–524). Oxford, UK: Pergamon Press.

Silverman, L. K. (1989). The highly gifted. In J. F. Feldhusen, J. Van Tassel-Baska, & K. R. Seeley (Eds.), *Excellence in educating the gifted* (pp. 71–83). Denver, CO: Love.

Vygotsky, L. S. (1978). *Mind in society: The development of higher mental processes.* Cambridge, MA: Harvard University Press.

Part 2: Purposeful and authentic assessment practices

Chapter 4: Assessment for learning with young gifted children

Jo Dean and Valerie Margrain

Introduction

Assessment is an essential part of quality teaching and learning for young children (Drummond, 2012). In the context of this book, assessment is a process of intentionally gathering information about children's learning. In the early years context in Aotearoa New Zealand, assessment is often referred to as "work in progress" (Ministry of Education, 2004, p. 3) and "assessment for learning" (Ministry of Education, 2011). The different assessments should "inform decisions about 'what next' as teachers, children, and families look back in order to look forward in the process of considering pathways of learning" (Ministry of Education, 2004, p. 3).

Drummond (2012) describes the approach as "the ways in which, in our everyday practice, we observe children's learning, strive to understand it, then put our understanding to good use" (p. vii).

Assessment can be viewed as either formative or summative, although some assessment is both. Generally it is the formative type of assessment that is used in the early childhood sector. This is because teachers are usually concentrating on supporting children to learn in the current situation (McLachlan, Edwards, Margrain, & McLean,

2013). On the other hand, summative assessment tends to focus on an end result, with teachers retrospectively looking back at what children have learnt at the end of an activity or experience, and this type of assessment is more often utilised in the school sector. However, both formative and summative elements are important (Absolum, Flockton, Hattie, Hipkins, & Reid, 2009).

Assessment findings are capable of generating a comprehensive picture of a child's strengths, enabling teachers to work more effectively with children. Also, through teachers' deepening understanding of each child, the choice of ongoing assessment practices can be purposeful. It is vital to ensure that selected assessment practices are relevant and age appropriate for all learners. For example, although some young children who are gifted may be highly advanced in reading skills for their chronological age, care should be taken with the choice of reading materials; not all material that a child *can* read matches their maturity or emotional development.

In the early years context, assessment is a major part of the planning process and should be ongoing, in a continuous cycle. Planning will usually begin by gathering observations of children's interests, strengths and behaviour (Ministry of Education, 1996). However, emerging interests and abilities will continue to develop and change, requiring further observations. These further observations inform reflection and influence decisions about the learning environment, necessitating the need for further observation. This is the planning cycle in action. Assessing is teaching in action, and teaching means constantly assessing. In this chapter we discuss early years approaches to assessment, a range of assessment methods, and the ways in which partnership is important for effective assessment.

Assessment approaches in the early years

There are many forms of inclusive assessment practices that can be utilised by teachers to enhance their understanding of a child's learning. In early years education, strengths-based assessment is valued (Carr, 2001), whereby assessment highlights "dimensions of strength" (Carr, 2006a). The assessment practices focus on what the child *can do* rather than what they *cannot do*. The teacher's view is based on the holistic development of children, meaning that all aspects of children are valued, not just the intellectual aspects.

Early years teachers ought to have a good understanding of children's learning and development at both the lower and upper ends of the learning spectrum. This is important when it comes to observation, because young children who are gifted may have strengths, interests (fixations perhaps) and sensitivities that are not particularly obvious in daily events. Allan (2002) suggests that "observing and listening to the underlying cause of frustration will help teachers to support the development of the child's behaviour" (p. 3). However, recognising 'potential' can be difficult when currents of inappropriate or unusual behaviour obscure the teacher's view.

In addition, a sociocultural lens guides current assessment practices, including collaborative partnerships with families. As well as gaining information from the parents and family/whānau, early years teachers can take the opportunities that arise to listen to children and include the child's voice and thinking in documentation (Ministry of Education, 1996). Indeed, the child's right to participate, to have a voice and to be respected is advocated by the United Nations *Convention on the Rights of the Child* (United Nations, 1989).

Both the early childhood curriculum, *Te Whāriki* (Ministry of Education, 1996) and *The New Zealand Curriculum* (Ministry of Education, 2007) advocate that assessment should incorporate the following approaches: assessment for learning, formative assessment, and use of holistic and strengths-based principles. Absolum et al. (2009) discusses the importance of using assessment approaches that have a focus on learner 'capability'. Despite these curriculum discourses relating to competence and capability, both in the school sector and in early intervention there is often a discourse on 'need'. In addition to identifying what children know, teachers and specialists may often focus on what the learners do not know, or cannot do, what the next steps ought to be, and how learning should be scaffolded for the child. While these elements of practice sound useful, they have also been in contradiction to the pedagogical discourse in early childhood which rejected any reference to or focus on 'need' (McLachlan, et al., 2013).

Assessment exemplars differ markedly between school and early childhood contexts. The early childhood use of learning story exemplars is considered later in this chapter and in the following chapter. The narrative nature of learning stories provides the opportunity to describe children's competence. In school, assessment exemplar resources include curriculum matrices, which provide detailed progress indicators and focus on samples of work that are moderated to a given 'level' (Margrain & Clements, 2007). The purpose of these exemplars in the school sector is to provide tangible reference points for levels and to support consistency of expectations. This helps teachers to decide the 'best fit' level in particular curriculum areas (maths, English, the arts, science, social studies, health and physical education, and technology). For gifted children, the focus on levels can provide an opportunity for assessment to confirm where achievement is well above the expected level for their age. The purpose of deciding on a level is more than mere assessment, though: it relates to selecting the most appropriate teaching and learning approaches for learners.

Identifying the best-fit level may also confirm for the teacher what learning is important at any given level. However, the increasing focus on 'needs' within school settings may also mean that children's competencies are overshadowed by a focus on the areas they are less skilled in. As we know, young children who are gifted are at times asynchronous in their development, so it should be expected that some areas of development would not be as advanced as others. As a result, the children can be made to focus on areas that are not strengths at the expense of their areas of ability. For example, a teacher might focus on writing rather than reading for a child who is above ability in reading but 'only' at age level for writing. This learner might then feel that their writing is problematic, even though it is not behind what should be expected for the age and year group. The learner might also be frustrated that they have less reading opportunity at school than they would enjoy.

The assessment emphasis on levels can be helpful for young children who are gifted because it clarifies how far ahead their development is in areas of strength. Teachers can be encouraged to use 'above-level testing', drawing on assessment tools and resources for older year groups in the school to more comprehensively assess the extent of a child's achievement potential. Although a child should be viewed holistically and valued as more than their assessment statistics (for example, "She's reading at age 10 ability"), having reliable evidence can help with advocacy for the child for whom additional programmes and resources would make a difference.

Methods of assessment

Observations are a way of 'watching' or 'looking to see' what children do—perhaps the way in which they behave and react within a spontaneous moment or learning experience (Podmore, 2006; Porter, 2005). Observations enhance teachers' and parents' understanding of children. Observations of children can be carried out in different places, situations and times of day to ensure teachers gain as authentic an overview of the child as possible. As we know, children have peaks through the day when they maintain a higher concentration span or retain a focus for a period of time. It would be unfair to carry out observations when a child is really tired or hungry, because the outcomes will not accurately reflect the capabilities of the child. It is also important that observations be carried out with familiar people, such as early years educators, rather than an unfamiliar stranger whom the child does not have a trusting relationship with. As Drummond (2012) clearly stated,

> In assessing learning, the act of seeing gives way to the act of understanding; the process of collecting evidence is followed by attempts to make the evidence meaningful. (p. 60)

It is important for teachers to utilise a range of techniques to give a rich, multiple perspective of the child's complex learning, and enough data for a thorough analysis.

Within Māori culture the involvement of parents, family/whānau and the Māori community is a large component of children's learning and background experiences. Bevan-Brown (2009) has suggested opportunities for whānau participation in identification, nomination, resource people, mentors, volunteers and role models. From a cultural perspective, she suggests that

> observation needed to be carried out within a culturally responsive environment by teachers who have a sound knowledge of Māori culture and Māori perspectives of giftedness. (p. 9)

Often, culturally diverse children may not be recognised as gifted because their cultural values may be disregarded or discouraged, causing low self-esteem in the children and low teacher expectations.

Specific methods of assessment are discussed in the following sections:

- observation methods
- narrative assessment / learning stories
- collection of artefacts
- checklists and scales
- standardised tests.

Observation methods

In this section a range of methods are described, all of which have validity in the early years context so long as the purpose is guided by constructively supporting the children's learning. These methods include anecdotal records, running record observations, time samples, event recording, frequency recording, duration samples and learning notes.

Anecdotes record children's participation through learning experiences, as well as their learning processes, such as problem solving and investigating topics. Anecdotes can be useful for recording verbal or non-verbal forms of interaction through play (Podmore, 2006). The records can be written by the early years teachers as well as by the parents/whānau, and they can be written after the event. These types of observations can help to reveal children's participation in a group or as an individual.

For example, a teacher may want to observe the social skills of a particular child who often isolates herself and plays away from others. It has been recognised that gifted children often play solo or prefer interaction with older children or adults more readily (Porter, 2005). As a teacher you would observe verbal interactions as well as body cues. Was there an opportunity for group entry? Did the other children try to engage the child by exchanging items with her? Did they reject the child? What about social interactions with adults? What vocabulary was used by the gifted child and her peers?

Running records form detailed and specific notes on what children do—their behaviour or actions in either spontaneous or structured activities (Hamer, 1999). Running record observations are useful for observing something in particular, such as children drawing or writing, because they capture more detail than other techniques. A specific focus may be on comprehension skills and the application of knowledge, which may highlight the advanced use of thinking processes through language, literacy or numeracy concepts (Porter, 2005).

If it is identified that further information would be useful on specific aspects of behaviour or interaction, this may warrant completion of time samples, or event, duration or frequency recording (Podmore, 2006). The level of detail from these observational tools is beyond what teachers complete on a regular basis, but it can illuminate details that anecdotal observations might miss, such as antecedents or influencing triggers. Thus, behavioural observations can be particularly useful for young children who are gifted. Some examples might include:

- conducting a time sample to find out the areas of play a child engages with in a given time (e.g., during the first hour of arrival, or after lunch)
- documenting the frequency of peer and adult interactions
- recording the duration a child persists with a challenging activity.

It is beyond the scope of this chapter to describe all the possible forms of observation, and we encourage wider reading on this topic. We do stress that having a diverse 'tool kit' of assessment approaches prepares teachers best for being able to assess holistically and responsively.

Narrative assessment / learning stories

Narrative assessment is a common approach in New Zealand early childhood settings. These types of assessment are usually termed learning stories (Carr, 2001). They are considered to be a sociocultural, holistic and meaningful approach to documenting the richness of children's learning. Learning stories involve the learning community of children, families, teachers and others. Many perspectives create a bigger picture of the child's learning and their learning context, and multiple voices are valid.

In Chapter 5 authentic learning stories of gifted children are analysed, illustrating characteristics of giftedness, teaching support, social context and engagement. The learning stories are available to download at www.nzcer.org.nz/nzcerpress/giftedness.

The dispositional focus of learning stories

Dispositions have become increasingly popular and recognised in relation to learning stories. They are usually the ways in which we behave on a daily basis, and they are often described as attitudes towards learning or 'quality attributes' (Carr & Claxton, 2002; Claxton & Carr, 2004). The early childhood curriculum, *Te Whāriki* (Ministry of Education, 1996), notes that "dispositions provide a framework for developing working theories and expertise" (p. 45). In the New Zealand context, dispositions have been drawn from the goals and strands of the early childhood curriculum, such as curiosity, perseverance and responsibility.

Dispositions that focus on children's thinking are referred to in the literature as habits of mind (Costa & Kallick, 2000), thinking dispositions (Perkins, Jay, & Tishman, 1993; Ritchhart, 2001), or learning power (Claxton, 2002), to name just a few. If key dispositions are connected to gifted characteristics, then teachers really begin to identify the potential of a gifted child. Linking thinking dispositions to gifted children's learning brings a different lens to observations. The focus becomes more about the child's thinking. However, with regard to assessment methods, teachers look to recognise the disposition. Continuity of a certain disposition (such as perseverance) may be evident through a range of experiences that require physical activity, or more structured activities such as writing.

Supporting children's learning involves recognising positive dispositions towards learning. Ritchhart (2001) has identified three thinking dispositions—creative, reflective and critical skills.

- Creative dispositions can "include imaginativeness, being open to new ideas and experiences, having tolerance of ambiguity, curiosity, adventurousness, exploration, being playful, seeking alternatives".
- Reflective skills include the use of metacognitive strategies of self-awareness, self-control and self-monitoring to regulate one's own thinking.
- Critical thinking skills may include "planning, and being strategic, inquiring, investigative, and logical" (Ritchhart, 2001, p. 144).

Margrain (2005) considered dispositions in her study of precocious readers. The study identified both learning dispositions, drawing on the frameworks developed by Carr (2001) and the thinking dispositions of Perkins et al. (1993). It was evident that the trait of 'passion' was a key disposition in young children who were gifted, because they displayed eagerness, delight and a real 'hunger' for reading (Margrain, 2005).

The key competencies in *The New Zealand Curriculum* (Ministry of Education, 2007) align with early childhood dispositions. This strengthens the continuity of assessment between the two sectors and negates the argument that dispositional-focused assessment is something that only occurs in early childhood. Table 4.1 illustrates the dispositions evident from the analysis of a group of young gifted children (Margrain, 2005). These dispositions are broader than the dispositions commonly connected to the early childhood curriculum, and Table 4.1 also illustrates potential connections to both the early childhood and school curricula.

Table 4.1. Dispositions and curriculum connections

Learning & Thinking Dispositions	Links to *Te Whāriki*	Links to *The New Zealand Curriculum*
Perserverance	Well-being, Exploration	Thinking, Managing self
Confidence	Exploration, Well-being	Relating to others; Using language, symbols & text
Responsibility	Belonging Contribution	Thinking, Relating to others
Courage & curiosity	Exploration	Managing self, Participating & contributing
Trust & playfulness	Communication	Thinking
Logical & ordered	Exploration	Thinking, Using language, symbols & text
Inquiry	Exploration	Thinking; Participating & contributing
Passionate	Well-being, Belonging	Managing self
Internal control	Contribution	Managing self

Source: Dispositions adapted from Carr, 2006a, 2006b and Perkins, Jay and Tishman, 1993 reported in Margrain, 2005.

Learning notes

Blaiklock (2010) has advocated the use of 'learning notes' as a descriptive assessment approach. Blaiklock argues that learning notes "can be used to provide an accurate description of an event, an interpretation of the learning that occurred, and ideas for future learning", and that "unlike Learning Stories, Learning Notes do not follow a story format or focus on dispositions to learn" (p. 5). The learning note could be as simple as a brief Post-it anecdotal note, or it could be a richer description, but it should always be written immediately after the event. Blaiklock (2010) claims that learning notes provide a useful approach for those who are concerned about issues of validity, reliability and manageability, though in New Zealand the dominant approach to assessment continues to be learning stories (Education Review Office, 2007; Mitchell, 2008). It is important that gifted children have strong and frequent assessment records, and the use of learning notes may be a manageable technique for teachers in busy early years settings, in which it is difficult to keep up with learning stories or formal assessment routines.

Collection of artefacts

In this section a range of artefacts are considered: digital media; samples of drawing, constructing and writing; and transcripts of conversations. These artefacts all add to the breadth and validity of a child's portfolio, contributing authentic evidence of competence.

Digital media such as photos and digital video recordings are a valuable tool to support other observations such as narratives or checklists. Photos are often useful to place alongside a running record or child's narrative, because the picture tells the story (Palaiologou, 2012). Photos can be an excellent visual observation tool to capture expression, or a child's advanced creativity, for example through dance.

Video recording can be valuable evidence of learning with very young children too, particularly when they have very little verbal communication. Non-verbal cues and responses are valuable and can be captured in documentation: children have many languages to express their feelings, thoughts and interests (Edwards, Gandini, & Forman, 1998). The camera can also be a wonderful tool for children to capture their own experiences. Children may enjoy taking photos of their work or their peers' work. Gifted children may have a different perception to other children through an experience, and taking photos of their own work can often expose the teacher to their views and understanding of their world.

A sample of a child's drawings over time can really show progression and mastery of techniques. For gifted children this can be an outlet for them to demonstrate their understanding of complex themes and processes. The research compiled by Harrison (1999) demonstrated the importance of collecting children's work, in that she found

> the processes involved in the completion of such drawings also indicated characteristics such as intrinsic motivation, persistence and perfectionism with some children completing many, many drawings of similar objects in the process of refinement. (p. 82)

Children enjoy revisiting their own work and recognising the changes that occur.

Samples of writing can be anything from scribbling marking, to letters, numbers or words created on paper or any other medium. This can show a child's interest in symbol making, which often leads on from drawing and encourages early stages of literacy learning and development. Some gifted children are able to write text independently, either by traditional pen and paper or with technology such as computers.

Capturing children's interactions and conversational skills is helpful for understanding their thinking, along with hearing their ideas, questions and contributions to play. This can highlight children's ability to negotiate and co-operate in a group situation, too. As Drummond (2012) points out, it becomes difficult to assess children's learning without considering the part that spoken language plays:

> Our attempts as teachers to get inside children's heads, and understand their understandings, are enriched to the extent that children themselves are prepared to give us, through their talk, access to their thinking. (Drummond, 2012, p. 51)

Through small group discussions, teachers should promote critical thinking skills and allow children to express and listen to ideas. Teachers can encourage children to indicate aspects of learning through showing concrete examples of abstract thinking, humour and imagination, and thinking logically. Through the research that Harrison (2004) conducted it is evident that the child's voice was a key component in the data collecting, because they were able to articulate their thinking during play. It can also be valuable to have evidence of the vocabulary and richness of dialogue used by verbally precocious children.

Talking with the child was also part of the approach in a case study carried out by Dean (2011). Advanced reading, comprehension skills and thinking skills were evident through talking about the 6-year-old child's interest in books. The child explained in detail why she liked particular chapter books, certain authors and sequel books. Teachers would not otherwise have gained this rich information through observations.

Checklists and scales

Checklists often focus on a particular behaviour or developmental characteristics. Traditionally, checklists have been recognised as a limited method, particularly in the early childhood context, with a number of flaws (Hamer, 1999). They can be misleading if interpreted inaccurately. As Porter (2005) highlights, "checklists rely on children's performances to identify giftedness" (p. 132), but there are traits and types of behaviour or dispositions that are not recognised through checklists, and it must be remembered that young children are diverse learners.

Despite these reservations, checklists can usefully be added to a teacher's toolkit of assessment resources. Although a checklist of common characteristics of giftedness (such as those reported in Chapter 2) will not apply to all gifted children, it can be a useful resource to alert teachers and parents to the possibilities of giftedness, or to alert them to the importance of further investigation. Most importantly, it can remind teachers of the skills and competencies of children, and for gifted children a reminder that learning experiences ought to be differentiated (see Chapter 8 of this book).

In her study of early readers, Margrain (2005) used a 15-item screening checklist (based on Jones, 1988). The two items of most consistent relevance to the children in the study, according to their parents, were "asks a lot of questions" and "shows interest and aptitude in many areas". The *Giftedness in Early Childhood Scale*, developed by Barbara Allan, has proven to be a valuable identification and assessment tool and is retrievable from http://gifted.tki.org.nz/Early-Childhood-Education-ECE/

Identification as part of the *Identifying and Providing for Giftedness in the Early Years* resource (Allan, 2002). Use of the scale was introduced in Chapter 2 of this book in terms of its contribution to identification approaches. It is unlikely that early years teachers would complete the scale for all children; rather, it would be completed for those children they have already observed to be displaying some characteristics of giftedness, and the scale allows teachers to gather more information. In this way the scale can be seen as contributing to holistic assessment.

Standardised testing

Standardised tests claim to have strong reliability and can therefore be useful to include in a learning portfolio. In Chapter 2 we noted the use of psychometric testing for identification purposes. As Margrain (2011) clearly points out, a limitation with standardised intelligence (IQ) tests is that they are generally completed out of context, place gifted children in an unfamiliar environment, and have a narrow focus on academic intelligence rather than a fuller range of giftedness. It is important that assessment for learning include a broader range of domains, such as physical, artistic, musical or leadership areas.

However, there are other forms of standardised testing than psychometric IQ testing. These include a range of areas of academic performance, including reading, spelling, maths, problem solving and receptive language. In Margrain's (2005) study she included several such tools:

- *British Picture Vocabulary Scale* (Dunn, Dunn, Whetton, & Burley, 1997), a test of receptive language
- *Neale Analysis of Reading* (Neale, 1999), assessing reading accuracy, comprehension and fluency
- *Coloured Progressive Matrices* (Raven, Raven, & Court, 1998), a test of problem solving
- running records of reading and the 6-year net literacy assessment (Clay, 1983), assessing a range of early reading and writing competencies
- the *Burt Word Reading Test* (Gilmore, Croft, & Reid, 1981), a test of non-contextual word reading.

Some of these tools, such as the *Burt Word Reading Test*, running records of reading, and the 6-year net, are assessments that primary school teachers use on a regular basis. Early childhood teachers can work in partnership with their local school teachers to identify assessment tools that could be useful for gifted children, particularly for maths and literacy. These tests can help teachers to identify just how far advanced the gifted child is compared to their age peers. More importantly, the assessment results can indicate specific aspects of strength and challenge, document progress over time, and clarify the next learning steps. These outcomes validate the use of the tools to support learning.

Assessment partnership

There must be more than one perspective when assessing for learning, which means that building reciprocal positive relationships with whānau and outside agencies is essential. Gaining information from whānau provides a valuable insight into outside experiences and provides further information about a child's learning. Hamer (1999) has pointed out that

> parents' insights provide a perspective not only on the behaviour but also on the child's cultural background and on the context of the child's life within their family and community. (p. 57)

Harrison (2004) has raised concerns from the parent's point of view, however. For example, lack of understanding of giftedness within the community and among teachers is still evident, even though some positive changes in attitude and understanding have made a difference. Further provision is still required for teachers and the wider community. As noted by the Ministry of Education (2000), "failure to recognise and meet the need of the gifted and talented can result in their boredom, frustration, mediocrity, and even hostility" (p. 6).

Assessment is not the sole responsibility of the teacher: it is a collaborative commitment between the teacher and whānau to build a positive, respectful and trusting partnership. When whānau feel they are valued, a sense of trust is built, and usually they feel confident and empowered to be able to contribute their knowledge to their children's learning. Furthermore, parents and whānau have specific expertise and knowledge to contribute as knowledgeable partners, not only about their own child but also about giftedness. Sharing information and knowledge can only be beneficial to the team supporting the child.

Through inclusive and collaborative practices teachers can also gain information from specialists such as education support workers and speech–language therapists. Dunn and Barry (2004) support the inclusion of different lenses: different people will observe different behaviours, so gathering information as a collective will be valuable. This applies to young children who are gifted, because often there may be an underlying behaviour that will mask their characteristics of giftedness. Allan (2002) highlights the point that

> uneven development, characteristic of young children, is particularly significant for gifted young children and should alert adults to be especially careful interpreting children's behaviour. (p. 11)

Building positive relationships with other agencies can be a useful source of support for teachers striving to understand these children.

Once a range of observations has been completed and artefacts collected, they need to be interpreted and analysed "before they can serve as a tool for learning" (Hamer, 1999, p. 56). Assessment documentation can inform an individual plan (IP). An IP is

> a plan that forms the basis for programmes designed specifically for an individual child who, in order to benefit from their learning environment, requires resources alternative or additional to those usually available. (Ministry of Education, 1996, p. 99)

IPs are commonly used for children with special learning needs, but they can be equally valid for young children who are gifted. Through such plans children's learning can be enriched and accelerated, and additional, more complex and stimulating educational challenges can be provided. Also, the parents and whānau may request that their child be provided with further support in other areas of development. Social skills, as one example, are key attributes that parents tend to become concerned about.

Conclusion

Assessment should always be purposeful and connected to learning. By drawing on a diverse range of assessment tools, teachers have the potential to understand children more deeply and teach more effectively.

This is particularly important to support the transition from early childhood to school. In the next chapter a range of case studies that demonstrate different assessment techniques will be shared. These case studies highlight the learning dispositions and characteristics of giftedness that were evident across various learning and curricular areas.

References

Absolum, M., Flockton, L., Hattie, J., Hipkins, R., & Reid, I. (2009). *Directions for assessment in New Zealand: Developing students' assessment capabilities*. Retrieved from http://www.tki.org.nz/r/assessment/research/mainpage/directions/

Allan, B. (2002). *Identifying and providing for giftedness in the early years: The early years research and practice series (1)*. Palmerston North: Kanuka Grove Press. Retrieved from:http://gifted.tki.org.nz/Early-Childhood-Education-ECE/Identification

Bevan-Brown, J. (2009). Identifying and providing for gifted and talented Māori students. *Apex, 15*(4), 6–20. Retrieved from http://www.giftedchildren.org.nz/apex/

Blaiklock, K. (2010). Assessment in New Zealand early childhood settings: A proposal to change from learning stories to learning notes. *Early Education, 48*(2), 5–10.

Carr, M. (2001). *Assessment in early childhood settings: Learning stories*. London, UK: Paul Chapman.

Carr, M. (2006a). *Dimensions of strength for key competencies*. Retrieved from http://www.tki.org.nz/r/nzcurriculum/docs/dimensions-for-ki.doc

Carr, M. (2006b). Learning dispositions and key competencies: A new curriculum continuity across the sectors. *Early Childhood Folio, 10*, 21–26.

Carr, M., & Claxton, G. (2002). Tracking the development of learning dispositions. *Assessment in Education, 9*(1), 9–37.

Claxton, G. (2002). *Building learning power: Helping young people become better learners*.Bristol, UK: TLO Limited.

Claxton, G., & Carr, M. (2004). A framework for teaching learning: The dynamics of disposition. *Early Years, 24*(1), 87–97.

Clay, M. M. (1983). *An observation survey of early literacy achievement*. Auckland: Heinemann.

Costa, A. L., & Kallick, B. (2000). *Discovering and exploring habits of mind*. Alexandria,VA: Association for Supervision and Curriculum Development.

Dean, J. (2011). A profile portraying a contemporary young gifted child. *Apex: The New Zealand Journal of Gifted Education,11*(1). Retrieved from http://www.giftedchildren.org.nz/apex/

Drummond, M. J. (2012). *Assessing children's learning.* London, UK; New York, NY: Routledge.

Dunn, L., & Barry, S. (2004). *Inclusive assessment for children with early intervention support: Final report to the Ministry of Education.* Wellington: Ministry of Education.

Dunn, L. M., Dunn, L. M., Whetton, C., & Burley, J. (1997). *British Picture Vocabulary Scale* (2nd ed.). Windsor, Berks, UK: NFER-Nelson.

Education Review Office. (2007). *The quality of assessment in early childhood education.* Wellington: Author.

Edwards, C., Gandini, L., & Forman, G. (Eds.). (1998). *The hundred languages of children* (2nd ed.). Greenwich, CT: Ablex.

Gilmore, A. M., Croft, A. C., & Reid, N. A. (1981). *The Burt Word Reading Test (NZ rev.).* Wellington: New Zealand Council for Educational Research.

Hamer, C. (1999). *Observation: A tool for learning.* Lower Hutt: The Open Polytechnic.

Harrison, C. (1999). Visual representation of the young gifted child. *Roeper Review, 21*(3),189–194.

Harrison, C. (2004). Giftedness in early childhood: The search for complexity and connection. *Roeper Review, 26*(2), 78–84.

Jones, R. (1988). The gifted preschool child. *Apex: The New Zealand Journal of Gifted Education, 2*(1), 3–8.

Margrain, V. (2005). *Precocious readers: Case studies of social support, self-regulation and spontaneous learning in the early years.* Unpublished doctoral thesis, Victoria University of Wellington.

Margrain, V. (2011). Assessment for learning with young gifted children. *Apex: The New Zealand Journal of Gifted Education, 16*(1). Retrieved from http://www.giftedchildren.org.nz/apex/

Margrain, V., & Clements, S. (2007). Exemplar assessment for all learners in Aotearoa New Zealand. *Kairaranga, 8*(2), 39–45.

McLachlan, C., Edwards, S., Margrain, V., & McLean, K. (2013). *Children's learning and development: Contemporary assessment in the early years.* South Yarra, VIC: Palgrave Macmillan.

Ministry of Education. (1996). *Te whāriki: He whāriki mātauranga mō ngā mokopuna o Aotearoa: Early childhood curriculum.* Wellington: Learning Media.

Ministry of Education. (2000). *Gifted and talented students: Meeting their needs in New Zealand schools.* Retrieved from http://www.gifted.tki.org.nz

Ministry of Education. (2004). *Kei tua o te pae: Assessment for learning: Early childhood exemplars: Book 7: Assessment and learning: Continuity.* Wellington: Learning Media.

Ministry of Education. (2007). *The New Zealand curriculum framework.* Wellington: Learning Media.

Ministry of Education. (2011). *Ministry of Education position paper: Assessment.* Wellington: Learning Media. Retrieved from http://www.minedu.govt.nz/theMinsitry/PublicationsAndResources/Assessment PositionPaper.aspx

Mitchell, L. (2008). *Assessment practices and aspects of curriculum in early childhood education: Results of the 2007 NZCER national survey for EC services.* Wellington: New Zealand Council for Educational Research.

Neale, M. D. (1999). *Neale analysis of reading* (3rd ed.). Melbourne, VIC: Australian Council for Educational Research.

Palaiologou, I. (2012). *Child observation for the early years* (2nd ed.). London, UK: Sage Publications Ltd.

Perkins, D. N., Jay, E., & Tishman, S. (1993). Beyond abilities: A dispositional theory of thinking. *Merrill-Palmer Quarterly, 39*(1), 1–21.

Podmore, V. (2006). *Observation: Origins and approaches to early childhood research and practice.* Wellington: NZCER Press.

Porter, L. (2005). *Gifted young children: A guide for teachers and parents* (2nd ed.). Crow's Nest, NSW: Allen & Unwin.

Raven, J., Raven, J. C., & Court, J. H. (1998). *Coloured progressive matrices* (rev.). Oxford, UK: Oxford Psychologists' Press.

Ritchhart, R. (2001). From IQ to IC: A dispositional view of intelligence. *Roeper Review, 23*(3), 143–150.

United Nations. (1989). *Convention on the rights of the child.* Retrieved from http://www.ohchr.org/english/law/pdf/crc.pdf

Chapter 5: Looking at learning: Narratives of young gifted children

Jo Dean, Carola Sampson, Annette Preston
and Emma Wallace

Introduction

The purpose of this chapter is to share some authentic work written by the authors from their work as teachers in early childhood settings. The discussion looks in depth at the learning of young children who are gifted through the lens of three case studies. Case studies are a research approach used to gather information and capture holistic and meaningful events in individual or group real-life contexts (Yin, 2009).

The teachers followed research procedures that complied with the Code of Ethical Conduct for Research (Massey University, 2014) and that were endorsed by the Massey University Committee of Ethics before collecting information. Ethical considerations were met through the following principles and actions.

- Each teacher spoke to individual parents/whānau and children, and gained formal written and informed consent for their child to be involved in this research project.
- Each teacher considered the rights of each child and their family, ensuring confidentiality and privacy were maintained (Smith, 1998).

- All individuals had the right to withdraw from the research at any time.
- Information was kept secured and confidential.
- Parents and children gave permission for children's photos and first names to be shared with other teachers and to be included as resources for the purposes of this book. In one case study a pseudonym was used.

The information was gathered in 2011 by the above qualified teachers within their working contexts, located at various early childhood settings throughout Aotearoa New Zealand. The observations undertaken have been documented mainly through the use of learning stories, but also with anecdotal records, notes and photos (Carr, 2001; Dahlberg, Moss, & Pence, 2013). The key characteristics of giftedness and learning dispositions have been identified in each case study. All learning stories in this chapter are available to download at www.nzcer.org.nz/nzcerpress/giftedness.

Case study 1: Jackson

Age span of child during observation period: 6 months to 3 years 6 months

Curriculum links: *well-being, belonging, communicaton, contribution, exploration*

Gifted characteristics: advanced language and knowledge; highly imaginative, abstract, conceptual thinking; curiosity; heightened interpersonal awareness and an independent problem solver

Context

Jackson started at the Early Childhood Education and Care mixed-age centre at 6 months, and continued there until he was 5 years old. The strength of the mixed-age group was apparent in the positive way Jackson worked with others across the ages, learning through observation, peer tutoring, leadership and role modelling. As teachers noticed and recognised Jackson's learning, they responded to and shared this knowledge among the children, family/whānau and teachers, and used this as the basis for the programme to increase the complexity of Jackson's learning.

Jackson's portfolio provided an opportunity to work in partnership with parents and extended family as the teachers shared in his life and the community, documenting the learning while acknowledging and working with his skills, interests and dispositions to extend and challenge his understanding of the world he lives in. Jackson's portfolios were easily accessible for him to look at, enabling him to revisit and respond to his own and his peers' learning. This practice of ensuring access to portfolios encouraged child self-assessment and reflection.

Looking at learning: Jackson

Teachers noticed from the beginning that Jackson would become intensely interested in his surroundings and was able to sustain his interest when focused on a piece of equipment as he figured it out (see Figure 5.1). This continued throughout the time he attended the centre.

Giftedness in the early years: Informing, learning and teaching

Look at me walking

7/2/08

Jackson was walking along the barriers and stretching out to hold onto my legs. This made moving around difficult for both of us.

I brought the trolley over for him to see what happened. He stood up and was ready to push, I hovered close by ready to intervene if it moved too fast for him to control. Luckily the carpet slowed the speed of the trolley and Jackson walked from one end of kura to the other.

When he couldn't go any further he would turn his head to face me and then call out for assistance. I would help him to turn the trolley and then he would head in the other direction. By the end of the week he was starting to pull the trolley back and trying to turn its direction himself.

His perseverance is amazing as he completes the goals he sets himself. He sets himself very high expectations and challenges Wendy to help facilitate his achievement to his satisfaction.

Observer Wendy

How did Ben get up here?

Oct 2nd 2008

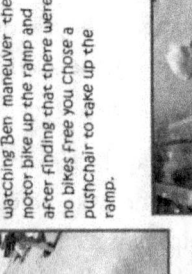
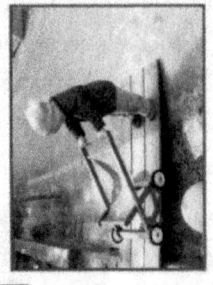

Jackson you had been watching Ben maneuver the motor bike up the ramp and after finding that there were no bikes free you chose a pushchair to take up the ramp.

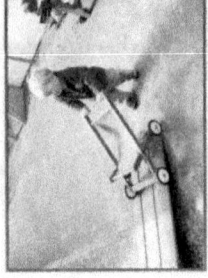
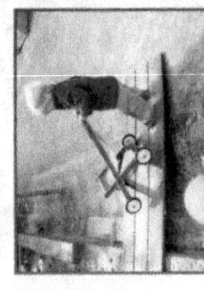

This was quite a challenge for you as the wheels kept falling over the edge. You brought this to Wendy's attention several times as you tested some of your own theories and strategies and Wendy's suggestions

Pulling, twisting and turning you finally managed to get to the top of the ramp.

Figure 5.1. Documenting the physical capabilities of a young toddler (age: 8 months)

The strength of Jackson's determination and belief in himself is shown in the narrative related to using the walking trolley at 8 months old. He demonstrated his belief in himself by pulling himself up to the handles, then, when in position, balancing his body, and with caution pushing the trolley forward by moving his feet one at a time, ensuring he maintained his balance as he moved. When there was an obstacle he took his time, moving the trolley in controlled movements to reposition it to move forward.

Jackson demonstrated his ability to persevere, concentrate intently on the task at hand and complete a goal he set himself. This was evident throughout the time he was at the centre, including the week following this narrative, when he noticed an interesting event at the other end of the centre. He stood up and walked to it, and continued to walk from this point on.

In the second narrative, Jackson at 16 months observed a 4-year-old riding a toy motorbike up and down a plank. Jackson watched until the child had finished, and followed up this idea by getting a pram and adapting the idea. He then tried to push it up the ramp. This took a great deal of patience, persistence, determination and belief that he could achieve this goal. Teacher support was provided through talking with Jackson when he became frustrated, and after repeating an action several times appeared to be going to give up. By providing suggestions on how the pram could be manoeuvred to resolve the problem, the teacher acknowledged that there was a problem while demonstrating respect and belief that Jackson had the ability to solve the problem himself. Many authentic learning experiences occurred at the centre, because the children were able to build respectful and trusting relationships across the age groups. The children were, building strong tuakana–teina (peer support) relationships, and were observed working alongside each other or with older children. Jackson, at only 16 months, was very advanced for his age to walk with the pram while negotiating the ramp and problem solving.

At around 3 years of age Jackson developed an intense interest in dinosaurs. This became incorporated into all aspects of his play and his relationships with the world around him as he took on the persona of different dinosaurs, in particular *T. rex*. Teachers recognised this interest and shared in his ever-growing knowledge, incorporating it into his literacy and technology skills through books and posters and introducing YouTube videos of dinosaurs and their living world. Jackson quickly picked up many names of different dinosaurs that were complex and hard to pronounce. He learnt about which dinosaurs were herbivores or carnivores and the defensive characteristics herbivores possessed to fend off attacking carnivores. Through his research and sharing his knowledge there were many opportunities for children and teachers to increase their understanding of these creatures, which provided opportunities for all the children to increase their understanding. Jackson enjoyed typing the names of the dinosaurs onto the computer, and after shared discussion with his parents he was provided with access to the family computer to extend his learning.

The learning story (Figure 5.2) written by one of the teachers showed that role play was a very intense part of the play used by Jackson to develop his understanding of the reality of being a dinosaur. He intently researched their size, shape, what they ate and how they interacted with each other, and dressing up became a daily ritual. In addition, Jackson increasingly demonstrated very strong feelings of right and wrong, showing very acute hearing and stepping in to right a perceived injustice. This combination of intense emotions required ongoing shared discussions with teachers and Jackson's family as teaching strategies were developed to support his learning while respecting the rights of other children.

The main effect for the children was that when Jackson dressed up as a *T. rex* he 'became' the dinosaur, with all its defences and fighting characteristics included. Through observation and recognising that this was occurring, it was negotiated with Jackson that he could be a *T. rex* as long as children were able to work with it, and that if they became frightened then he would need to be Jackson. This took time to negotiate and work through with the children, Jackson and parents, and provided the opportunity to talk together as a team in partnership with parents about the intensity of children's emotions and how this could be worked with. For gifted children this can be a very strong characteristic that takes time to understand and work with, as the child, family and teachers work together to develop a shared understanding.

Chapter 5: Looking at learning: Narratives of young gifted children

Figure 5.2. Jackson's teachers support literacy skills and technology interests

Giftedness in the early years: Informing, learning and teaching

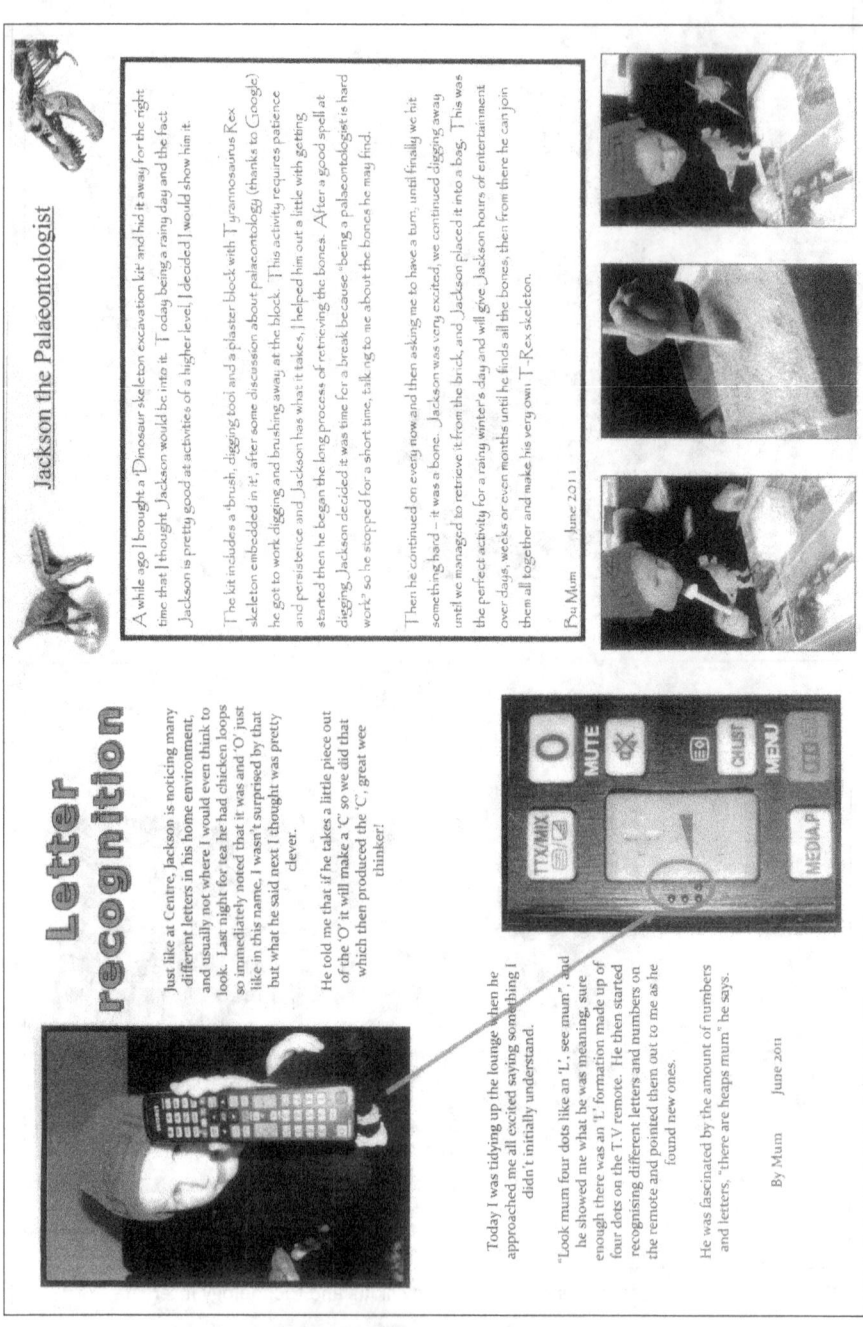

Figure 5.3. Jackson's parents share his interests from home with his teachers

The parent voices in the learning story narratives shown in Figure 5.3 demonstrate the link with home and centre, in terms of both listening to Jackson and following through on his understanding of the world around him. The learning stories also show the connections he was making as he worked in the different environments (Ministry of Education, 1996).

Parent voice was welcomed and valued, and involved daily discussion of Jackson's day from when he first started at the centre. This provided the opportunity to identify gifted characteristics and develop effective strategies, which ensured he was empowered to learn at his own pace through recognition of his dispositions, interests and strengths in order to provide a stimulating and challenging programme to support Jackson.

Jackson was recognised as being complex, capable, curious and intensely motivated in pursuing his search for complexity and connection in his learning during the time he attended the centre. The characteristics which were identified over this time included early achievement of developmental milestones, keen observation of the environment, deeper knowledge than other children, and quick learning. Jackson demonstrated his ability to use numbers in advanced ways, including the following characteristics of giftedness amongst those provided by Porter (2005); imaginative, creative problem solving; early comprehension; advanced speech; enjoyment of role play; early ability to play games with rules; leadership skills; early development of moral reasoning and judgment; non-conformity; emotional sensitivity; and intensity and responsiveness.

Assessment records had a strong focus on knowledge, skills, attitudes and dispositions, and the teaching team were able to provide continuity and increasingly complex provocations to extend his learning. Depth, intensity and quality of learning required varied and interesting experiences. This was provided through open-ended experiences, autonomous learning, experiences for discovery, and investigation with the opportunity of developing strategies for problem solving and to learn how to access reference resources (Harrison, 2004). Developing a partnership with the parents over the 4½ years he attended the centre provided opportunities to share and deepen the teachers' understanding of the child by linking home and centre. Teachers provided support and encouragement while respecting the parents' perspective, recognising that parents and families are experts who have extensive and significant knowledge and experience to contribute to the education and care of the young child (Porter, 2005). It was essential that all teachers were able to understand Jackson's thinking, depth and strength of emotions and how he worked with other children. His acute hearing was acknowledged and worked with in order to support his social development.

Communication began with non-verbal interactions as a young infant of 6 months, and evolved to Jackson being able to clearly articulate ideas and working theories, which he developed over the time he attended the centre. The portfolios of narratives were used by the child to revisit prior learning and to continue to develop or repeat experiences with other children and teachers as he engaged with the learning environment.

Support for the gifted child requires observant teachers, and parents and whānau to support the child's interests while developing a shared understanding and holistic view of the child. The reciprocal nature of constructive relationships between teachers, parents, whānau and children empowers all individuals as they increase their knowledge and understanding of learning, and in the process children's learning can be deepened and widened.

Case study 2: Dereck

Age span of child during observation period: 4 to 5 years

Curriculum links: *contribution, communication, exploration*

Gifted characteristics: leadership skills, intense interest, with sustained concentration, creativity, cultural abilities and qualities

Context

Dereck started kindergarten at the age of 4 years. He already knew a few other children because the kindergarten was close to his home, and he settled in well at first, but then he started getting upset more often. He liked to be the leader in group games, but his age peers did not listen to his many ideas, which at times involved a lot of talking. His peers began to ignore him and walk off, which threw him into despair and seemingly exaggerated grief every time this happened.

His prolonged crying was occasionally accompanied by aggressive behaviour, which the teachers found difficult to handle. Often this type of behaviour can mask the child's true characteristics, but it also indicated Dereck's more intense experiencing of these situations during his time at kindergarten.

Looking at learning: Dereck

One of Dereck's teachers knew about giftedness, in particular overexcitabilities (intensities – see Piechowski, 2006), noticed Dereck's prolonged distress, and decided to talk to his parents to find better ways to support him in situations he found stressful. The teacher followed the parent's example of removing him gently from the scene, acknowledging his sadness and calming him. This change of approach both acknowledged and supported Dereck: he felt safe and understood. With his well-being adjusted, Dereck opened up and began to look at the activities and resources the kindergarten had to offer, and he became increasingly interested in the Māori legends the teachers read to the children during mat times (see Figure 5.4). Bevan-Brown (2009) advocates for culturally responsive practice, and Dereck's case study documents an example of this practice in action.

The Battle of the Mountains

15-09-11 Dereck and Margot It began last week when Joseph wanted to read the legend of the Battle of the Mountains. At the back of the book were templates that could be photocopied and coloured and made into little models of the mountains. Jaquaydis insisted on making them so April photocopied them and various children coloured and made them. Dereck became interested in what was going on. At first he just asked to have the story read to him but by Tuesday this week he was getting the mountain models and using them to act out the story with a teacher or just with his friends. Dereck and the book became inseparable. He would carry it around with him all day long. By now he was getting to know the names of all the mountains and he knew exactly what was coming next in the story.

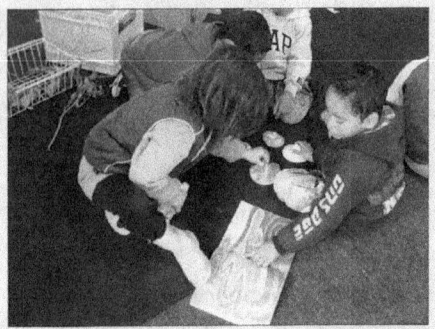

Today Dereck asked me to read the story again. He found the models and as I read the words, he would tell me which mountain had which name. The mighty Tongariro was his favourite. As the mountains in the story moved to different parts of New Zealand, Dereck moved the models into position on the carpet. When we finished the story I asked Dereck if he wanted to make his own mountains. He was very keen and brought me the book to photocopy the templates. I suggested that he draw his own and he wasn't too sure about that. I drew a circle on a piece of paper and gave it to him to cut out. He made a really great job of the cutting and then he found a coloured pencil that matched the colours of the picture of Tongariro that was in the book. He studied the picture closely and then began to draw beautiful koru patterns. Then he found a yellow pencil for Tongariro's eyes. I helped him cut a slit and staple Tongariro into a mountain shape. "I want to make that one now" he said and so he repeated the process all over again to make Taranaki. He chose the colours to match the book and added the details of eyes, mouth and snow on the peak. "I'm making the ones with the teeth now" he announced and Tauhara and Putauaki were created.

 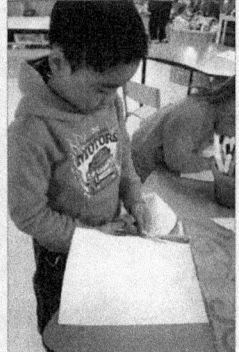

When your Mum came to pick you up this afternoon you very proudly showed her your work. She told us that you tell them all the story at home. Lucky family to have such a great storyteller.

16-09-11
Today Dereck asked me to read him the story again. He realised he was missing some of the models so I asked if he wanted to make a new one. He wanted to make a really big Tongariro so together with Tyson we sellotaped two pieces of paper together and drew and cut out an enormous circle. Tyson and Dereck added all the colours and details by studying the book. Tyson lost interest but Dereck stayed and added some coloured cellophane for the lava flows. What an amazing effort.

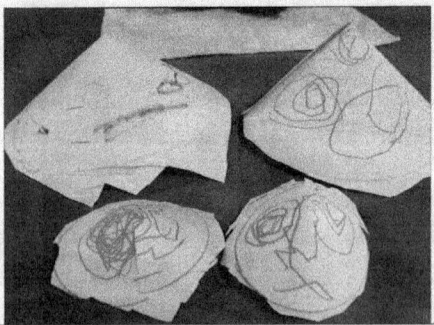

Dereck, you have found a real passion in the Legend of the Mountains. Every day you are keen to revisit the story and to make new models. You are taking your knowledge back home and sharing with your family too. I wonder if there is someone in your family who tells you about the legends of Aotearoa. You are a boy who is able to become deeply interested in a subject and then who can pursue that interest to deepen and build on his knowledge.

I have loved working with you and learning about the mountains. Next time your family goes to Taupo ask them to point out all the mountains and where they stand today. You can borrow our camera.

Figure 5.4: Dereck's intense interest and understanding of Māori legends

Interest in Māori legends

The children's book *The Battle of the Mountains* (Gossage, 2012), a story about the mountain group on the central plateau of New Zealand's North Island, became a favourite of Dereck and the other children. It included an activity with templates to cut out and decorate, and the children were able to act out the story. Dereck's strong interest was recognised, and a teacher encouraged him to make his own templates, which, after some initial hesitation, he did. He became increasingly captivated by the story and its description of mountains (volcanoes). He created and decorated them, and added features like lava flow, then he would re-enact the story with the props he had made. Extending on Dereck's interest further, one of the teachers suggested lending one of the kindergarten cameras to the family the next time they went for a visit to the town of Taupo so that Dereck could take photos of the volcanoes nearby there, since those mountains were at the heart of the story.

Through this focused interest Dereck displayed many characteristics that alerted the teachers to his giftedness. These included his long concentration span, his need to revisit learning experiences, and his desire to use newfound knowledge to other areas, such as literacy, numeracy, art, photography, geography and leadership. These characteristics connected to the teachers' reading of researchers in gifted education by Allan (2002), Bevan-Brown (2009) and Silverman (2013).

A couple of weeks after the initial conversations about New Zealand mountains, Dereck circled around the water tub at kindergarten and discovered a toy stingray. He took it out and went to the teacher to show her the 'North Island' of New Zealand, referring to the book *The Fish of Maui* (Gossage, 2011), another Māori legend that had been read at kindergarten. Together they placed the stingray on a large New Zealand map, and from there Dereck predicted the location of the kindergarten. Dereck also created a stingray out of play dough. He then formed a waka (Māori canoe), which he explained was "the South Island".

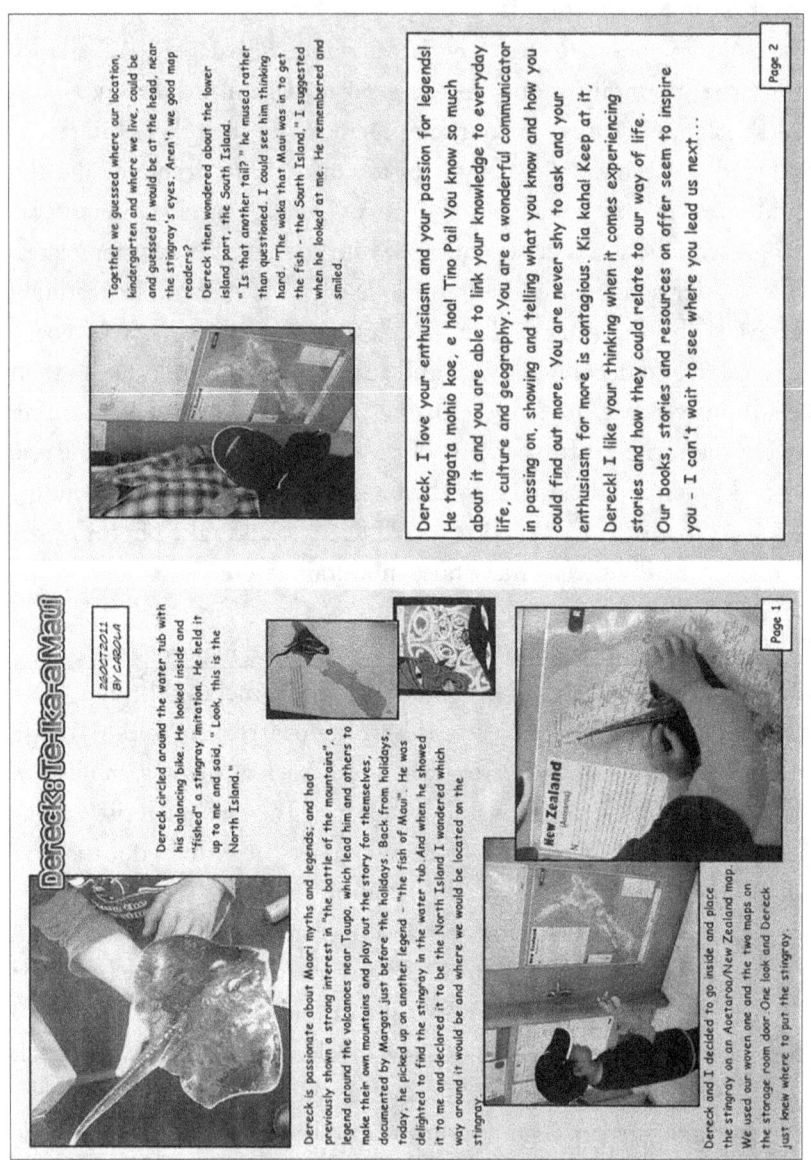

Figure 5.5. Dereck learning about the legend of the stingray

Dereck intensified his strong interest in Māori legends (see Figure 5.5). While the other children at kindergarten also had a passion for the legends, he was the only child taking it to this level. He played, created, analysed, and even questioned and performed the legends; for example, being Hatupatu from the book *Hatupatu and the Bird Woman* (Bacon & Dickinson, 1988). The teachers recognised his way of learning: making meaning of the world around him through the knowledge he had gained from Māori myths and legends—the stories of his culture (Ellwood, 2010; Mahaki & Mahaki, 2007). The teachers valued and supported his learning, and Dereck took pride in involving his peers, his family, his teachers and the community at kindergarten. The kindergarten's responsiveness made it possible for Dereck to explore his interest in and passion for Māori legends, which are important expressions of his culture.

Dereck's learning stories documented his outstanding abilities in storytelling, his knowledge and delight in the stories of his ancestors (which can be linked to whakapapa, or Māori genealogy), and his knowledge of the land of his people. These competencies can be linked to kaitiakitanga (guardianship), a specific characteristic of Māori giftedness (Mahaki & Mahaki, 2007). His teachers acknowledged and responded to Dereck by drawing on his interests, and by involving all the children at kindergarten and the family, as the early childhood curriculum expects for all children (Ministry of Education, 1996). Dereck's kindergarten has a high proportion of Māori and Pasifika children and aims to be a culturally responsive environment where teachers and families work closely together to achieve outcomes like Dereck's.

Dereck's interests and learning were promoted and documented with learning stories, anecdotal records, notes and photos, which were shared among his peers, teachers, family and community through his portfolio, and displays on tables (zigzag boards) and walls. Learning stories, together with all the other documentation in the portfolios as formative assessment, provide powerful tools for noticing, recognising and responding to interests, exceptional skills and ongoing learning if they are shared among all parties and include their voices (McLachlan, Edwards, Margrain, & McLean, 2013). For Dereck, this meant that his teachers, other adults working with him and other children were able to provide, adapt and modify learning experiences, and thereby provide appropriate challenges for further learning.

Case study 3: Emma

Age span of child during observation period: 3 - 4 years of age

Curriculum links: *Communication, Exploration*

Gifted characteristics: Very creative, intense interests, very articulate through oral langugae, long concentration span, persistence

Context

Emma commenced kindergarten at the age of 3 years. To begin with, at least once a week she would bring in a type of plant from her home garden or one that she had found on her way to kindergarten. Emma was outstanding at identifying plants as well as being able to label them and provide the correct name (see Figure 5.6). Some plants carried names that were two or three words long, and often the teachers had to ask Emma to repeat these names. This was an intense interest that stood out. Teachers began asking more questions about Emma's plants, which encouraged her to bring in more until it became a daily ritual. Often the reference books would be made available nearby, so that further investigation could continue with Emma. Other times a stroll around the kindergarten grounds would reveal a new plant or one similar to the one Emma had found.

Through developing this relationship during the plant interest, Emma showed other interests, and gifted traits started to become more evident. Because she could see that her interests were valued, this also created a sense of belonging within the setting for Emma, connecting to the early childhood curriculum strand of Mana Whenua – Belonging (Ministry of Education, 1996).

Chapter 5: Looking at learning: Narratives of young gifted children

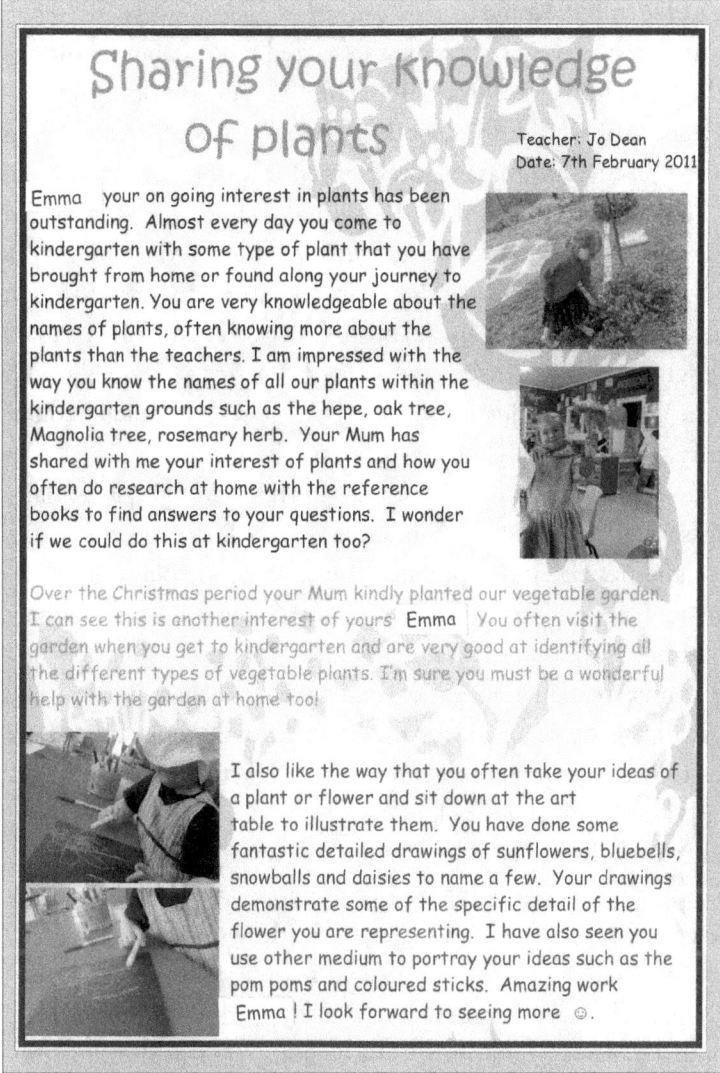

Figure 5.6. Emma shares her interest and knowledge of plants

Looking at learning: Emma

Emma was close to 1 year old before she started talking, but by the age of 2 she had a word bank of over 200 words. Through building a trusting and respectful relationship, vital information like this was shared between the teacher and parent, drawing on information recorded in Emma's Plunket book. One of the key gifted characteristics is a child displaying advanced skills in language development (Porter, 2005). Emma's advanced language development continued to grow through her intense interests, such as in plants and arts. When Emma talked about designing or painting, she was very descriptive, notably with clothes: the dress wasn't just pink or yellow; it was a "peach" colour with "puffy sleeves" and a "bodice with a twirly skirt".

Emma's approach to learning was through doing, particularly involving sensory experiences. Emma especially liked to create with paint, dye and pastels, and experiment through messy play with shaving foam and gloop. The transformation schema was very evident through Emma's exploration. Emma would often use a medium in a different approach than that anticipated by the teacher. Rather than applying paint to paper or an art medium, Emma would often have her hands fully covered in paint, embracing the tactile feel through her senses and transforming the look of her skin.

Emma was a holistic, visual learner, and she was drawn to experiences including art, drawing, cooking and creating things. Holistic learners often see things as a whole and prefer to do things as a whole, rather than breaking them down into components in order to understand them (Porter, 2005). This meant Emma could easily work on a project for 3 hours without a break. The stories below demonstrate this thinking process. Often when Emma was interrupted for tidy-up time, the undesirable behaviour would emerge. When teachers only see the consistent misbehaviour it can be difficult to make connections to the gifted traits.

Through the arts, Emma demonstrated a very good memory and could quickly recall stories and songs heard some time before. She enjoyed getting involved in dramatic play with props and her dolls and teddies. Through this dramatic play there emerged an interest in sewing and making clothes for her dolls and teddies (see Figure 5.7). Some clear dispositions were noted, such as her attention to detail, extended concentration and being highly attentive in terms of artistic expression.

Chapter 5: Looking at learning: Narratives of young gifted children

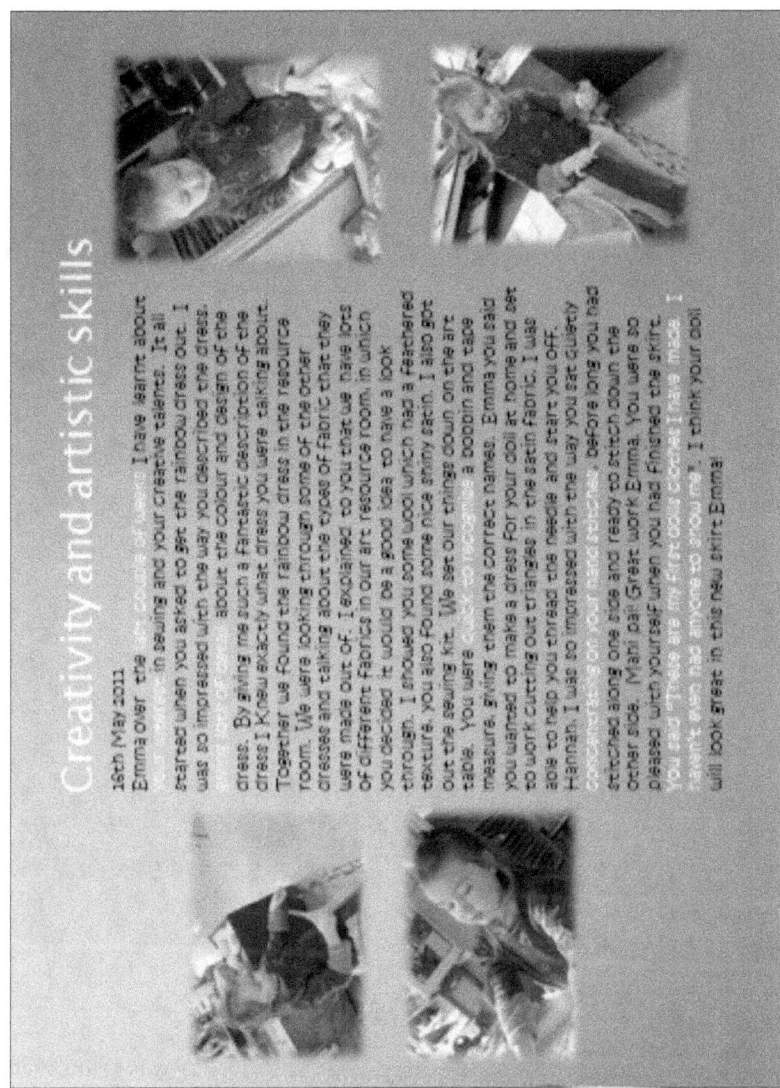

Figure 5.7. Showing a strong sense of creativity

Giftedness in the early years: Informing, learning and teaching

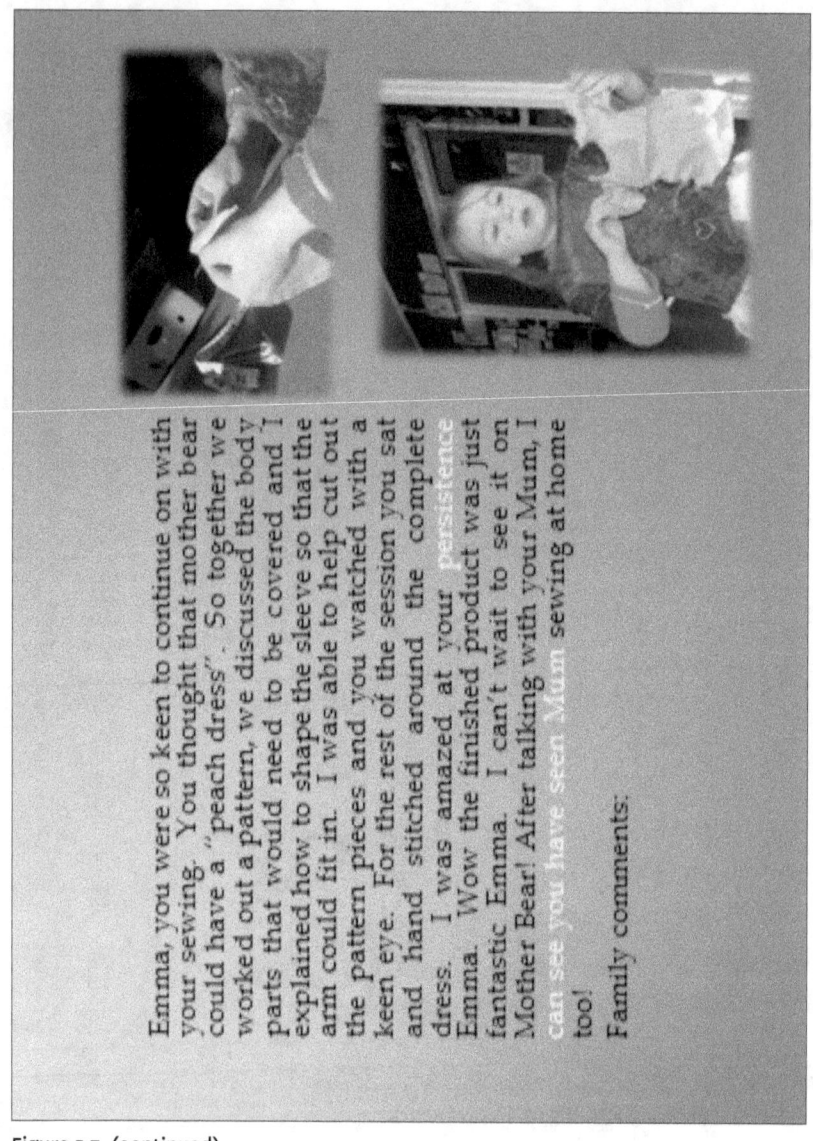

Emma, you were so keen to continue on with your sewing. You thought that mother bear could have a "peach dress". So together we worked out a pattern, we discussed the body parts that would need to be covered and I explained how to shape the sleeve so that the arm could fit in. I was able to help cut out the pattern pieces and you watched with a keen eye. For the rest of the session you sat and hand stitched around the complete dress. I was amazed at your persistence Emma. Wow the finished product was just fantastic Emma. I can't wait to see it on Mother Bear! After talking with your Mum, I can see you have seen Mum sewing at home too!

Family comments:

Figure 5.7. (continued)

Emma frequently showed an ability to be an independent problem solver, using prior knowledge and experiences to deepen her understanding. For example, she displayed a high level of planning and advanced thinking when it came to her interest in sewing. Planning would often start with a hand-drawn design, and then the tape measure would be located so that fabric could be measured (see Figure 5.8). Sometimes teddy would be placed on a piece of paper and traced around to create a pattern. Emma would carefully cut the fabric accordingly and then begin to start hand sewing. This creative interest continued to develop over a period of weeks. Emma returned to her hand sewing work—as well as planning and designing—almost daily. As the sewing advanced, Emma progressed to using the actual sewing machine confidently.

Emma could articulate her ideas and thinking very clearly. One way in which she demonstrated her understanding was through drawing. The example below shows Emma understanding the abstract concept of distance (see Figure 5.9). Through the narrative of 'Cinderella', which Emma had drawn, she showed Cinderella close up, so "you can't see her shoes here," but on the next page Emma went on to inform the teacher that "you can see the ceiling and the floor because Cinderella is far away". As Harrison (2010) notes, gifted children will often show an understanding of complex ideas, not always verbally but through visual representations. "Drawing is sometimes used as a means to explore the subtleties and complexities of human emotion, relationships and societal structures" (Harrison, 2010, p. 193).

Giftedness in the early years: Informing, learning and teaching

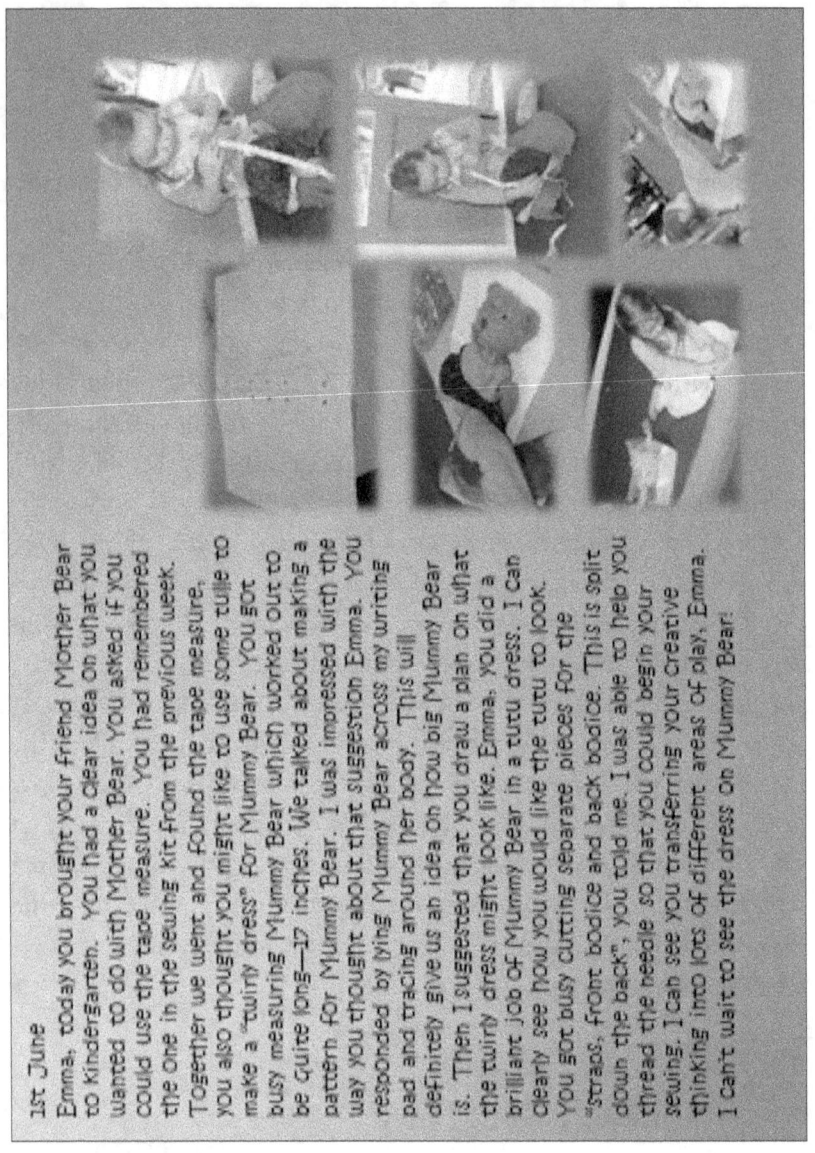

Figure 5.8: Developing a plan for Emma

The teachers recorded their observations and documented Emma's interests through narratives in learning stories. Over time they were alerted to some interesting behaviours, and it was then the suggestion was made to undertake further observations by using scales from *Identifying and Providing for Giftedness in the Early Years* (Allan, 2002). Only one teacher in the teaching team of five was familiar with this scale. The scale was used over a period of 3 months to capture Emma's learning style and strengths. The teachers worked alongside the parent because there were some indicators that were not as obvious within the setting but would be seen at home. It was also a way to compare information gathered in two different contexts. For example, the interactions between siblings showed that Emma had some understanding of things well enough to teach someone else. This was not evident in the educational setting, but was extremely consistent in the home environment.

Although the parents were beginning to realise that their child was quite advanced in a number of learning areas, the scale was a true record of Emma's gifted potential. This was something that could be shared with the new entrant teacher when it came time for Emma to transition to school.

Conclusion

Overall this chapter has provided insights for teachers to understand how gifted children's learning can be documented. It is not different from the strengths-based and holistic early years approach to children's assessment documentation in general, as discussed in Chapter 4:

> The curriculum builds on a child's current needs, strengths and interests by allowing children choices and by encouraging them to take responsibility for their learning. (Ministry of Education, 1996, p. 20)

This curriculum intent can be most effectively realised when teachers use dispositions, specific language and resources effectively to enhance children's learning. The learning stories and portfolio entries shared in this chapter are examples of the ways in which teachers can notice, recognise and respond to potential.

Giftedness in the early years: Informing, learning and teaching

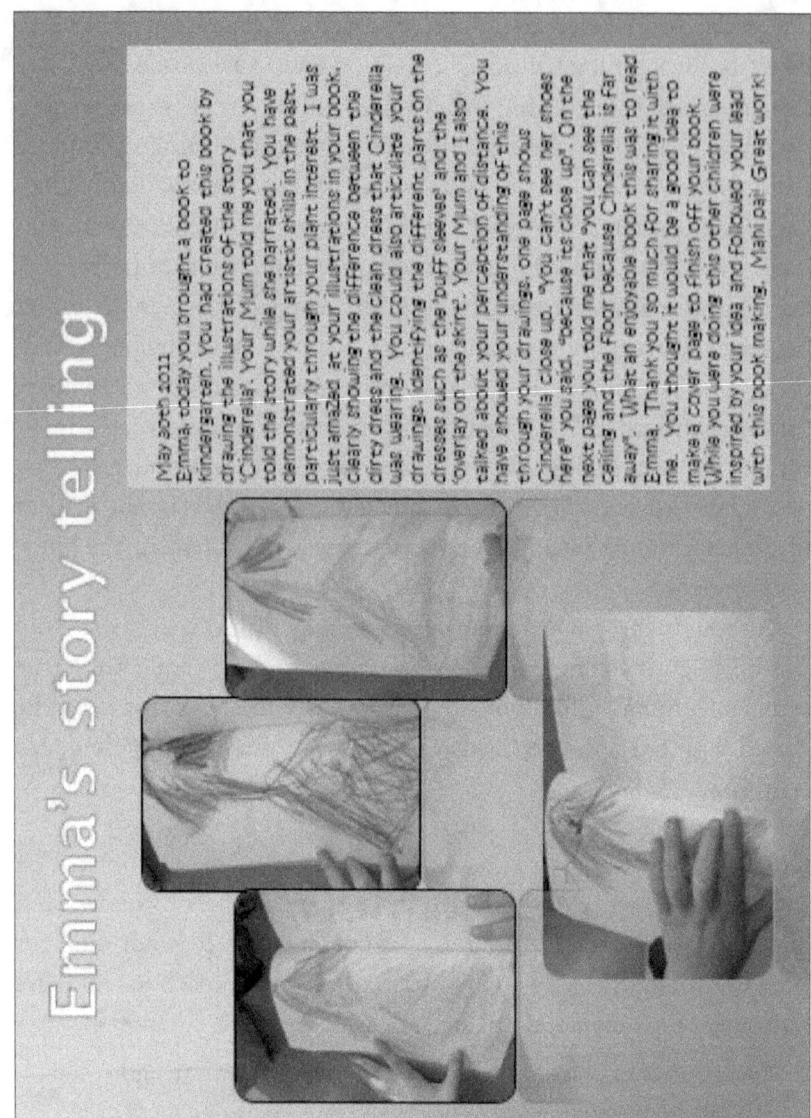

Figure 5.9: Demonstrating the concept of distance

References

Allan, B. (2002). *Identifying and providing for giftedness in the early years: The early years research and practice series.* Palmerston North: Kanuka Grove Press. Retrieved from http://gifted.tki.org.nz/Early-Childhood-Education-ECE/Identification

Bacon, R., & Dickinson, S. (1988). *Hatupatu and the bird woman.* Wellington: Waiatarua Publishing.

Bevan-Brown, J. (2009). Identifying and providing for gifted and talented Māori students. *Apex: The New Zealand Journal of Gifted Education, 15*(4), 6–20. Retrieved from http://www.giftedchildren.org.nz/apex/

Carr, M. (2001). *Assessment in early childhood settings: Learning stories.* London, UK: Paul Chapman.

Dahlberg, G., Moss, P., & Pence, A. (Eds.). (2013). *Beyond quality in early childhood education and care: Languages of evaluation* (3rd ed.). Abingdon, Oxon., UK: Routledge.

Ellwood, A. (2010). Caring for Papatuanuku: Yesterday, today and tomorrow. *Early Education, 47,* 19–22.

Gossage, P. (2011*). The fish from Maui.* Auckland: Puffin Group.

Gossage, P. (2012). *The battle of the mountains.* Auckland: Puffin Group.

Harrison, C. (2004). Giftedness in early childhood: The search for complexity and connection. *Roeper Review, 26*(2), 78–84.

Harrison, C. (2010). Visual representation of the young gifted child. *Roeper Review, 21*(3), 189–194.

Mahaki, P., & Mahaki, C. (2007). *Mana tu, Mana ora: Identifying characteristics of Māori giftedness.* Retrieved from http://gifted.tki.org.nz/For-schools-and-teachers/Cultural-considerations/Maori-students

Massey University. (2014). *Massey University code of ethical conduct for research, teaching and evaluations involving human participants.* Retrieved from http://humanethics.massey.ac.nz/pdf/muhec_code.pdf

McLachlan, C., Edwards, S., Margrain, V., & McLean, K. (2013). *Children's learning and development: Contemporary assessment in the early years.* Melbourne, VIC: Palgrave Macmillan.

Ministry of Education. (1996). *Te whāriki: He whāriki mātauranga mō ngā mokopuna o Aotearoa: Early childhood curriculum.* Wellington: Learning Media.

Piechowski, M. (2006). *"Mellow out," they say. If I only could: Intensities and sensitivities of the young and bright.* Madison, WI: Yunasa Books.

Porter, L. (2005). *Gifted young children: A guide for teachers and parents* (2nd ed.). Sydney, NSW: Allen & Unwin.

Silverman, L. K. (2013). *Giftedness 101.* New York, NY: Springer.

Smith, A. (1998). *Understanding children's development* (4th ed.). Wellington: Bridget Williams.

Yin, R. K. (2009). *Case study research: Design and methods* (4th ed.). Thousand Oaks, CA: Sage Inc.

Part 3: Supporting quality practice

Chapter 6: The myth busters: Fearless, inclusive teaching for young gifted children

Melanie Wong and Valerie Margrain

Introduction

As long ago as 1975 the New Zealand Association for Gifted Children's founding president, Peter Walters, provided the example of a 5-year-old whose teacher placed him with other children who were using emergent reading materials, despite the child having already taught himself to read to an advanced level. The teacher's reasoning was that the boy had to learn to participate with children his own age. What she failed to appreciate was that his advanced intellectual abilities made it very difficult for him to relate to other 5-year-olds, and that exposure to too-easy material was preventing him from learning at an appropriate level. This example provides an enduring lesson that we need to professionally critique and question our practices so that we do not continue to needlessly replicate history and perpetuate myths.

This chapter explores some common myths that teachers encounter in their daily practice in early years settings and considers some responses. Young children who are gifted come from all cultural and socioeconomic backgrounds, and so these children may be present in any educational setting. While many teachers are willing to cater for the individual needs of children, their practice can be impeded by myths and misconceptions about giftedness (Davidson, Davidson, & Vanderkarn, 2003), which create barriers for teaching and learning.

Common myths and responses in the early years

In addition to specific myths about giftedness (Porter, 2006; Zeigler & Raul, 2000), there is a more general myth that inclusive practice is effectively and universally implemented in early years settings. Inclusive practice is promoted by teachers, teacher educators and other professionals in the field as practice that includes everyone, but according to Wong (2013), the reality is that gifted children are nearly always overlooked. The New Zealand Government acknowledges 'priority learners' as children who have not successfully achieved in the school system, such as Māori and Pasifika learners, students from low socio-economic backgrounds, and children with special education needs (Education Review Office, 2012). So while inclusive practice accepts children who have disabilities or English as a second language, and those from diverse cultural backgrounds, it seldom extends to young children who are gifted (Kay, 2000; Kearney, 1996; Wong, 2013).

Why might teachers be overlooking gifted children and failing to meet their needs, despite applying the principle of inclusive practice? Insights can be found in the teachers' personal backgrounds, teaching experiences, cultural differences and/or levels of understanding of giftedness. All of these factors result in myths or erroneous beliefs being constructed in each teacher's personal understanding of giftedness. Our research, based on conversations held with teachers (Wong & Margrain, 2012), identified 16 dominant myths in the early years. These 16 myths, which are discussed in this chapter, were identified by teachers and sector leaders in the early years as being those most pertinent to giftedness within the early years sector. Our research included focus groups conducted in Auckland, Wellington and Christchurch in 2011 (Wong & Margrain, 2012), and analysis of a national survey of the early years sector (Margrain & Farquhar, 2012). In this chapter, to support early years teachers we describe the 16 myths, offer some responses to these myths, and connect the myths and responses to the research and literature. The aim is for this information to give teachers and child advocates the opportunity to re-frame their ideas about giftedness. (A summary of the myths and responses is given in Appendix F.)

Myth 1: Teachers know it all

Response: Learning is life-long, and information is being updated all the time.

Research: Under the "Commitment to the profession" requirement of the Code of Ethics for Registered Teachers (New Zealand Teachers Council, 2004), teachers need to continually develop an open and reflective professional culture. Furthermore, one of the registered teacher criteria developed by the New Zealand Teachers Council (2010) states that teachers need to reflect on their practice through engaging with evidence and literature. If a teacher thinks they know everything, then how can they be reflective, open to learn and able to meet the registered teacher criteria?

Myth 2: Preschoolers and new entrants are too young to be gifted

Response: Giftedness is evident in early childhood, and teachers should expect to find young gifted children across a range of domains.

Research: Gagné's (1995) Differentiated Model of Giftedness and Talent (DMGT) differentiates between innate, hereditary giftedness and talent that develops through practice, opportunity, experience and motivation. Therefore, giftedness is more likely to be seen in the early years than talent.

Myth 3: Teachers get adequate training

Response: Teachers deserve to receive professional development, support and resources to enable them to make a positive difference, but not all teacher education providers cover gifted education in their courses.

Research: The Ministry of Education (2012) has articulated a commitment to gifted and talented learners in its gifted education policy. However, little of the professional development provided has included the early childhood sector; for example, the earlier provision of gifted and talented advisors is for the school sector only. Kane et al. (2005), Riley and Rawlinson (2008) and Wong and Hansen (2012) found that very few New Zealand teachers had received explicit pre-service information about gifted children. In order to fulfil the commitment of meeting the principle in the revised 2012 policy it is our hope that this resource will provide a positive difference in terms of supporting teachers.

Myth 4: Very bright children don't need to be taught—they know everything already

Response: Gifted children may know more than their peers, but they don't know everything. They still need teachers to teach and guide them, and deserve enrichment and extension. Their passion for learning means they want to learn new things.

Research: Gifted children are able to develop a range of skills earlier than other children, but this does not mean they do not need to be taught. Gagné's (1995) DMGT highlights that if gifted children do not receive appropriate environmental support their giftedness may not develop and the children may not realise their potential.

Myth 5: Parents who think their children are gifted usually aren't right

Response: Parents are far more effective than teachers at correctly identifying giftedness.

Research: Porter (2006) cites a range of research studies that have accurately correlated parent identification with giftedness. Parents do not tend to 'over-nominate', whereas teachers do tend to 'under-nominate'. In Margrain's (2005) study of precocious readers, there were no parents who overestimated their child's reading competence.

Myth 6: Every parent wants their child to be gifted

Response: Parents are proud of their child and they want their child to do well at school, but this does not mean they want their child to be gifted.

Research: In Margrain's study of young gifted learners, parent expectations were not found to be élitist or even focused on academic success: the parents wanted their children to be happy, to have a positive childhood and to learn (Margrain, 2010).

Myth 7: Every child is gifted

Response: All children have areas of strength and competency, but these do not necessarily mean the child is gifted. While all children are unique, and all are able to learn, some are born with a predisposition towards exceptional performance in at least one area.

Research: Wong (2013) and Beresford (2008) describe the differences between children who are gifted and those who have strengths. Strengths can be developed over time, but giftedness is a natural ability that cannot be trained. Gagné's (2014) DMGT suggests that 10 percent of all individuals are innately gifted.

Myth 8: Gifted children have social problems and can't socialise

Response: Like-minded peers do not need to be the same chronological age. Gifted children often form strong relationships with adults and older children.

Research: Sampson (2013) has pointed out that young children who are gifted tend to have different characteristics from other children and often prefer the company of adults or older peers. While older children and adults are more willing to accept advanced abilities, younger children appear to have difficulties understanding the intense passions often associated with giftedness. Teachers play an important role in recognising the social and emotional characteristics of giftedness, facilitating interactions with like-minded peers and encouraging wider social acceptance and respect.

Myth 9: Gifted children's needs can be met by giving them more challenging resources

Response: Responding to gifted children requires engagement as well as resources.

Research: Breen (2008) encourages teachers and parents to prepare many hands-on activities and discussion topics, so that children are exposed to lots of different concepts and curriculum areas through interaction with their teachers and peers. This is effective pedagogy for all learners (Ministry of Education, 2007). Needham (2012) argues that teachers need to be aware of the characteristics of gifted and talented children, support social and emotional dimensions and well-being. Thus, understanding the individual child is important: it is not simply a matter of giving challenging resources.

Myth 10: Gifted children are difficult and challenging to teach

Response: Gifted children are no more difficult or easy to teach than others. All children need to be able to learn at their own pace and level. When young children engage in their learning they are likely to operate more autonomously.

Research: Gifted children bring passion, innovation, inspiration and leadership to early years settings (Davidson, 2012; Tomlinson, 2003). Nevertheless, some teachers find working with gifted children challenging because they do not understand them, or misunderstand challenging behaviour (Margrain & Farquhar, 2012; Murphy & Margrain, 2007). If teachers work on understanding the special characteristics of gifted children, and are willing to accept differences, then appreciation of gifted children should result. The Ministry of Education (2008) states that gifted children are like all other children: they need to be loved and supported in a nurturing, responsive learning environment so that their potential can be extended.

Myth 11: The parents of gifted children are usually challenging and demanding

Response: Parents are their children's advocates, but asking for an appropriate education for their child is often interpreted as being demanding.

Research: In *A Nation Deceived*, Colangelo, Assouline and Gross (2004) argue that although the parents of gifted children are entitled to expect curriculum differentiation, few parents approach schools with their concern due to the fear of being labelled "pushy". Margrain (2010, 2012) did not support the idea of parents as "pushy", hothousing or overly ambitious for their children, presenting these views as misunderstandings. Instead, the parents in her research were responsive, supportive advocates of children. However, they were fearful of the label "pushy" and of community misunderstanding.

Myth 12: Early years teachers know how to respond to children's strengths and interests

Response: Early years teachers need ongoing professional learning to understand the phenomenon of giftedness and to be exposed to current research in order to strengthen their teaching.

Research: Wong and Hansen (2012) and Margrain (2010) have argued that the strengths, interests and needs of young gifted children are not universally well understood or responded to in the early years. Breen (2008) has provided a range of practical approaches that early childhood teachers can use in their work with gifted children. Combining specific knowledge about giftedness with the inclusive and strengths-based approach of *Te Whāriki* (Ministry of Education, 1996) offers positive opportunities.

Myth 13: Children in junior primary can't be accelerated.

Response: There are many valid ways to appropriately accelerate children's learning at any age.

Research: Acceleration approaches can include: ensuring that the child has access to content at a more advanced level within the class; accepting that content will be mastered more rapidly than for age-peers; and supporting the child in advanced placement for all or part of the day. In Margrain's (2005) study of early readers, she followed four of the children in the study as they transitioned to school, and three of the children had diverse but positive experiences of acceleration. One child was placed with older children for literacy and numeracy components of the day. Two of the other children worked on advanced and enriched content, but within a class of same-age peers. In each of these three cases the teachers considered the emotional needs of the child as well as their academic capability, but ensured that advanced content was offered in some form. The fourth child was not given any opportunity for acceleration due to the beliefs of the class teacher.

Myth 14: Gifted children have to do the basics in case they miss out on something important

Response: Gifted learners learn faster and make connections in ways that others don't. Learning "the basics" should be part of complex conceptual thinking, not the focus of the learning.

Research: Frustration experienced by gifted children has long been highlighted, with Hollingworth noting back in 1942 that in the regular primary school classroom, moderately gifted children wasted almost half their time and exceptionally gifted children almost all their time. Gifted children often 'catch on' to the basics well ahead of other learners of the same age, and are able to apply basic knowledge in a way that appears almost intuitive (Colangelo, et al., 2004).

Myth 15: Giftedness only relates to academic success.

Response: Giftedness manifests itself across many areas, including physical, spiritual and cultural areas, the arts and the interpersonal domain.

Research: The Ministry of Education (2012) states, "It is now generally accepted that the gifted and talented are not only those with high intelligence" (p. 23). Current approaches to gifted education recognise that giftedness includes general intellectual abilities, specific academic aptitude, cultural abilities and qualities, creative abilities, social and leadership abilities, physical abilities, emotional and spiritual qualities, and abilities in the visual and performing arts.

Myth 16: Young children should be playing and having fun, not being 'hot-housed'

Response: When young gifted children are able to acquire early and advanced knowledge without this being induced by adults, this is not hot-housing.

Research: Sigel (1987, cited in Margrain, 2007) defines hot-housing as "the process of inducing infants to acquire knowledge that is typically acquired at a later developmental level" (p. 212). Parents who respond to their children are being supportive, but Margrain (2005) found that teachers often negatively misunderstood parent support. Furthermore, young children who are gifted do play, but in complex ways (Murphy, 2005). See Chapter 3 of this book for further discussion on play.

Case study: Why inclusive, evidence-based response is important (a case study from Margrain, 2005)

David loved computers with a passion. At his kindergarten he helped the teachers when they had trouble setting up the computer for other children. At home he cracked the password on his mother's work laptop. When David was 4 years old he told his parents that he wanted to go to the same computer-based maths after-school classes that his sister attended. His mother asked the organisation if he could enrol, but was told that no enrolments were accepted under the age of 7. David's mother explained that he was a gifted child with a strong ability in maths and using computers, and with a strong attention span, but the organisation still said no. Eventually, after further negotiation, the organisation accepted David on a trial basis, on condition that if he did not stay focused then he would be asked to leave but his mother would still have to pay the full term's fee.

That never happened and David loved his classes, talking about them to all who would listen, including his kindergarten teachers. When the kindergarten teachers heard about David's attendance at these classes they assumed that he was being 'forced' into academic after-school activities as 'hot-housing.' They felt sorry for him that he was being 'deprived' of his childhood and not having any time to play. The reaction of the kindergarten teachers showed their assumption that a maths computer activity was oppositional to play, although in fact it provided exactly the conceptual and advanced play with ideas that David craved. The reaction of the maths computer class organisers showed their misunderstanding of the capabilities of gifted children. The actions of David's mother as a supportive, responsive advocate for her child were misunderstood, and it was assumed that she was both coercing him to overachieve and depriving him of age-appropriate activities.

Becoming fearless as an inclusive early years advocate

This section is informed by the current doctoral research of the first author (Wong). Her doctoral study investigates how associate teachers support practicum student teachers in their work with gifted and talented children. Associate (supervising) teachers are the focus of her project because evidence clearly demonstrates that associate teachers have a significant impact on the professional development of student teachers (Clarke & Jarvis-Selinger, 2005). Wong's in-progress preliminary findings indicate that once teachers realise they should cater for gifted children, they seem to agree with the notion that they should provide support and differentiate practice—though more often than not they initially don't know how to proceed.

Wong's research also investigates an ITE (initial teacher education) programme that prepares student teachers to work with gifted and twice-exceptional children while continuing to work with children who do not have identified special needs and abilities. This ITE programme is being developed in partnership with early years practitioners and teacher educators in Aotearoa New Zealand. Information gathered from Wong's current research—and from the views of parents of gifted children in several different countries, including the US, Canada, Australia, Indonesia and Aotearoa New Zealand (e.g., Chellapan & Margrain, 2013)—supports the view that it is essential that early years settings have a flexible approach to delivering the curriculum, and an inclusive philosophy.

Inclusive philosophy

Best practice is based on an inclusive philosophy: that is, all children have a right to learn, and to be accepted, respected and supported. The data analysed thus far from Wong's current research suggest that whether the special learning needs of gifted children are being met very much depends on the teachers' understanding of and attitudes towards gifted education. This situation is even more so for twice-exceptional children, who not only are gifted but also have some disability.

An early years practitioner participating in Wong's in-progress research said that it is important that

> gifted children and their families have access to flexible learning environments; for example, technology and that the centre provide avenues for appropriate pacing, acceleration, and adequate growth.

Another participant said that teachers need to understand

> inclusive approaches towards ensuring that these children are offered appropriate learning programmes and the importance of this; also

the way that gifted learning can be disguised or misunderstood. ... however, I also think that the teacher's view of the child, that of a capable and competent learner, is fundamentally important.

A programme leader in an ITE programme said that responsive teaching is not just about setting out general resources, but also about knowing the children well, responding individually, and ensuring that learning opportunities are open ended.

> I mean by truly responding to the needs of the child. Whereas often you go into centres and things are already set up on tables, and while we [teachers] respond to your [children's] needs as long as they are kind of fitting in with the things that I've got available ... on the tables. The resources and set-up need to be open ended, depending on children's interests and needs.

The early years sector is one that espouses a commitment to principles of inclusion, respect, partnership and competence throughout almost all policy and research. We argue that "all" must indeed include everyone. Evidence shared throughout this book, including the Chapter 10 case study, indicates that we still have more work to do.

Curriculum commitment to inclusion for all

New Zealand's curriculum for early childhood education, *Te Whāriki* (Ministry of Education, 1996), does not explicitly mention gifted education, even though it does provide some information about inclusive education. Instead, it advocates for meeting the learning needs of a diverse range of children with the statement that "equitable opportunities for learning" need to be provided that "recognise, acknowledge, and build on each child's special strengths" (Ministry of Education, 1996, p. 64). Bevan-Brown and Taylor (2008) suggest that references to special needs in *Te Whāriki* could also be considered to refer to gifted children. Meanwhile, *The New Zealand Curriculum*, which is written for school-aged children, aims to "be flexible enough to encompass ... the need for challenge as a medium for growth" (Ministry of Education, 2007, p. 21).

The importance of promoting inclusion is not just about welcoming all children to the setting. It is also about access, participation and support (Division for Early Childhood of the Council for Exceptional Children, 2009). Children in early childhood settings, for example, can be included in all learning opportunities and their families included too, so that they feel a sense of belonging in the setting. Teachers should celebrate children's differences regardless of each child's ability to extend their potential.

In the school sector, in addition to the curriculum documents, the New Zealand Government has set out its National Education Goals (NEGs) in its National Education Guidelines (Ministry of Education, 2009c) and directed how it expects these goals to be met through its National Administration Guidelines (NAGs) (Ministry of Education, 2013). NAG 1 states that each board of trustees, through the principal and staff, is required to foster student achievement by providing teaching and learning programmes and assessment practices that incorporate *The New Zealand Curriculum*. A commitment to inclusion is inherent in NEG 1, which refers to "the highest standards of achievement through programmes which enable all students to realise their full potential" (Ministry of Education, 2009c). The reference to "all students" requires schools to provide learning opportunities that will allow children with different backgrounds and abilities to satisfactorily participate in the classroom environment.

Some researchers have noted that despite understanding the inclusive intent of the curriculum, many teachers have had limited explicit instruction in their initial teacher education programme on how to cater for gifted children (Kane et al., 2005; Riley & Rawlinson, 2008; Wong & Hansen, 2012). The consequence of having little guidance in the curriculum documents, along with teacher education programmes that pay scant attention to introducing gifted education, is that many teachers are wary of the concept of giftedness. Murphy (2004) argues for the importance of teacher education programmes, including relevant, current information regarding gifted education, in order for student teachers to gain a deeper understanding. Many teachers may not be able to recognise gifted children with whom they work, let alone include them in their current suite of professional practices.

Enacting the philosophy of inclusion
Every teacher has their own teaching philosophy and beliefs, which are influenced by their knowledge and experiences with children, and so a philosophy should evolve with experience and over time.

A teacher's attitudes towards gifted and twice-exceptional children are directly influenced by their philosophy (Kemp, 2014; Sutherland, 2012; Tungaraza, Sutherland & Stack, 2013). Early years teachers and academics who are passionate about gifted education have usually had personal or teaching experiences with gifted and twice-exceptional children.

Teachers in the early years commonly use the three-step practice of 'notice, recognise and respond' when assessing for learning (Ministry of Education, 2009a). Many teachers believe they are capable of working with all children, but if they don't know how to identify gifted and twice-exceptional children and their characteristics, how can they properly notice, recognise and respond to these children? Some teachers don't feel confident working with gifted children, even when they know these children have different learning needs. Teachers may feel overwhelmed because they don't have a working understanding of the concepts of the giftedness, or they may see these children as challenging because they don't understand the characteristics of these children. Instead, many teachers prefer to ignore such children, or look at their needs negatively. Negative attitudes and practices of avoidance may affect children's interest in learning and cause challenging behaviours. Both authors of this chapter have heard negative attitudes and comments about gifted children and families from schools, early childcare settings and communities.

A number of participants in Wong's doctoral research so far indicate that ongoing professional development is essential if teacher attitudes are to change and if the needs of gifted children are to be met. V, an initial teacher education programme leader, stated:

> So, certainly professional development as a structure to help teachers who are now in the field; they [be]come familiar with the concept … able to think about how we can go back into our centre and develop a policy and look at our practices, those sorts of things with that kind of PD [professional development] is probably really helpful to early childhood teachers.

Another teacher educator explained:

> We do it [learn about giftedness] in such a small part of our programme. It's just this teeny drop in their programme that, unless it's a particular student's passion, they didn't go on to do anything with it after graduation.

Thus, in-service training and professional development have an important role in fostering the growth of teachers to improve children's learning. Educational settings need to support professional development so that teachers can continue to strengthen their practice throughout their careers. Again, we suggest the Government needs to demonstrate its commitment to inclusive education by ensuring professional development is available for teachers who work with gifted children in the early years.

Becoming fearless in supporting gifted children: an illustrative model

The model provided in Figure 6.1 illustrates the point that teachers need to be supportive of gifted children The model was developed after analysing data collected from Wong's doctoral research. The model includes different dimensions of how teachers may be able to better understand how they can effectively support the special learning needs of gifted children. Although this model may be relevant to other education sectors, the specific focus here is on teachers working in early years education. The original stimulus for creating this model was an appreciation that the catalysts noted in Gagné's (2004, 2014) Differentiated Model of Giftedness and Talent (DMGT) could be drawn upon to better understand the challenges inherent in teaching gifted children.

Chapter 6: The myth busters: Fearless, inclusive teaching for young gifted children

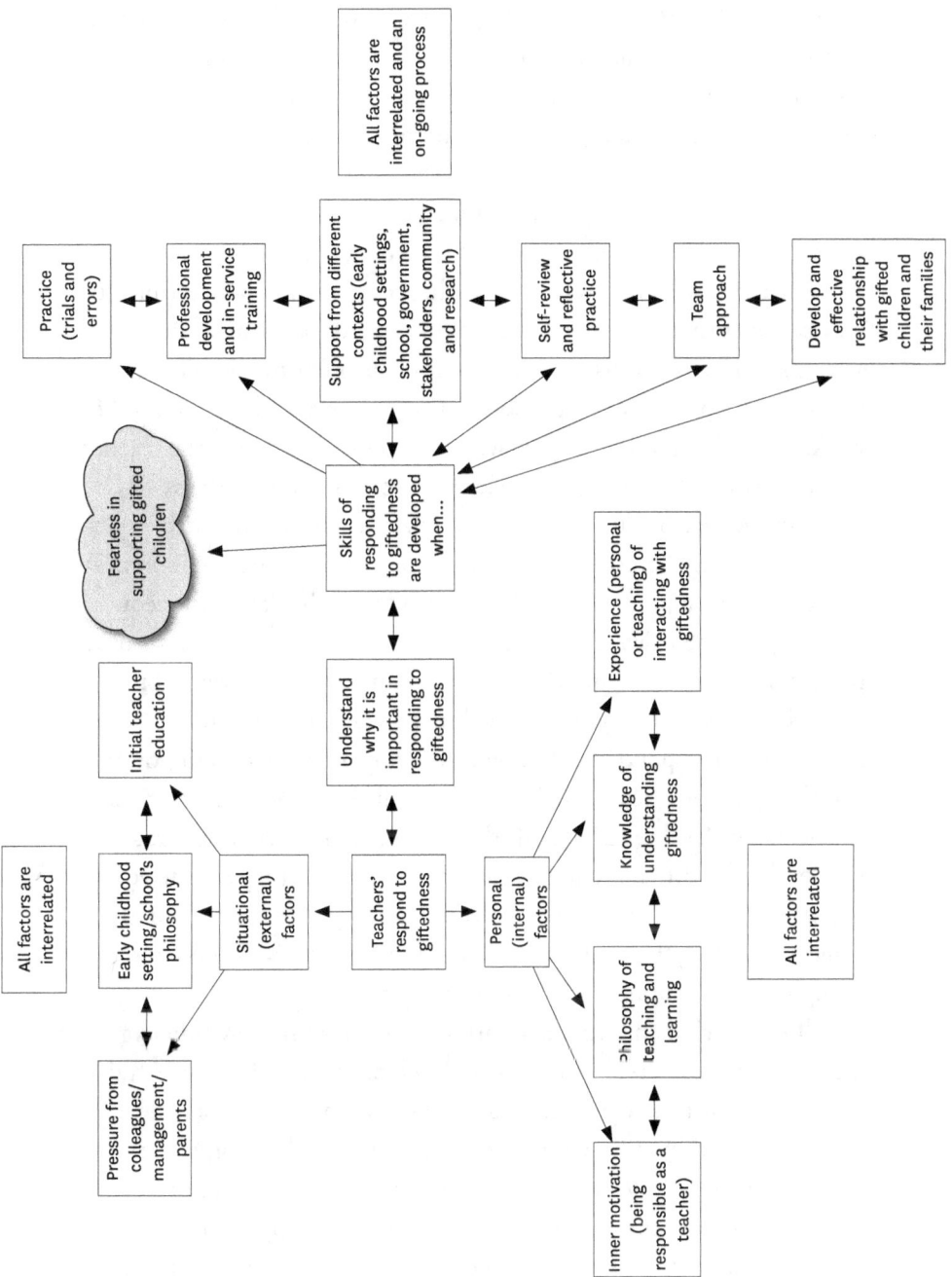

Figure 6.1. Becoming fearless in supporting gifted children: an illustrative model
Source: Wong, 2014 ©

Figure 6.1 illustrates that both personal (internal) and situational (external) factors influence early childhood teachers' realisation that they need to respond to gifted children. Various factors and diverse experiences tend to shape a teacher's initial starting point in their journey in gifted education. For example, the teacher may be puzzled by a child's behaviour, or notice that a child has more intense demands than other children. Perhaps the parent of a gifted child wants to make sure that her child will be catered for in their early childhood settings, or may consider that her gifted child's needs are not being met. Or maybe a parent raises concerns or asks for different help for her child. The philosophy of the early childhood setting or school where the teacher works, as well as guidance by colleagues, might also inspire the teacher or management to develop practice in responding to giftedness.

Figure 6.1 also illustrates the fact that teachers start with a personal philosophy and their current knowledge about gifted children. A teacher's starting point may be influenced by the initial teacher education programme in which they trained, and/or it may be informed by their own experiences, and this starting point could be positive or negative. Teachers on this journey need first to develop their understanding of how to respond to giftedness and why a response is important, and then gain practical experience. Through their teaching experience, teachers can develop skills and ideas about useful teaching strategies for developing differentiated learning experiences. They also have the opportunity to reflect on sociocultural stereotypes, stigma and challenges, including the mistaken belief that giftedness is limited to those of high socioeconomic background (Ballam, 2013)

All of the elements that support skills development within Figure 6.1 must be considered. Professional development and in-service training are needed to strengthen teaching and learning. Teachers deserve to be supported by different contexts, such as their colleagues, the settings in which they teach, the government, and their community and stakeholders. A team approach is important for supporting teachers' development, and it should be noted that if the team is not continually focused on providing for giftedness, a single teacher is unlikely to be able to effectively support gifted children and their families. Teachers can draw on their broader skills as reflective practitioners, using a self-review approach (Ministry of Education, 2009b) and reflective practice to grow and improve their quality of practice. As part of that reflection they can consider whether planned practices are informed by sound research and evidence (Walsh, Kemp, Hodge & Bowes, 2012).

Finally, another important element in the provision of quality gifted education is to create and maintain an effective relationship with gifted children and their families. If teachers want to support gifted children and their families, then the teachers must first know about them. Key aspects of effective pedagogy include understanding who the gifted children are, and acknowledging their individuality (Cathcart, 1994). Letting all involved in the support partnership (families, teachers and children) know that others are there to provide support is also fundamental Once a relationship is established, teachers can respond efficiently to the needs of young children who are gifted.

Case study of student teacher learning

Giselle is a student teacher on the final practicum of her initial teacher education programme. Her teaching philosophy for this practicum includes supporting inclusive practice. Giselle has attended several hours of classes about giftedness during her programme of study. During this practicum Giselle realised there was a 3½-year-old child in the kindergarten who learns differently from other children. This child has advanced language abilities and is able to talk about different sea creatures in great detail. Also, the child tends to play with older children or teachers and gets annoyed when presented with repeated activities. Giselle spent some time with this child and wrote down her observations. She discussed this child's learning and interests with other teachers and suggested they search for more information about giftedness in preschool children. However, none of the teachers at the kindergarten believe that giftedness can be found in the early years. One teacher said to Giselle that if the child is gifted, she does not need help—she can learn by herself.

Giselle strongly believes that in terms of supporting inclusive practice—as well as acknowledging her own teaching philosophy—she believes that she needs to notice and recognise gifted children as well as respond to each child based on their needs and interests. Giselle searched for information on the Ministry of Education websites about identifying and supporting gifted children. Before she finished her practicum she had developed a very positive relationship with this child and very much enjoyed the time interacting with them. Other teachers at the kindergarten were amazed with Giselle's practice, and the teachers are now beginning to look for professional development opportunities relating to gifted education. Giselle also made a commitment to herself that, after completing her initial teacher training, she is going to enrol in a postgraduate qualification in gifted education.

Conclusion

Misunderstandings undoubtedly work against opportunities to support gifted children in early years settings and can create harmful constraints to learning and the development of relevant and meaningful provision. Misplaced beliefs, such as those identified in this chapter as being dominant in the early years, can limit the ability of well-intentioned teachers to meet the individual needs of gifted children. If teachers had better professional learning opportunities to support the development of a stronger understanding of giftedness and relevant research, they would be more empowered to tackle the aforementioned myths. Through the enactment of an inclusive philosophy and the development of professional assessment and teaching skills, teachers can recognise and respond to young children's strengths and abilities. Teachers who respond constructively to every child's strengths and abilities will make a positive difference. The model shared by Wong in this chapter illustrates that when experience, philosophy, reflection, research evidence, professional learning, expert guidance and support are present, teachers have the potential to be influential, and to be fearless in their advocacy for and practice with young gifted children.

References

Ballam, N. D. (2013). *Defying the odds: Gifted and talented young people from low socioeconomic backgrounds*. Unpublished doctoral thesis, The University of Waikato. Retrieved from http://researchcommons.waikato.ac.nz/handle/10289/8424

Beresford, L. (2008). *The need for recognition of gifted new entrants*. Paper presented at the New Zealand Association for Gifted Children Conference, Auckland. Retrieved from http://www.giftedchildren.org.nz/agm08/lynntxt.pdf

Bevan-Brown, J., & Taylor, S. (2008). *Nurturing gifted and talented children: A parent–teacher partnership.* Wellington: Ministry of Education.

Breen, S. (2008). *How to cater for very bright pre-schoolers: The Small Poppies way*. Retrieved from http://www.giftededucation.org.nz/artandpub.html

Cathcart, R. (1994). *They're not bringing my brain out*. Auckland: REACH Publications.

Chellapan, L., & Margrain, V. (2013). "If you talk, you are just talking. If I talk is that bragging?": Perspectives of parents with young gifted children in New Zealand. *Apex: The New Zealand Journal of Gifted Education, 18*(1). Retrieved from http://www.giftedchildren.org.nz/apex.

Clarke, A., & Jarvis-Selinger, S. (2005). What the teaching perspectives of cooperating teachers tell us about their advisory practices. *Teaching and Teacher Education, 21*, 65–78.

Colangelo, N., Assouline, S. G., Gross, M. U. M. (2004). *A nation deceived: How schools hold back America's brightest students.* Iowa City, IA: Connie Belin & Jacqueline N. Blank International Center for Gifted Education and Talent Development, University of Iowa.

Davidson, J. E. (2012). Is giftedness truly a gift? *Gifted Education International, 28*(3), 252–266. doi:10.1177/0261429411435051.

Davidson, J., Davidson, B., & Vanderkarn, L. (2003). *Genius denied: How to stop wasting our brightest young minds.* New York, NY: Simon & Schuster.

Division for Early Childhood of the Council for Exceptional Children. (2009). Early childhood inclusion: A summary. *Young Exceptional Children, 53*(1), 52–53.

Education Review Office. (2012). *Evaluation at a glance: Priority learners in New Zealand schools.* Retrieved from http://www.ero.govt.nz/National-Reports/Evaluation-at-a-Glance-Priority-Learners-in-New-Zealand-Schools-August-2012/Background

Gagné, F. (1995). From giftedness to talent: A developmental model and its impact on the language of the field. *Roeper Review, 18,* 103–111.

Gagné, F. (2004). Transforming gifts into talents: The DMGT as a developmental theory. *High Ability Studies, 15*(2), 119–147.

Gagné, F. (2014). *Differentiated model of giftedness and talent* (DMGT). Retrieved 20 November 2014, from: http://www.gagnefrancoys.wix.com/dmgt-mddt

Hollingworth, L. S. (1942). *Children above 180 IQ Stanford-Binet: Origins and development.* Yonkers, NY: World Book.

Kane, R. G., Burke, P., Cullen, J., Davey, R., Jordan, B., McCurchy-Pilkington, C., et al. (2005). *Initial teacher education policy and practice.* Wellington: Ministry of Education.

Kay, K. (Ed.). (2000). *Uniquely gifted: Identifying and meeting the needs of twice exceptional students.* Gilsum, NH: Avocus Publishing.

Kearney, K. (1996). *Highly gifted children in full inclusion classrooms.* Retrieved from http://www.hollingworth.org/fullincl.html

Kemp, C. (2014). Inclusion in early childhood. In P. Foreman, & M. Arthur-Kelly (Eds.), *Inclusion in action* (4th ed., pp. 411–456). South Melbourne, Australia: Cengage Learning.

Margrain, V. G. (2005). *Precocious readers: Case studies of spontaneous learning, self-regulation and social support in the early years.* Unpublished doctoral thesis, Victoria University of Wellington.

Margrain, V. (2007). Inside the greenhouse: Hothousing, cultivating, tending or nurturing precocious readers? *New Zealand Research in Early Childhood Education Journal, 10*, 33–45.

Margrain, V. (2010). Parent–teacher partnership for gifted early readers in New Zealand. *International Journal about Parents in Education, 4*(1), 39–48.

Margrain, V., & Farquhar, S. (2012). The education of gifted children in the early years: A first survey of views, teaching practices, resourcing and administration issues. *Apex: The New Zealand Journal of Gifted Education, 17*(1). Retrieved from http://www.giftedchildren.org.nz/apex

Ministry of Education. (1996). *Te whāriki: He whāriki mātauranga mō ngā mokopuna o Aotearoa*. Wellington: Learning Media.

Ministry of Education. (2007). *The New Zealand curriculum*. Wellington: Learning Media.

Ministry of Education. (2008). *Nurturing gifted and talented children: A parent–teacher partnership*. Wellington: Learning Media.

Ministry of Education. (2009a). *Kei tua ō te pae—Background*. Wellington: Learning Media.

Ministry of Education. (2009b). *Self-review tools for teachers*. Retrieved from http://nzcurriculum.tki.org.nz/National-Standards/Self-review-tools/Teachers

Ministry of Education. (2009c). *The National Education Goals (NEGs)*. Retrieved from http://www.minedu.govt.nz/theMinistry/EducationInNewZealand/EducationLegislation/TheNationalEducationGoalsNEGs.aspx

Ministry of Education. (2012). *Gifted and talented students: Meeting their needs in New Zealand schools*. Retrieved from http://gifted.tki.org.nz/

Ministry of Education. (2013). *The National Administration Guidelines (NAGs)*. Retrieved from: http://www.minedu.govt.nz/theMinistry/EducationInNewZealand/EducationLegislation/TheNationalAdministrationGuidelinesNAGs.aspx

Murphy, C. L. (2004). Teachers' perceptions of the play patterns and behaviours of young children who are gifted, in an early childhood setting. *New Zealand Research in Early Childhood Education, 7*, 57–72.

Murphy, C. L. (2005). *Play patterns and behaviours of young children who are gifted in an early childhood setting*. Unpublished master's thesis, Massey University.

Murphy, C., & Margrain, V. (2007). Do roosters have chins?: Insights into parenting a gifted child. *The First Years Nga Tau Tuatahi: New Zealand Journal of Infant and Toddler Education, 9*(1), 16–20.

Needham, V. (2012). Primary teachers' perceptions of the social and emotional aspects of gifted and talented education. *Apex: The New Zealand Journal of Gifted Education, 17*(1). Retrieved from http://www.giftedchildren.org.nz/apex

New Zealand Teachers Council. (2004). *Code of ethics for registered teachers*. Retrieved from http://www.teacherscouncil.govt.nz/content/code-ethics-registered-teachers-0

New Zealand Teachers Council. (2010. *Registered teacher criteria*. Retrieved from http://www.teacherscouncil.govt.nz/sites/default/files/Registered-Teacher-Criteria-%28English%29.pdf

Porter, L. (2006). *Twelve myths of gifted education*. Retrieved from http://www.louiseporter.com.au/pdfs/twelve_myths_of_gifted_education_web.pdf

Riley, T., & Rawlinson, C. (2008). Gifted education in teacher education: Is it more than a one-off lecture? In C. M. Rubie-Davies & C. Rawlinson (Eds.), *Challenging thinking about teaching and learning* (pp. 209–213). New York, NY: Nova Science Publishers Inc.

Sampson, C. (2013). Social and emotional issues of gifted young children. *Apex: The New Zealand Journal of Gifted Education, 18*(1). Retrieved from http://www.giftedchildren.org.nz/apex/pdfs18/Sampson.pdf

Sutherland, M. (2012) Paradigmatic shift or tinkering at the edges? *High Ability Studies, 23*(1). pp. 109-111.

Tomlinson, C. A. (2003). *Fulfilling the promise of the differentiated classroom*. Alexandria, VA: Association for Supervision and Curriculum Development.

Tungaraza, F., Sutherland, M., and Stack, N. (2013) Universal education or open education opportunities for all? *Compare: A Journal of Comparative and International Education, 43*(6), 822-824. (doi:10.1080/03057925.2013.850285)

Walsh, R. L., Kemp, C.R., Hodge, K. A., & Bowes, J. M. (2012). Searching for evidence-based practice: A review of the research on educational interventions for intellectually gifted children in the early childhood years. *Journal for the Education of the Gifted, 35*, 103-128. doi: 10.1177/016235321440610

Wong, M. (2013). Finding the lost treasure: A literature review of defining and identifying gifted and talented children in early childhood settings in

Aotearoa New Zealand. *Te Iti Kahurangi School of Education e-Journal, 1,* 93–101. Retrieved from http://edjournal.manukau.ac.nz/

Wong, M., & Hansen, J. J. (2012). Pursuing the pot at the end of the rainbow?: Provision for gifted and talented education in early childhood teacher education programmes in Aoteaora New Zealand. *Tall Poppies Magazine of the New Zealand Association for Gifted Children, 37*(2), 16–17.

Wong, M., & Margrain, V. (2012). *Myths and misconceptions about teaching gifted children in the early years.* Paper presented at giftEDnz conference, Wellington.

Zeigler, A., & Raul, T. (2000). Myth and reality: A review of empirical research studies on giftedness. *High Ability Studies, 11*(2), 113–136.

Chapter 7: Social and emotional issues for young gifted children

Carola Sampson

Introduction

The recognition of the social and emotional aspects of giftedness in the early years is critical. This chapter provides some specific behavioural examples and associated support strategies.

Giftedness and social–emotional development are closely linked, which makes the holistic and comprehensive definition of giftedness from Harrison (2005) so appropriate to early years contexts:

> a gifted child is one who performs or has the ability to perform at a level significantly beyond his or her chronologically aged peers, and whose unique abilities and characteristics require special provisions, and social and emotional support from the family, community and educational context. (p. 87)

Emerging outstanding abilities can be seen more easily in young children through their fast pace of learning and the fact that learning at this young age is often more intrinsically motivated—which also means that any linked emotions and experiences might be more noticeable, depending on the child's intrapersonal expressions, such as temperament, determination and resilience (Gagne, 2012; Probst & Piechowski,

2012). More than 50 years ago Kazimierz Dabrowski, a Polish psychiatrist and educational psychologist, coined the term 'overexcitabilities', which describes the inherent compulsion to react intensely to individually different stimuli, which can increase emotional growth (Daniels & Piechowski, 2009). Overexcitabilities are essential aspects of highly gifted individuals and equally as important as their cognitive abilities (M. Piechowski, personal communication, 25 March 2010).

Overexcitabilities embody essential qualities and expressions of personality, temperament and resilience, and as such can be related to intrapersonal traits that influence young gifted children's emotional and talent development from within (Daniels & Meckstroth, 2009; Gagné, 2012, 2013; Piechowski, 2014). This chapter focuses on overexcitabilities in young children who are gifted. It attempts to provide insights and ideas for early childhood teachers in practical situations, keeping in mind that there is no one recipe that fits all young children (Needham, 2012). Dabrowski's overexcitabilities are grouped into the following five areas (Piechowski, 2014):

- psychomotor intensity
- sensual intensity
- intellectual intensity
- imaginational intensity
- emotional intensity.

Each of these five intensities will be discussed in this chapter and a supporting case study provided.

Psychomotor intensity

Introducing psychomotor intensity: theory and practice

Psychomotor intensity can be seen as an overload of energy (Piechowski, 2014). Young children who are gifted may appear very busy and restless, and as having a need to fiddle with their fingers and to move around while thinking. They might have problems sitting still on the mat or keeping their hands to themselves while trying to concentrate. Further expressions and signs are compulsive talking, acting out, nail chewing and finger picking (Daniels & Piechowski, 2009). It is of great help to allow young children exhibiting these behaviours to have something in their hands while sitting on the mat, such as a small bean bag or soft toy, or have the child go on an errand such as getting a book from the shelf. In the classroom a small, soft ball or deflated balloon, filled with rice, kept in the child's pocket to allow them to fiddle with it while thinking and concentrating, provides the same relief.

It is beneficial when addressing the needs of children with psychomotor intensity to consider changes to the structure of the mat time: shorten the duration, or divide a large group of children into two or three smaller groups, depending on the number of teachers available, who can then each take a group. It is also useful to plan for movement opportunities in the classroom, especially following activities that require sitting still for a longer time, such as reading, writing or listening to stories (Daniels & Meckstroth, 2009).

> **A case study of psychomotor intensity: Oliver, age 7**
> The class were discussing painters who also had other professions and passions, such as Leonardo da Vinci, who was a mathematician and an inventor, among other occupations. The whole class was engaged when Oliver, who was very taken by Leonardo's work, began to wiggle on his chair, stood up and sat down again, flicked wads of paper off his table and began talking to himself. After a few more minutes he raised his hand and asked his teacher quietly if he could be excused for a while and go for a walk. The teacher agreed and suggested he do a couple of rounds of the school's sports field next to the classroom. After Oliver had his quick walk outside he went back to the classroom and remained fully engaged until the bell rang. The teacher had previous conversations with Oliver's mother and understood Oliver's need for movement to relieve tension when excited about something.

Sensual intensity

Introducing sensual intensity: theory and practice

Sensual intensity involves a heightened emotional reaction to sensory experiences, often manifested by the intense expression of emotions and heightened tension (Piechowski, 2014). Piechowski (2014) and the seminal work by Dabrowski (1972) use the term 'sensual' differently to ordinary usage of the term, and in terms of giftedness is related to sensory intensity. Children might experience intense seeing, hearing, smelling, touching, and tasting. Highly gifted children's reactions can be extreme and seemingly out of place. Intense reactions might be prolonged crying, anxiety, hiding, screaming, scratching, vomiting, extreme addictiveness and euphoria. The stronger and more intense the experience, positive or negative, the more extreme the reactions can be (Daniels & Meckstroth, 2009).

In my teaching practice I have seen individual children tearfully covering their ears during mat times involving musical instruments while everyone else had fun; another child could not cope with the noise of the Christmas carol singing, although he was supposed to participate. Some children experience difficulties with food when texture or taste appears unpleasant to them; others are overly sensitive to light or smell. Some children might be absorbed by a certain type of music, or the way a ray of light or a sun beam falls through coloured glass. Many children (and adults) can have reactions to the above, but because young children who are gifted might have more intense emotions, their reactions can be quite extreme and severe.

Giving young children who display sensual intensities support to develop self-help skills and strategies to cope (especially in situations where their senses simply take over and cause them excessive emotional stress) is of the utmost importance. It is helpful to find a solution together *with* the child, involving the parents as well. We can talk with children about things they like and don't like, thereby constructing a place where children can recognise and express their feelings about what feels beautiful, stimulating, or not.

In the early years, environments that are aesthetically pleasing to all the senses are important. Learning environments should be comforting and inviting for children, and should include quiet spaces and cushioned corners to cater for those moments of sensual overload. The feel of smooth rocks and pebbles, the sparkling sunlight captured in coloured glass beads and mirrors, the smell of flowers in the garden, the sound of bird song in spring—these sensory experiences instil a sense of happiness in some, a world of immeasurable wonder in others.

> **Case study[1] of sensual intensity: Tom, age 4**
>
> Tom wriggled intensely, arching his shoulders and flailing his arms. Although it was mat time and the children were expected to sit still during the group discussion, Tom's teacher understood his physical cues well enough to recognise that something was seriously bothering him. After some discussion with him it was realised that he was wearing a new sweatshirt given to him by an extended family member who did not realise his intolerance for the sensation of certain fabrics. While many individuals may notice unfamiliar textures, Tom was particularly sensitive. He did not want to take the sweatshirt off, however, as it was a present. His teacher re-oriented his senses by giving him a small piece of silk fabric to stroke. Stroking this fabric soothed him and diverted his senses away from the feeling of the unfamilar clothing on his arms. Tom was then able to focus on the mat time discussion. After Tom's teachers shared this strategy with his family they often put a small piece of silk into his pocket so that he could soothe himself by stroking it unobtrusively when stressed.

Intellectual intensity

Introducing intellectual intensity: theory and practice

Intellectual intensity is a combination of a superior activity of the mind and a passion for problem solving, keen observation, avid reading, high concentration, a hunger for knowledge and voracious curiosity (Piechowski, 2014). There can be a strong streak of perfectionism evident, which may promote excellence and outstanding intellectual achievements, but can also lead to anxiety, fear of failure, avoidance, feeling their work is not good enough, and spiralling down the path of never-ending frustration. Acceptance and acknowledgement of these feelings will support children exhibiting intellectual intensity and provide the groundwork for the development of coping strategies (Daniels & Meckstroth, 2009). For example, a high concentration span and perfectionism can prevent the completion of a product or task in the time allocated. To avoid this, teachers can plan for extra time, discuss with the child possibilities to complete their work, and/or provide storage so

---

1   Case study provided by Valerie Margrain.

that further work can be done later or another day, or to allow completion at home. Flexibility in teachers' attitudes and approaches is the key.

Discussions with children about failure and misjudgements—which are necessary for learning—are invaluable. Examples can be the bridge in the sand pit not being stable enough, or the tower of blocks that toppled too early, as well as the drawing depicting a horse that resembles something other than intended. Young children who are gifted often know exactly what it is they want to create but might lack a certain skill, or their hands might be too small, or they simply don't know how to put their 'plan' into practice.

Talking, modelling and demonstrating that we all learn from our mistakes (even teachers) support young gifted children when they experience failure and can help prepare them for future challenges (Daniels & Meckstroth, 2009). Coping with failure, and being able to learn from non-accomplishment as part of mastering a skill, are invaluable lessons for gifted children with intellectual intensity and perfectionism. The earlier in life a young gifted child gets support to find coping strategies, the less the risk of poor self-esteem, because he or she sees failure as just another challenge or opportunity to improve, fostering resilience (Daniels & Meckstroth, 2009).

Intellectual peers—who are often not age peers—might be able to give extra support and advice here. It is very beneficial for gifted children to mingle with like-minded peers of different ages for socialising, further learning, sharing experiences and feeling understood and accepted (Daniels & Meckstroth, 2009; Porter, 2011). Intellectual peers for gifted youngsters are not easily found in early childhood settings, where all children are a similar age, which might explain why gifted children may turn to the next best thing—the adult in the setting (Porter, 2011). Young children who are in mixed-age settings may find interaction with older children valuable. Depending on a child's age and interests, intellectual peers can be found in Explorer camps (run by local associations for gifted children); local extra-curricular programmes such as holiday programmes, junior memberships at zoos and wildlife parks or museums and sports clubs; or Small Poppies, an extension programme discussed in Chapter 2.

> **Case study of intellectual intensity: Emily, age 3 years 8 months**
>
> I was sitting with a group of children at the art table. We all had paper and pens and talked about our favourite animals. Emily wanted to draw her cat but did not know how to. She watched the other children drawing, and then stared at her piece of paper. Eventually she gave it a go, but when she noticed that the cat she was drawing appeared to have too many legs and the head looked too small, she gave up. Emily wasn't happy. Finally she asked me if I could draw the cat for her. I knew that she had a clear picture of her cat in her mind, so I suggested closing her eyes and 'looking' at her cat more closely, and only then starting drawing, because I didn't know her cat. I asked about the shape of the head, the eyes and the ears of the cat and Emily described them to me, one by one—and was able to draw, bit by bit, until she had drawn the whole cat all by herself. Breaking the task down in this way gave support to Emily, who had previously been overwhelmed by her self-expectations and perfectionism.

Imaginational intensity

Introducing imaginational intensity: theory and practice

Imaginational intensity is seen in spontaneous imagery as an expression of emotional tension (Piechowski, 2014). Highly creative children often have a vast imagination and the ability to immerse themselves in imaginary adventures, play and worlds, and to create a range of imaginary friends, pets and animals. Many children know the difference between reality and imagination, and may even involve others in their imaginary play. If in doubt, careful questions about 'the story' might shed light on this, and may clarify if scaffolding is needed to help children to distinguish between fantasy and reality (Daniels & Meckstroth, 2009).

Not all imaginary events are positive and taken lightly. One example is the imaginary play of a group of 5-year-olds, who had invented a mining company and then 'fired' the chief executive officer, who was then heartbroken for several days. It took his family nearly a week to find the reason for his withdrawal and silent grieving.

It is wonderful when children share their imaginary adventures with others. It is a great opportunity for learning stories and anecdotal observations to be recorded in children's portfolios, documenting children's creative potential from a young age. Imagination can be encouraged for all kinds of problem solving and challenges, so why not use imaginary play to tackle a problem?

> **Case study of imaginational intensity: Reese, 4 years 6 months**
> Reese had been busily 'working' in the kindergarten sandpit all by himself, creating a city with infrastructure and road map on a carefully swept and prepared area of levelled sand. It was all there in his mind. Another child came along with good intentions and a rake, going over the area with the tool to help, thereby destroying the other child's 'masterpiece' unknowingly. Reese was very upset, and his despair turned into rage and aggression. He grabbed a shovel and wanted to hit the other child with it. A teacher nearby was able to stop Reese, holding him and calming him until he dropped the shovel and sobbed. Another teacher led the 'helping' child away from the scene. The first teacher acknowledged Reese's hurt feelings, and then talked to him about what had happened. Recognising that the other child had only wanted to help, the teacher wondered aloud how a situation like this could be handled better next time, and Reese had a few ideas, such as explaining to the other child what he was doing and maybe letting him (or her) know that he does not need help, or calling a teacher for help if it's not working.

Emotional intensity

Introducing emotional intensity: theory and practice

Emotional intensity consists of strongly intensified feelings and emotions, which can be positive or negative. Young children who are gifted can be very aware of other people's feelings and emotions and may identify with their feelings. This form of overexcitability is the most extensive one because of its complexity (Daniels & Meckstroth, 2009; Piechowski, 2014).

For the child, emotional intensity can feel like being on a rollercoaster, because emotions run high and low, in extremes. Deep-felt sadness can turn into anguish and despair. Relationships are important and are felt deeply. Strong emotional attachments to specific people, things, rituals and traditions, and environments often make change emotionally heartfelt and intense (Piechowski, 2014). Loss and grief can be traumatic, and rejection a serious pitfall.

A child who feels like this will not understand why the friend he played with yesterday is no longer a friend today, a situation that happens quite frequently in early childhood settings as children begin to establish for themselves what friendship actually means. An adult in the teaching environment can be the friend for a while, and then gradually include other children, who can then become playmates and even friends, that way making it inclusive. This might take a long time, but it is worth it.

Emotions can be complex, deep and difficult for children to understand, so they might not always be able to explain what they are feeling (Piechowski, 2014). It is important that these feelings are acknowledged by a teacher through active listening. The teacher might be able to recognise these emotions and support the child by explaining them, so that the child is eventually able to identify them without help in future situations (Daniels & Meckstroth, 2009).

Active listening is also important when it comes to behaviour management. We do children a disservice by letting them act out negative feelings in ways that are socially inappropriate. How can children survive in a society where social skills are necessary and where the lack of such skills may close doors (Fertig, 2009)?

A good management strategy for teachers is to calm the child, acknowledge the feeling (not the reaction) and discuss calmly with the child how the situation could have been handled more positively, working out strategies for similar future situations. The child might also learn about how others feel, which fosters the development of empathy and may lead to a better understanding of social skills (Daniels & Meckstroth, 2009).

Case study of emotional intensity: Oscar, age 4

Oscar was sitting at the gate, crying inconsolably and reaching through the bars. His crying grew louder as he became increasingly more upset, so I walked over, sat next to him and waited. He stopped crying when he noticed me, but it took him some time to be able to talk. He wanted to go home, he said. I was wondering why, so he eventually told me that he had been playing with a rope, which he had tied to the fort structure. The rope was his 'snake'. He had to leave his 'snake' when he needed to use the toilet inside, and when he came back he found the 'snake' had been untied and other children were using it. Being very angry that the children took his snake, he had lashed out at them and was sent away to calm down by another teacher, but how could he calm down when they took the rope, 'his snake'?

He shook his head and began crying again. He just wanted to go home. I gave him a box of tissues so that he could blow his nose, then asked him if he knew how many children we had at kindergarten. He wasn't sure about the number but thought quite a lot. I told him that we had 40 children attending, and that while we had plenty of toys, we only had one rope that was strong and long enough to be used for pulling and tying to the fort structure. He didn't know that, and by then he had stopped crying. Oscar thought for a moment and said that he could understand that the children need to take turns, but his turn wasn't finished. He just had to use the toilet. I told him that the children probably didn't know that and must have found the rope while he was away. That seemed to make sense to him. He said that now he understood, but he couldn't do anything about his feelings. He was just so sad. I asked him what would help. Oscar looked around and then pointed at a shrub beside a tree within the kindergarten. He was wondering if he could go behind the shrub and cry a little more, because he was still so sad. I answered that this would be quite all right, and that he could take his time. Oscar promised to be back and play again in 5 minutes. And he was.

Overview of excitabilities and strategies

The five areas of excitability presented in this chapter have been summarised in Table 7.1, including common behavioural indicators and useful strategies (see also Appendix G).

Table 7.1. Excitabilities and support strategies

Social–emotional focus	Behavioural indicators	Useful support strategies
Psychomotor intensity: oversupply of energy	Busy, restless, moving while thinking, difficulty sitting still on the mat, chatting, talking out of turn, nail biting, picking	Give children something to hold (e.g., a bean bag or soft toy). Fill a balloon with rice or corn flour. Include outside and physical learning. Limit the time for sitting still.
Sensual intensity: heightened sensory and sensual expression of emotional tension	Intense seeing, hearing, smelling, touching and tasting: either beautiful and soothing and pleasing, or offensive, disturbing, hurting and distasteful. Dislikes clothing labels and tight clothing.	Support self-help skills and strategies. Create aesthetically pleasing environments and positive sensory experiences. Provide comfort and discussion, help children identify likes and dislikes, remove clothing labels and scratchy fabric.
Intellectual intensity: superior activity of the mind	Passion for problem solving, hunger for knowledge, avid reading, voracious curiosity, keen observation, high concentration, perfectionism, fear of failure, avoidance, anxiety, frustration	Give children time and space to complete projects, discuss mistakes, share own experiences of mistake making. Arrange meeting with like-minded peers, extra-curricular activities such as chess, or join gifted support groups.
Imaginational intensity: spontaneous imagery as an expression of emotional tension	Immense ability to be immersed in imaginary worlds, create imaginary friends and pets. Differentiates between imagination and reality. Able to involve others in play and amuse self.	Talk through the stories the child has created. Record learning stories. Document examples of creativity. Use imaginative skills to problem solve real-life situations. Involve other children in play activities.
Emotional intensity: strongly intensified feelings and emotions.	Aware of own and others' feelings. Rollercoaster emotions (extreme): anguish, despair, anger, compassion, misery. Deep relationships, though not necessarily with age peers. Strong attachments, rituals. Change is challenging. Blushing, sweating, heart racing, 'knot' in stomach.	Accept that adults can be friends. Help children recognise and understand feelings and physical reactions. Help children learn self-control and manage anger and behaviour. Respond to behaviour calmly. Teach empathy.

(Table 7.1 is based on Piechowski, 2014)

Overexcitabilities and temperament

Temperament is also an important aspect to consider. Although the temperamental expression of characteristics can differ in every child, depending on environment, temperament affects overexcitabilities in young children who are gifted (Probst & Piechowski, 2012). Many gifted children are introverts, needing time to themselves to recharge (Probst & Piechowski, 2012). It is not in their nature to have a large number of friends, and they may be happy with just a few who will be close to them (Porter, 2011). It should be acceptable for a child to play alone for a while, but often teachers think that solitary play is something to be concerned about.

Gifted young children who are introverts often appear shy and should not be pushed towards socialising, but instead should be given some space and the opportunity to join at any time (Fertig, 2009; Probst, 2008). Social assurance from others is definitely supportive, but there is a fine line between pressuring and encouraging; trusting relationships are the key for teachers knowing when to help and how much support is needed (Fertig, 2009; Probst, 2008; Probst & Piechowski, 2012). Teaching empathy, respect and tolerance is important for all children, but for those with intensities, particular support is necessary to help children manage tragedies, cope with distress and communicate feelings.

Conclusion

Overexcitabilities, temperament, advanced and complex interests, as well as the need for advanced social interactions with older peers can definitely challenge adults who live with, care for or work with gifted young children in early years settings. Out of context the child may seem to be annoying and difficult, and perhaps even unmanageable, aggressive, hyperactive or a 'drama queen'. Although not all gifted children have excitablities, for many children it is the case that whatever it was that triggered a display of unusual behaviour, or any upset can be felt with significantly more intensity (Piechowski, 2014).

Young children who are gifted deserve support and acceptance from adults (parents, family and caregivers) who care for them and from those who work with them (teachers). They need to know that it is okay to move around or play unobtrusively with a squishy small toy if it helps them think (*psychomotor*); that it is safe to ask for help when emotions are just too hard to bear (*emotional*); that we can't be perfect every time (*intellectual*); that it is acceptable to be lost in the taste and texture of an apple or to be repelled by it (*sensual*; and that it is fine to play imaginary adventures with "your spaceship in a different solar system" at the back of the kindergarten all by yourself (*imaginary*) (Sampson, 2013). It is essential for teachers to establish good and trusting relationships with the children and families they work with, and to accept children's overexcitabilities as their specific innate expressions of how they experience the world around them (Probst & Piechowski, 2012). Active listening and collaborative relationships, paired with openness to alternative ideas, will make it easier to work together on individual strategies that support their social and emotional development.

References

Dabrowski. K. (1972). *Psychoneuroses is not an illness*. London: Gryf.

Daniels, S., & Meckstroth, E. (2009). Nurturing the sensitivity, intensity, and developmental potential of gifted young children. In S. Daniels & M. Piechowski (Eds.), *Living with intensity* (pp. 33–56). Scottsdale, AZ: Great Potential Press.

Daniels, S., & Piechowski, M. (2009). Embracing intensity: Overexcitability, sensitivity, and the developmental potential of the gifted. In S. Daniels & M. Piechowski (Eds.), *Living with intensity* (pp. 3–17). Scottsdale, AZ: Great Potential Press.

Fertig, C. (2009). *Raising a gifted child: A parenting success hand book*. Waco, TX: Prufrock Press.

Gagné, F. (2012). Differentiated model of giftedness and talent. In T. L. Cross & J. R. Cross (Eds.), *Handbook for counsellors: Serving students with gifts and talents* (pp. 3–19). Waco, TX: Prufrock Press.

Gagné, F. (2013). The DMGT: Changes within, beneath and beyond. *Talent Development & Excellence*, 5(1), 5–19.

Harrison, C. (2005). *Young gifted children: Their search for complexity and connection*. Sydney, NSW: Inscript Publishing.

Needham, V. (2012). Primary teachers' perceptions of the social and emotional aspects of gifted and talented education. *Apex: The New Zealand Journal of Gifted Education*, 17(1). Retrieved from http://www.giftedchildren.org.nz/apex

Piechowski, M. (2014). *"Mellow out", they say. If I only could: Intensities and sensitivities of the young and bright* (2nd ed.). New York, NY: Royal Fireworks Press.

Porter, L. (2011). Giftedness in the early years. In R. Moltzen (Ed.), *Gifted and talented: New Zealand perspectives* (3rd ed., pp. 111–156). Auckland: Pearson.

Probst, B. (2008). *When the labels don't fit: A new approach to raising a challenging child.* New York, NY: Three Rivers Press.

Probst, B., & Piechowski, M. (2012). Overexcitabilities and temperament. In T. L. Cross & J. R. Cross (Eds.), *Handbook for counsellors serving students with gifts and talents* (pp. 53–73). Waco, TX: Prufrock Press.

Sampson, C. (2013). Social and emotional issues of gifted young children. *Apex: The New Zealand Journal of Gifted Education, 18*(1). Retrieved from http://www.giftedchildren.org.nz/apex

Chapter 8: Opening the treasure chest: Differentiation for young children who are gifted

Caterina Murphy

Introduction

Curriculum involves everything children experience in an educational setting. Young children who are gifted are likely to need individual adaptations to the curriculum. These children need the intellectual stimulation typically given to older children, yet their physical size and individual social–emotional developmental needs may mean that some activities for older children are not suitable for them (Porter 1999).

According to Tomlinson (1999), "Children already come to us differentiated. It just makes sense that we would differentiate our instruction in response to them" (p. 24). With this in mind, it is obvious that a 'one size fits all' kind of curriculum delivery is just not going to work for everyone (Riley, 2002). It was Cathcart (1996) who asserted:

> It remains a source of astonishment ... that the same sane and caring adults who would not dream of forcing a child [who was] growing at a faster rate than average into shoes too small for her feet, will nonetheless insist on forcing a child whose mental growth is faster than average into a learning programme too small for her mind and imagination—and see no harm. (p.124)

A priority for teachers is to remember that at the centre of curriculum planning is a young child, and that the *whole child* must be seen before the giftedness. Jones and Jones (1995) remind us that children will not learn until their emotional needs are met; therefore, an emotionally supportive and responsive learning environment is a crucial aspect of teacher response to these children. Environmental responsiveness includes physical factors such as resources and space, and affective factors such as a warm and secure environment that encourages well-being and belonging. In this chapter, approaches to providing differentiation are discussed, supported by authentic examples from my teaching experiences.

Explaining differentiation

If programme planning is viewed simply as what we (teachers) do, why we do it and how we do it, then differentiating the curriculum will involve making changes in our plan of what we teach, how we teach it and why we teach it. Therefore, being a flexible teacher, who is open to change and responsive to individual diversity, is one of the core 'essentials' of qualitative differentiation.

Personalising learning

Differentiation involves young children experiencing a flexible, challenging and adaptable curriculum, one that is responsive to individual learning interests, needs and aspirations (Riley, Bevan-Brown, Bicknell, Carroll-Lind, & Kearney, 2004). It is a positive response so that young children who are gifted are fully engaged in learning that is stimulating, interesting, challenging and not boring. Differentiation is all about *personalising* education with the aim of maximising each child's individual potential. It is not about more of the same thing (quantitative differentiation): it is about moving the educational programme to different levels and adapting it to accommodate those children who have already acquired the knowledge that you or others are trying to share. Teachers must take into account the children's *atypical* interests and constellation of abilities (Wolfe, 1990), intentionally invite these differences and actively seek out children's preferences for learning (Riley, 2014).

Personalising education involves allowing for differences in development and a particular child's approach to learning, understanding and interests, and ensuring sufficient variety in order to meet the child's needs (Dodge & Colker, 1992). Children who are gifted may be more vulnerable to stress reactions because their environments may not meet their atypical needs (Porter, 1999).

Differentiation also involves cultural considerations for Māori; for example, teachers and family/whānau together need to encourage and develop Māoritanga in their children, enabling them to develop pride in who they are and in their culture (Bevan-Brown, 2011). Using learning methods that are culturally appropriate for young Māori children is vital, and these must be created in order to cater for the different needs and learning styles of young Māori children, recognising the validity of their skills, knowledge and whānau values (Bevan-Brown, 2011).

Essential elements of effective differentiation

Effective differentiation encompasses aspects such as higher-order thinking, open-ended tasks, research skills and methods, and the integration of curricular ideas. Porter (1999) suggests the following general curriculum guidelines for working alongside young children who are gifted:

- encourage higher-level thinking skills, such as analysis, synthesis, evaluation and problem solving
- allow the children to pursue their own interests to a depth that satisfies them
- involve less repetition and a faster pace than are usual for their age
- promote intellectual risk taking (i.e., creativity) and divergent thinking
- offer a high degree of complexity and variety in their content, process and product (which expresses their learning).

Qualitative differentiation involves a number of key elements, according to Van Tassel-Baska (1994) and Patterson (2000). These include:

- complexity
- novelty
- challenge

- acceleration
- enrichment
- evaluation
- self-understanding
- choice
- depth
- breadth
- independence
- diversity
- advanced content relating to conceptual themes
- comprehensive, related and reinforcing learning experiences.

Understanding the terminology

There are a number of different terms in the literature on curriculum and gifted education, and it is helpful for early years teachers if the language they use reflects the terms used by the majority of international educators in gifted education. 'Core curriculum', 'complex curriculum', 'extension', 'differentiation', 'enrichment' and 'acceleration' are all curriculum terms that are discussed in this chapter. This section begins by discussing two key terms, 'enrichment' and 'acceleration', although the concepts are not mutually exclusive (Ministry of Education, 2000), and young children who are gifted are best supported when the two approaches are used together. There are advantages and disadvantages to each approach, but by blending the two, a balance of good practice in the education of these children can be achieved (Ministry of Education, 2000). We then go on to look at other terminology using metaphor and examples.

Enrichment

Townsend (2011) emphasises that enrichment concerns deeper and broader applications within regular teaching, taking into account each child's abilities and learning needs. Although many teachers in the early years might argue that we have enrichment happening all the time, enrichment activities normally occur in addition to the regular programme or core curriculum being offered. Enrichment would involve modifying the regular sessional or all-day learning experiences by offering challenge, novelty, critical thinking, skill development, advanced creativity development, or an individual investigative approach—to name a few. Enrichment can occur in many ways. In this resource we focus on aspects of content, the process of learning or the teaching strategies used, the learning environment, and the expressions of learning produced.

Acceleration

Acceleration is instruction that aims to align the abilities and learning needs of the young child more closely with the curriculum. Townsend (1996) emphasised this by stating:

> In practice, acceleration occurs when children are exposed to new content at an earlier age than other children or when they cover the same content in less time. (p. 361)

For early years teachers it could mean allowing the 2-year-old into the 3-year-old area early, working with an individual school to achieve earlier transition into a formal learning environment for a particular child, or teaching a particular skill for mastery at a faster pace than you normally would in the junior school classroom. It most often means that content for some children is 'taught' over a shorter period of time.

Acceleration differentiates the timing of the introduction of content and/or the rate of coverage (Ministry of Education, 2000). Townsend (2011) suggests that acceleration, when well planned and individualised, can provide young children who are gifted with the mental stimulation and opportunities to interact with like-minded children.

Differentiation, metaphor and practice

The terms in Table 8.1 are explained through the metaphor of a multi-storey house, and with application to a typical early years activity: play dough (see Appendix H). When reflecting on this activity, consider the following questions: What about the child who is bored at the play dough table? What about the 3-year-old who is tired of the same old equipment? Some children quickly lose interest, and activities soon lack novelty and challenge. What about the ones who want to do something different with materials? Do we extend the play? How? These considerations are explored in Table 8.1.

Table 8.1. Differentiation, metaphor and practice connections

Term	Explanation	Metaphor of a house	Practice example: play dough
Core curriculum	Content that teachers routinely cover	Exploring a room on the ground-floor level of a house	Talk, roll, pat and pound, sing, add glitter, cut shapes, share tools, add water, stick things into the dough, mould it, laugh about it, smell it, taste it and squeeze it.
Quantitative differentiation	More of the same thing	Exploring the room next door	
Extension	Application to new areas of activity	Finding out how you can use downstairs belongings in new ways in second-floor discoveries	Make play dough, grate it, bake it, paint it, stamp on it, glue with it, add more to it, print with it and build with it.
Complex curriculum	Ensuring that learning opportunities are deeper, richer and more complex	Climbing up to the loft, where there is a bottomless treasure chest. The content on the ground floor is still there, but the journey has moved on.	Find out how flour is made, experiment with dyes, test the salt in science experiments, visit a bakery, bake bread, design new printing materials, make new cutters, compare it to clay, analyse it, try to move it, break it down, boil it, find out what else can be done with it, read about salt lakes, try and squeeze oil out of things, examine the shapes of oil bottles, draw the shapes, find out what happens when we make it without oil; examine wet and dry, microwave it, sun dry it, and much more!
Qualitative differentiation	Open-ended adaptation and application	The treasure chest in the loft is used in diverse and novel ways that capture interest. Wings are made and the child may choose to fly beyond the loft.	

Roberts and Roberts (2001) suggest that planned learning experiences need to make accommodation for each child to continuously progress. They argue that these experiences must be differentiated so that the learning 'ceiling' is removed, allowing a child who is ready to learn at a more complex level and/or at a faster pace to continue learning each day. This is the ultimate analogy to complete the metaphor I have been using of climbing within a multi-storey home. Not only might the ceiling be removed, but the child sufficiently empowered to build their own wings and fly forth, with confidence, further researching topics of interest to them and seeking new knowledge at a complex and advanced level.

Differentiating content, process, product and learning environment

Children with advanced abilities require opportunities to be exposed to and use the vocabulary and concepts typically used by much older children. They need to study subjects in depth because they have an unusually keen power to make connections and perceive relationships. In this section we illustrate several different elements of differentiation: content, process, product, and learning environment.

These four elements require close examination. Kulik and Kulik (1997) remind us that curriculum differentiation refers to the provision of different learning activities for same-aged children who have different learning needs and preferences. When planning to differentiate the curriculum, we need to consider what it is that we want to cover—for those identified as gifted—that is additional to what is already provided for everyone (Eyre, 1997). Caution needs to be taken to ensure that teachers educate with authenticity rather than forge ahead with the latest new ideas. Thus any curricular differentiation needs to be educationally justifiable (Callahan, 1996). However, any richness added to the programme through curriculum differentiation will not only benefit those children identified as gifted but other children as they may show interest in a particular topic or new equipment being utilised, share knowledge that teachers did not realise they had, be educationally stimulated in a new direction or through a different mode of learning.

Case study: Toby

Imagine that you have a small group of young children who are fascinated with space. There has been a movie on in town that you suspect has generated enthusiasm for this topic of learning, and you want to be responsive to that. You find out from this group what it is that intrigues them about space and what they want to learn more about. Using your curriculum framework as a guide, you may brainstorm ideas on how you will deliver this teaching unit or how you will incorporate the concept of space into the children's day.

But what about Toby? He knows more about space than the teacher. How can the programme accommodate Toby? Differentiation supports Toby to learn at another level than his age peers. A range of specialist teaching techniques can be used to manipulate the knowledge he has already acquired and to provide a curriculum that is less core and more complex for him. Toby's teacher might ask, "How can I stretch that information in another direction for Toby?"

The outcome of that manipulation will be evident in how Toby demonstrates his learning. Toby's 'product', or expressions of learning, may be quite different to that of other children. For example, other children may be producing flat paintings of a night sky with planets, or moulding models of planets out of clay, whereas Toby may be outside on the concrete placing planet cut-outs he has made in relative position, or he may have instigated the making of a 3D model of a planet. Other children may give a fairly accurate account of their learning about space, but Toby may give a longer, deeper and more meaningful account.

The learning environment should also be reflected upon. What resources, materials and environmental changes will be needed in order to enrich Toby's learning? Extra posters may be required, computer software could be borrowed, extra boxes may be needed, or more space in the room provided as Toby creates his paper mâché 'Pluto'.

Content differentiation

In order to differentiate content, consideration needs to be given to how the more complex and more abstract dimensions of teaching and learning can be included. Content modification necessitates reflecting on:

how children can be assisted to manipulate the knowledge they have already acquired, how children understand, and how further investigation of that understanding can be accommodated within programmes.

To differentiate what is taught, more complex learning experiences are required so that young children can comfortably understand the things that matter to them. Modifying content includes getting the child to develop higher thinking skills, perhaps at a more abstract level. Harrison (1999) argues that

> content modifications focus on the ideas, concepts and information, which are presented to the child. For the young child who is gifted, this may be at a surprisingly complex and abstract level not typically presented in early childhood settings. (p. 59)

Take this example of a dialogue I had with a 2-year-old child at an early childhood centre:

Child: Caterina, did you know that there was this thing on the radio and granddad will have to move his lettuces?

Teacher: What was it on the radio that you heard?

Child: Well I heard that all the ground where we live has this stuff in it which could be poisonous.

Teacher: I wasn't listening to my radio this morning. Can you tell me about it?

Child: Well, there is this stuff called 'oxydoxydiny' which someone has found and I don't know what Granddad is going to do because I don't want him to eat his lettuces from his garden.

Teacher: Did you tell Granddad about what you heard on the radio?

Child: No I didn't see him this morning because he doesn't live at my house.

Teacher: Are you feeling a bit worried about granddad this morning?

Child: Yes, because I don't want my granddad to die.

Teacher: Would it make you feel better if you rang granddad up today and told him all about it?

Child: Yes, and I want to ring those other people up because they need to bring all their big diggers in and move all the soil and take it away somewhere; but they can't put it in the sea, they have to put it somewhere where no one will ever be able to find it again, cos it's *bad* stuff ['bad' was dramatically emphasised].

Teacher: I wonder where they could put it all? I'm trying to think of lots of ideas as to what the people with the diggers could do.

Child: Well they need to put it in one of those big rockets and blast it out into the sky. It will make the stars all dirty though [child laughs].

Teacher: Let's see what we can find out about the dioxin together. I'll need to listen to the radio tomorrow morning to see what is going to happen to all the soil won't I?

Child: We don't have any rockets in New Zealand, Caterina, but we have lots of granddads growing lettuces.

Walker, Hefenstein and Crow-Enslow (1999) emphasise that curriculum for any child should be meaningful, and that this meaningful curriculum needs to furnish children with opportunities to address content at many different levels. Morelock and Morrison (1996) addressed this by getting us to reflect on the following questions:

- Is the topic conceptually complex enough to be meaningful to gifted children?
- Is the content based on the children's interests?
- Does the content meet the social and emotional needs of the children?
- Does the content begin with the children's direct experiences and then extend to proximal experiences (scaffolded by teachers to achieve and be challenged at differentiated levels), thereby enabling the children to explore the topic in greater depth?

Conceptual themes are addressed by Riley (1997), who suggests that a common thread in enrichment options is the teaching of conceptual themes, and that these can be tools for increasing the complexity of content. We already know that young children who are gifted have an unusual capacity for processing information and a need for tackling challenging and diverse learning experiences. Children need to actively participate in making choices about what they want to learn.

Process differentiation

Process in this context relates to how children are taught and the ways in which children use the information they have acquired. A critical consideration is open-ended discussion. This strategy can be incorporated not only into direct conversation with children, but also with children as to how materials are presented in different ways, including learning centres and areas of play. Open-ended communication benefits all children, but in order to make learning and thinking processes more appropriate for young children who are gifted, teachers need to consider the pace of instruction or knowledge sharing, and modify the types of thought processes and approaches to reasoning in their teaching (Maker & Nielson, 1996). This includes co-constructed discussions with children concerning the setting up of the learning environment in order to drive pedagogy.

The process of learning and teaching should be real and meaningful for the child. Maker (1982) emphasises that modifications to 'process' address the way the child thinks and learns, the way information is presented, the experiences in which children participate, and the teaching strategies used. According to Maker and Nielson (1996), a key necessary modification is structuring learning activities that allow children to choose content or projects for study in order to enrich their thinking.

These authors highlight the differences between convergent versus divergent thinking, as follows.

- In convergent thinking an individual attempts to give the right or best answer.
- In divergent thinking an individual attempts to generate many, varied and unique possibilities or answers.

Both types of thinking have an important place in everyday life. Open-endedness, however, requires a sustained commitment by teachers in their teaching practices. Maker and Nielson (1996) argue that this is reflected in:

- questioning techniques and the content of questions
- the design of learning activities and materials
- evaluation of children's responses to questions.

Open questions encourage children to give a response and encourage group interaction rather than teacher–child interaction. They elicit more complete and more complex responses, allowing children to give knowledgeable answers and encouraging children to question themselves (Maker & Nielson, 1996). In other words, open-ended discussion stimulates further thought, learning and exploration. A teacher who always provides answers or asks closed questions limits the opportunities for young children to celebrate the joy of discovery (Maker & Nielson, 1996). Open-endedness implies that it is acceptable for a child to know more about a certain topic than the teacher. Creativity concerns a child's fluency, flexibility and originality of thought (Renzulli & Reis, 1986). Open-ended discussions stimulate the creative 'juices' of a child, encourage playfulness and the full use of imagination, and promote openness to new experiences. Take this example of a conversation I had with a 3-year-old child early in my teaching career. Critique it. Reflect on how you would have answered the initial question.

Child: Caterina, why is the sky blue?

Teacher: I'm not sure why the sky is blue. How do you think we could find out?

Child: We could ask the birds!

Teacher: What a great idea! How will we understand what the birds are telling us?

Child: We'll listen to their chirping noises.

Teacher: Sounds like fun. What other ideas have you got?

Child: We could take rides on their backs and see for ourselves.

Teacher: I wonder what we would see once we are up there?

Child: I'd see lots of houses. We could fly over them and sit on top.

Teacher: What a great idea! I almost feel like flying now just thinking about it.

Child: Let's pretend. I'll be the big bird and you be the little one. You've got a bad wing.

Teacher: OK. I wonder what I need to help me fly.

Child: You need two good wings silly! [Lots of giggling.]

Teacher: Mmnn. I think I might need to make my own. What sort of things could I use?

Needless to say, I never did get to find out why the sky is blue, and neither did the child. But we did go on a fabulous journey. By the time we had made our wings, other children had joined in. We painted our faces, stuck feathers in our hair, decided on a launching point (great debating going on there!), jumped into puddles, investigated the puddles, pretended to drink them, stamped our 'clawed feet' in them and created a new flying song.

Product differentiation

Common to all children is their need to demonstrate what they have learnt (Porter, 1999), and expressions of their learning and their creations do this. In the early years there are countless opportunities for children to accomplish this. However, the example of Toby during the space unit illustrates that the end product has to be satisfying to the child. We all know how important it is not to throw away by mistake that piece of wood with one nail hammered into it, because when a child's parent comes to pick him/her up, that piece of wood will be looked for by the child until it is found. However, just as important is the child's dance that he/she has created, the song he/she has learnt, their collection of stones, or the experiment enjoyed that morning. Young children demonstrate their learning through product development in hundreds of different ways.

Porter (1999) raises the important point that in the early years children's reading and writing skills will limit their ability to record and express what they have learnt. This is where teachers need to be flexible and divergent thinkers themselves and seek to provide alternative methods for children to demonstrate their learning. Computers, cameras, and other areas of technology are some of the tools teachers can use to enhance those demonstrations.

The following case study illustrates product differentiation. I was working with a group of six 3- and 4-year-old children in an enrichment programme.

> **Case study: Amy**
> A 3-year-old, Amy, was at the drawing table. We had been discussing transport. The children in the room started to discuss rockets, and she demonstrated her learning through a drawing and its evaluation.
>
> Teacher: Amy, I really like your drawing.
>
> Amy: It's a rocket with me in it.
>
> Amy then very hurriedly coloured in the bottom of the rocket in black felt pen. She was vigorous and pushed the end of the felt into the plastic so that it couldn't be used anymore.
>
> Teacher: Your black colouring looks interesting. Is it something very important to do with your rocket?
>
> Amy: It's the ... it's the ... [her arms start making big circular movements in the air as she tries to think of the words] ... it's the ... it's the starting of the parting!

It is important that teachers closely observe children's creations in order to recognise what children are thinking about—what they are prioritising or emphasising. In Amy's drawing she was processing how a rocket 'parts' from the earth (lift off). She was emphasising what it is about rockets that was of most interest to her.

Learning environment

Additional resources or adaptations to the learning environment are required to support young children who are gifted. Teachers of course are an important and driving facet of a child's learning environment. For young children to have the freedom to be creative, consideration needs to be given to physical, intellectual, creative and socio-emotional influences (Riley, 2014). This encompasses both the actual physical spaces in which learning occurs (e.g., the centre, classroom and outside areas), but also the feeling or atmosphere of those spaces. Greenman (1988) suggests that

> an environment is a living, changing system. More than physical space, it includes the way time is structured and the roles we are expected to play. It conditions how we feel, think and behave: and it dramatically affects the quality of our lives. (p. 5)

Meade (2000) argues that challenging young children involves more than just rearranging the physical environment: it is highly dependent on the quality of our interactions and the perception we carry of children's abilities. It concerns having an inviting learning environment which is psychologically and emotionally 'safe' for children. The intentions of the teacher in how they provide an inviting learning environment are paramount. "Invitational education is the process by which people are cordially, creatively, and consistently summoned to realize their potential" (Purkey & Novak, 2013, p. 7). As Riley (2014) provoked: imagine being invited to learn. Imagine what it would be for young children who are gifted to have teachers in their learning environment who are committed, with a persistent sense of purpose, imaginative resourcefulness and courage (Purkey & Novak, 2013).

Some important questions for teachers to consider include:

- Is there an area where I can talk quietly, one to one, with a child?
- Can I listen to children in this space?
- Is there room for the many and varied group activities that we share (e.g., story times, brainstorming times, group sharing times)?
- Is there a good *feeling* in this room?

It is critical to consider how children perceive their learning environments. Encouraging children to be part of the evaluation, ensures that the spaces around them and the atmosphere of them, give young children who are gifted opportunities to play and work in places that promote well-being and belonging. It is also critical that teachers assess the learning environment (Riley, 2014) in response to young children who are gifted.

Clark (2013) asserts that teachers will know that the learning environment is responsive when:

- The atmosphere is free of undue pressure and stress
- The lessons present novel challenges appropriate for the student's stage of development
- Stimulation to all of the senses is involved in the lessons
- Students have exposure to a broad range of skills and interests
- There is social interaction among intellectual peers
- Choices and the opportunity to choose are evident
- Exploration is an on-going part of students' learning.

Where to from here?

There are a number of useful curriculum models that readers wanting additional reading can find out about. In this section two models, by Bloom and Cathcart, are briefly introduced, followed by some reflective questions for those who work with children to ponder.

Bloom's taxonomy

Bloom's taxonomy (Bloom, 1956) is a cognitive model which focuses on intellectual behaviours and development. It provides a mechanism to apply the higher-level thinking skills, critical thinking skills and creative thinking skills advocated in gifted education literature. This taxonomy allows teachers to be guided through a step-by-step system to help them acknowledge the stages of learning a child can work through during the 'process' stage of an experience. It is called a taxonomy because of the hierarchy of levels. A strength of the model is that elements of it can be utilised with all learners, while the advanced aspects particularly meet the needs of young children who are gifted. Table 8.2 provides an illustration of Bloom's taxonomy applied to the content area of zebras (see also Appendix I).

Table 8.2. Bloom's taxonomy applied to young children and zebra learning

Stage	Explanation of stage	Zebra example
Knowledge	Young children acquire knowledge through play, exploration, manipulation, and with the assistance or guidance of the teacher or others in their environment.	"This animal is called a zebra" (a teacher reading from a book).
Comprehension	Young children gain an understanding of the information they have acquired.	"I know that is a zebra because it has black and white stripes and looks like a horse."
Application	Young children apply their understanding of the information they have acquired.	"I can draw and paint zebras on my own."
Analysis	Young children break a concept or idea, etc. down into components, elements or parts.	"Do zebras look like any other animal? Where do zebras live? What do they eat? Do we have them in New Zealand? Why don't we? Are there any other animals in the world with black and white stripes? How will we know if they are zebras?"
Synthesis	Young children put the parts together again and create something new, or adapt an idea to suit their needs or to answer their initial questions.	"Let's create our own black and white striped animals! What shall we call them? Where will they live? What will they eat?"
Evaluation	Young children make judgements about the value or purpose of something and make connections with internal or external evidence.	"What do zebras offer to our world? What do we need to do to conserve them? Should we care about them? How can we learn more about them?"

Cathcart (2010) offers a practical model that can particularly support less experienced teachers who may lack clarity in converting the theoretical principles of content, process and product differentiation as discussed earlier in this chapter, into effective teaching and learning opportunities for young children who are gifted. She writes about a series of steps designed to 'hook' or stimulate children's thinking around a topic. These steps promote engagement, offer hands-on learning experience, give freedom of choice as to how a learner will process information, along with the opportunity to develop research skills and explore issues deeply through open-ended inquiry learning.

Here is one example of the model's steps in action, focused on the topic of ancient civilisations:

Step 1: Mind-opening query
How old must a civilisation be, before we call it 'ancient'? Is there a rule?

Step 2: Establishing our data
How big was the biggest pyramid? How much land space did it occupy? How high was it? Can you find a building near where you live that is about the same size?

Step 3: Exploring our ideas
Write a news sheet to be read out to the workers who are building the next pyramid. Include news, announcements and advertisements.

Step 4: Examining our thinking
Ask students to consider whether archaeologists are simply modern-day tomb robbers. What's your view?

Conclusion

Qualitative differentiation is a crucial element of teaching young children who are gifted. Wise decisions are required by teachers so that children enjoy and are stimulated through opportunities for self-directed and discovery learning (Harrison, 1999) and so that they are intentionally invited to learn (Purkey & Novak, 2013). This freedom to self-select allows the child to act on their own intrinsic motivation and can be achieved through long periods of uninterrupted play, flexibility in centre routines, accessible resources and the self-selection of activities. In other words, by removing the ceiling that I talked about earlier and maintaining a flexible attitude, teachers can leave the learning world wide open for these children to use the higher-order thinking skills of analysis, synthesis and evaluation (Bloom, 1956).

Reflective questions

Opportunities for supporting young children can be enhanced when professional reflection is engaged in. Anyone working with young children may find it helpful to think of a particular child who is gifted and then ponder the following points of reflection, which evaluate programme differentiation (see Appendix J):

- What did the child learn?
- How did I facilitate and support their learning?
- How can I help the child to find the right level of challenge?
- In what ways does the learning environment need adapting in order to maximise learning opportunity?
- Were the experiences I planned for and provided of quality and at varying levels?
- Were the learning outcomes planned for? Were they realised? If not, why not?
- How challenged and supported am I feeling?
- Have I encouraged growth in all developmental domains?

References

Bevan-Brown, J. (1996). Gifted and talented Māori learners. In R. Moltzen (Ed.), *Gifted and talented: New Zealand perspectives* (3rd ed., pp. 82–110). Palmerston North: Massey University ERDC Press.

Bloom, B. S. (1956). *Taxonomy of educational objectives: The classification of educational goals: Handbook 1: Cognitive domain.* New York, NY: Longmans, Green & Co.

Callahan, C. M. (1996). A critical self-study of gifted education: Healthy practice, necessary evil, or sedition. *Journal for the Education of the Gifted, 19*(2), 148–163.

Cathcart, R. (1996). Educational provisions: An overview. In D. McAlpine & R. Moltzen (Eds.), *Gifted and talented: New Zealand perspectives* (pp.121–138). Palmerston North: Massey University ERDC Press.

Cathcart, R. (2010). *Differentiation made practical: Lessons to satisfy gifted learners, their classmates and teachers.* Invercargill: Essential Resources.

Clark, B. (2013). *Growing up gifted* (8th ed.). Boston, MA: Pearson..

Dodge, D. T., & Colker, L. J. (1992). *The creative curriculum for early childhood.* Mt. Rainier, MD: Gryphon House.

Eyre, D. (1997). *Able children in ordinary schools.* London, UK: David Fulton.

Greenman, J. (1988). *Caring spaces, learning spaces: Children's environments that work.* Redmond, WA: Exchange Press.

Harrison, C. (1999). *Giftedness in early childhood.* Sydney, NSW: GERRIC.

Jones, V., & Jones, L. (1995). *Comprehensive classroom management: Creating positive learning environments for all students* (4th ed.). Boston, MA: Allyn and Bacon.

Kulik, J., & Kulik, C. C. (1997). Ability grouping. In N. Colangelo & G. A. Davis (Eds.), *Handbook of gifted education* (pp. 230–242). Boston, MA: Allyn and Bacon.

Maker, C. J. (1982). *Teaching models in the education of the gifted.* Rockville, MD: Aspen.

Maker, C. J., & Nielson, A. B. (1996). *Curriculum development and teaching strategies for gifted learners.* Austin, TX: PRO-ED Inc.

Meade. A. (2000). If you say it three times, is it true?: Critical use of research in early childhood education. *Journal of Early Years Education, 8*(1), 15–26.

Ministry of Education. (2000). *Gifted and talented students: Meeting their needs in New Zealand schools.* Wellington: Learning Media.

Morelock, M. J., & Morrison, K. (1996). *Gifted children have talents too!: Multidimensional programming for the gifted in early childhood.* Highett, Vic: Hawker Brownlow Education.

Patterson, K. (2000). *What parents need to know about curriculum differentiation.* Retrieved from http://www.cagifted.org/partip3.htm

Porter, L. (1999). *Gifted young children: A guide for teachers and parents.* Sydney, NSW: Allen & Unwin.

Purkey, W. W., & Novak, J. M. (2013). *Invitational education.* Retrieved from http://www.invitationaleducation.net/ie/PDFs/Fastback1[1]%20Invitational%20education.pdf

Renzulli, J. S., & Reis, S. M. (1986). The enrichment triad/revolving door model: A schoolwide plan for the development of creative productivity. In J. S. Renzulli (Ed.), *Systems and models for developing programs for the gifted and talented* (pp. 216–305). Mansfield Center, CT: Creative Learning Press Inc.

Riley, T. L. (1997). Tools for discovery: Conceptual themes in the classroom. *Gifted Child Today, 20*(1), 30–33.

Riley, T. L. (2002). *Supporting and enhancing gifted education study guide four.* Palmerston North: Massey University.

Riley, T. L. (2011). Qualitative differentiation for gifted and talented students. In R. Moltzen (Ed.), *Gifted and talented: New Zealand perspectives* (3rd ed., pp. 276–303). Auckland: Pearson.

Riley, T. (2014) Differentiating learning environments for gifted and talented learners. Retrieved from http://www.giftedchildren.org.nz/massey14/Tracy%20Riley%20Differentiation%20NZAGC%202014.pdf

Riley, T. L., Bevan-Brown, J., Bicknell, B, Carroll-Lind, J., & Kearney, A. (2004). *The extent, nature and effectiveness of planned approaches in New Zealand schools for identifying and providing for gifted and talented students.* Wellington: Massey University.

Roberts, J., & Roberts, R. (2001). Writing units that remove the learning ceiling. In F.A. Karnes & S.M. Bean (Eds.), *Methods and materials for teaching the gifted*. Waco, TX: Prufrock Press.

Tomlinson, C. A. (1999). *The differentiated classroom: Responding to the needs of all learners*. Alexandria, VA: ASCD.

Townsend, M. A. R. (1996). Enrichment and acceleration: Lateral and vertical perspectives in provisions for gifted and talented children. In D. McAlpine & R. Moltzen (Eds.), *Gifted and talented: New Zealand perspectives* (pp. 361–376). Palmerston North: Kanuka Grove Press.

Townsend, M. A. R. (2011). The need to balance acceleration with enrichment in gifted education. In R. Moltzen (Ed.), *Gifted and talented: New Zealand perspectives* (3rd. ed., pp. 252–275). Auckland: Pearson

Van Tassel-Baska, J. (1994). *Comprehensive curriculum for gifted learners* (2nd ed.). Boston, MA: Allyn and Bacon.

Walker, B., Hefenstein, N. L., & Crow-Enslow, L. (1999). Meeting the needs of gifted learners in the early childhood classroom. *Young Children, 54*(1), 32–36.

Wolfe, J. (1990). Gifted preschoolers within the classroom. *Early Child Development and Care, 63,* 83–93.

Chapter 9: Talking together: Supporting gifted children and positive transitions to school

Monica Cameron and Valerie Margrain

Introduction

In this chapter we consider issues related to collaborative practice in early years education, including communication, support for the transition to school, and relationships between key stakeholders. These stakeholders include children, parents, extended family/whānau, teachers, early childhood setting and school management, specialist support staff, and community members. The Ministry of Education (2012) recommends the use of a collaborative inquiry planning model to improve provision for gifted children and students, including the step of reflecting on the question "who are our partners in addressing these students' needs?" (p.18). Collaborative relationships between these partners, including parents, teachers and children, provides a particular opportunity for those involved to give and receive support: no single partner has to be solely responsible for giving support.

Parent-teacher communication

Partnership—including respectful, reciprocal relationships between the early childhood setting, school and families—is a fundamental element of teaching in the early years (Ministry of Education, 1996, 2007). We begin by discussing the purpose of communication, then share case studies and research findings of positive and less-than-successful communication, and provide some communication strategies valued by the parents of young gifted children.

The purposes of communication
Good communication builds on understanding and a genuine desire to listen and share. It is ideal if parents and teachers—and, where appropriate, other educational experts—collaborate to share assessment information about the child (Rogoff, Goodman, Turkanis, & Bartlett, 2001). Each group is able to bring important information and assessment perspectives that contribute to collective understanding (Margrain, 2007). The child is central to these discussions and interactions. The purposes of communication vary, but for those supporting young children who are gifted (teachers, parents and others), these include a desire to:

- share information
- learn from one another
- mutually agree on goals and strategies
- advocate
- give feedback.

Parent information sharing
Building effective partnerships and welcoming authentic participation is universally important, and this involves teachers being open to learning from parents and specialists, because each partner has insight and understanding that add value and support. Mutual sharing and respect support the development of a constructive learning environment for children and enhance the knowledge base of the adults involved (Ministry of Education, 1996, 2007). Parents know their children and their strengths and interests very well, so it is important that their input is sought and acted upon. When teachers take steps to build collaborative relationships with parents and whānau, they are better able to access such information, which can then be used to more effectively meet the child's needs. Finding out about what the child does at home,

how the family is supporting their interests and any goals the child has set for themselves can provide rich information for teachers to utilise in their planning for future learning.

An authentic practice example comes from the first author (Cameron).

> **Case study: rugby**
>
> The parents of a 4-year-old boy told the teachers that he had displayed significant skill in playing rugby on the weekends. The boy regularly spent hours outside practising with his father and had decided he wanted to learn how to kick the ball over the goal posts. The kindergarten teachers were already aware of his gross motor abilities, and with this new information they were able to plan to regularly take the child, and others who were interested, to the rugby field nearby. The teachers provided lots of opportunities for skill development, including providing tees for kicking practice, along with verbal feedback and encouragement. Rugby players from the local high school were invited to come along and demonstrate practice drills, modelling skills and better equipping the teachers to support this interest.

Although communication and collaboration are generically important, it is especially critical that parents and those working with children who are gifted have opportunities to communicate, because these children are so often misunderstood and there continue to be many myths surrounding giftedness (Porter, 2006). In addition to knowledge about their own child, many parents have particular knowledge and expertise in the area of giftedness. Genuine opportunities are needed for parents to share information about their child's unique traits and characteristics, as well as effective support strategies. This has multiple benefits, including supporting the work of teachers and empowering parents as advocates. Examples of valuable parent–teacher information sharing include:

- multiple perspectives on giftedness
- profiles of the community of educators and learners
- sharing literature about giftedness
- newsletters on events and professional development

- identification procedures and tools
- contact information for others, such as psychologists or support groups
- forums for discussions and support
- celebrations of children's work.

Parent experiences

In this section the experiences of parents of early readers are described, based on two studies by Margrain (1998, 2005). Although Margrain (2005) found that in some settings teachers were negating, disbelieving or negative about the children's giftedness when told of it by parents, it is critical that such information is used to inform teaching rather than being dismissed.

The 1998 study of precocious readers (Margrain, 1998) reported that parents focused their energy on supporting teachers and building relationships. For example:

> A parent explained that she made sure that she gave affirming and positive comments to the teachers about their work. She washed paintbrushes and put away resources, helped clean at the end of the week, helped in the library, was on the fundraising committee, and helped with class trips. This parent hoped that the teacher would be more willing to communicate with her if ever there was an important issue about the child because of the parent's contribution of time and because she had resisted approaching the teacher with small concerns.
> (cited in Margrain, 2010, p. 42)

Parents reported that they made an effort to support teachers, both in early childhood and at school, "building the foundations of a positive relationship for the benefit of their children" (Margrain, 2010, p. 42). Because constructive parent–teacher relationships contribute to children's learning (Mitchell, Haggarty, Hampton, & Pairman, 2006), teachers need to ensure they have a repertoire of strategies for initiating and maintaining positive working relationships with families. Making sure that such relationships are forged for families of gifted children should be a core responsibility of the teacher, and not one that is left for families to instigate.

Parent attempts to communicate: research findings

One of the three research questions addressed in Margrain's (1998) study by way of a survey was, "What happens when children who can already read go to school?" Responses were received for children from 44 sets of parents. Some examples of reading ability in children, reported by their parents, included:

- being able to read whole chapter books in a day
- one child who read five chapter books concurrently, reading a chapter of each one in turn, yet retaining comprehension of the individual stories
- reading Tolkien's *The Hobbit* and *The Lord of the Rings*
- reading *Encyclopaedia Britannica*, newspapers and a range of non-fiction texts.

In their survey responses most of the parents described making efforts to liaise with the school before their child turned 5 to share the extent of their children's reading ability, such as the examples given above. Parents reported three kinds of responses from school staff:

- interest and support (e.g., lending reading materials to a family of a 4-year-old, and providing an individual education plan)
- reserved caution (e.g., listening to parents but being non-committal until the school staff had evaluated the children themselves, even when the families provided full assessment documentation from specialists)
- diffidence, hostility or suspicion—sadly, these were the majority of comments.

The parents were asked, as part of the survey, to explicitly describe *effective* communication strategies from schools. Shockingly, 14 of the families (32 percent) were unable to state *any* effective communication strategies experienced during the transition process, and others qualified any positive strategies by reporting overall frustration with the communication approaches used. For example, a typical parent comment was, "I have to instigate all communication", and another parent stated, "On the whole there is NO communication apart from two reports a year, which let us know absolutely nothing. I always have to ask for feedback" (Margrain, 2003, p. 16).

School communication strategies valued by parents

Despite challenges and frustrations, two-thirds of parents in Margrain's 1998 study were able to report at least one effective communication strategy employed by schools. The school communication strategies were analysed and collated into four categories (informal interpersonal; formal interpersonal; written; and system-level), and they have been collated in Table 9.1 (Margrain, 2003; see also Appendix K). Of course, many of these strategies are not exclusive to working with gifted children or to school contexts and also could readily be used by teachers in early childhood settings.

Table 9.1: Teacher communication strategies valued by parents

Category	Strategy
Informal interpersonal	Informal comments, personal contact, questions, email
	Parent involvement in school, class or centre
	Teacher actively approachable
	Listening, acknowledgement and reassurance
Formal interpersonal	Formal parent–teacher interviews
	Meetings regarding an 'issue': 'awesome' or 'intense' meetings
	Individual education plan (IEP) or education plan (EP)
	Parent education evenings
Written communication	Written reports
	Portfolios or work samples
	General newsletter
	Certificates
	Comments notebook
	Homework
Systems-level communication	Open-door policy—parents able to observe
	Support for 1-day school for gifted students
	Principal/manager supportive
	Websites
	Advising parents of child's reading age or level, test results or grades

Source: Margrain, 2003

The following case study[1] illustrates the potential to include a range of key partners in discussion, the benefits of documenting strategies within an IEP, and a range of positive outcomes. The case study exemplifies the fact that utilising many concurrent strategies is important.

Case study of effective collaboration and communication

David's mum was worried about her son's performance and well-being at school. She spoke with his classroom teacher after school, who said she had also noticed this. They discussed and compared how he was at home and at school, and asked David how he felt about his schoolwork and friends. As a result of the conversation mum decided to have him assessed by a psychologist. The results indicated that he was a twice-exceptional gifted learner (gifted with learning difficulties). Mum shared the report with the teacher and a meeting was arranged with David, his mum, the GATE (gifted and talented education) teacher, the classroom teacher, the special needs facilitator and a SPELD tutor (working with specific learning difficulties).

The meeting encouraged an open forum for all involved, including David himself. Strategies were developed, including an IEP, inclusion in the school GATE programme and in school SPELD sessions. Everyone had a copy of the psychologist's report, which was examined and any recommendations included. The teachers discussed how to differentiate for his needs in their planning. A meeting date was set to follow up on the changes and check on progress in case any adjustments were needed.

The relationship between this team was collaborative, with a common understanding and vision. The GATE teacher included David in the mentor programme, which gives student voice through learning stories and collects data tracking any plateau effects or slipping of grade levels. As a result of this, David felt supported and understood by the community of people involved with his learning and has gained a greater understanding of himself, enabling him to develop healthy friendships and to have productive learning experiences.

---

1   Case study contributed by primary school teacher Brenda Thorrington.

Partnership with children

It is vital that we hear, understand and validate the voices, perceptions and feelings of children. Their interpretations and experiences should not be ignored. After all, although the teacher, family and community play an integral role in the process, it is the child that is at the heart of the matter (Sutherland, 2012). The growing awareness of the need to seek children's perspectives and opinions (Peters & Kelly, 2011) means that adults—both teachers and parents—need to consider and develop a range of strategies that encourage children to share their ideas, feelings and understanding. Talking with children—and really listening to them—is a great starting point.

Empowerment, agency and children's rights

The New Zealand Curriculum (Ministry of Education, 2007) talks about growing "young people who will be confident, connected, actively involved, lifelong learners" (p. 12). The term 'actively involved' has connections to transition, communication and collaboration. To support children to be actively involved, teachers need to think about the power they hold and explore ways to foster children's agency so that they know and feel they have some control of the situation. Of course this does not mean leaving everything up to the child, but rather establishing ways to support children to take some control, to share their views and understanding in ways that best meet their needs. These ideas are supported by Dockett and Perry's (2003) assertion that it is critical that teachers and researchers engage and interact with children if they wish to have any real understanding of what children are experiencing.

With regard to *Te Whāriki*, the principle of *empowerment* is particularly relevant in relation to transition, communication and collaboration. The early childhood curriculum talks about its role in "empowering the child to learn and grow" (Ministry of Education, 1996, p. 40). In order to empower children, teachers and parents must listen to them and really understand what they are saying, both verbally and non-verbally, so that they can respond appropriately. The importance of the relationships teachers establish with children is an important consideration, because it is through strong relationships that teachers will best come to know children and understand what they need at an individual level. This includes the social and emotional aspects of giftedness (Needham, 2012).

The need to access children's perspectives—their 'voices'—is inherent within the United Nations Convention on the Rights of the Child (United Nations, 1989), which is a set of standards and obligations that set out the basic rights of children and the obligations of governments to fulfil those rights. The convention is important because, according to UNICEF, more countries have ratified the Convention than any other human rights treaty in history: 194 countries had become state parties to the Convention as of November 2014.[2] Two articles from the convention are considered below.

The best interests of the child (Article 3): Laws, actions and decisions affecting children should put the children's best interests first and benefit them in the best possible way. This includes budget, curriculum, policy and practice. The best interests of a gifted child may not be the same as for all children of the same age.

A voice (Article 12): Children have a right to be able to voice their opinion about decisions that affect them, to use their voice to self-advocate, and to have their opinions taken into account. This does not negate the responsibility of parents and teachers to exercise leadership and responsibility, and the level of a child's participation in decisions will be influenced by their developmental maturity. However, it should be remembered that gifted children are likely to have deeper reflection, insight, communicative ability and conceptual understandings than their age peers, so may have a different voice to share.

Teachers enjoy a multitude of opportunities daily in which they can seek and respond to children's voices—their perspectives, choices and preferences. Opportunities for children to make meaningful decisions in relation to their learning are important. An example of this would be giving children opportunities to engage in ongoing projects and activities that do not have to be put away at the end of the day, or even at the end of the week.

The following case study draws on authentic experience of the first author (Cameron), although a pseudonym has been used for the child.

---

2   See http://www.unicef.org/crc/index_30225.html

> **Case study of child's voice: Lily**
>
> Lily at age 4½ years was displaying interpersonal and leadership skills well in advance of her peers. One day Lily chose to take on the teacher's role during a small group time when the teacher was responding to another child. Lily gathered the group of approximately 10 children together, sat in the chair usually used by the teacher and began singing a familiar song. Very quickly the other children joined in and Lily continued leading the group time by singing more songs after the teacher returned. Lily then chose to 'read' a story she was very familiar with to the children. Later that day the teacher and Lily had a discussion about whether Lily wanted to continue leading the group time, which she chose to do. Together, each day, they would decide on a plan for the approximately 10-minute-long session, gather the resources needed and collaboratively share the leadership of the group time.

Transition to school

Transition is generally understood as a process of moving from one setting to another, which is likely to include a change of status and culture (Fabian, 2007). The transition from early childhood educational setting to compulsory schooling is a time of significant change, which can be both positive and challenging for children, including children who are gifted. Just as no two children who are gifted are the same, the process of transition to school is not the same for any two children. While little is currently known about gifted children's experiences of starting school (Grant, 2013), the topic of transition to school is one that is of growing interest in New Zealand and around the world.

How children and their families experience the transition to school has the potential to have an impact, either positive or negative, on their future school success (Yeboah, 2002). This long-term influence means that it is important for children, families and teachers from both the early childhood and school sectors to work constructively together to ensure that transition is a positive and smooth experience for all children. For young children who are gifted, this is especially important to ensure that their unique skills, strengths and interests are fostered and further developed. It is also important for families, because when transition is not successful, it is the family that is left to support a frustrated, miserable or rejected child.

Because "transition to school needs to be based on collaboration between and amongst key stakeholders" (Mirkhil, 2010, p. 69), it is important that opportunities are created for sharing and working together with everyone involved in supporting young children who are gifted through the transition process. Of course how this collaboration looks will be different in each situation, but what is most important is that everyone is working together. In order for such collaboration to happen, their first needs to be communication. Through communication the unique strengths, interests and aspirations of each child can be shared and then used to support children's ongoing learning and development across all areas (Sutherland, 2012).

Successes and challenges when beginning school

Major difficulties with transition to school were reported by 24 out of 41 families in Margrain's 1998 study involving children who were already able to read before they started school. Some of these families described the transition experience as "traumatic". Parents reported over and over that their children were frustrated and bored, and also that their children were:

- "frequently depressed and unhappy"
- "bored, unhappy, miserable"
- "negative and baffled ('why are they always telling me things I already know?')"
- "kept back by other children in her group (seven years ahead of age)".

More recently, Gallagher (2008), reporting on findings from her earlier master's study, noted that parents often felt they had less access to teachers in the school sector and that some parents had to repeatedly prove to another set of teachers that their child was in fact gifted. These are not the transition experiences intended by either *Te Whāriki* (Ministry of Education, 1996) or *The New Zealand Curriculum* (Ministry of Education, 2007), as both documents make clear the need for continuity between the sectors and that education should be a positive experience. We assume that teachers do not intend for children to be miserable in their classrooms, but our experience and research tells us that some children are. Transition to school should be, and is assumed to be, a time of anticipation, excitement and new challenge.

A more positive and constructive experience is evident in the following case study, shared by the first author (Cameron).

> **Case study: Andrew**
>
> Andrew had demonstrated his skill as an early reader soon after starting kindergarten at approximately 3 years 7 months of age, when he picked up a disc in the office, read the label and asked the administrator, "What are you going to do with this March back-up disk?" This was when Andrew's key teacher first realised he could read and had an interest in computers. She talked with the family and found out more about his skills, strengths and interests and used these to support Andrew's learning while at the kindergarten.
>
> A few months before Andrew was due to start school, with his parent's permission the teacher contacted the new entrant teacher at the school he was going to attend and organised a time to talk about Andrew and his transition to school. This meant that valuable information was able to be shared between the teachers. The new entrant teacher also chose to visit Andrew at the kindergarten, to see him in an environment in which he was comfortable and to start building a relationship with him. The school teacher maintained contact with the kindergarten teacher and Andrew's family over the following months, ringing when she was unsure or required further information. Andrew's teacher was better able to respond to his individual strengths, skills, interests and needs because she knew about him and had a relationship with him, his family and previous teachers through the development of a collaborative working relationship.

Strategies to support the transition to school

The need to build strong and respectful partnerships between families, teachers (in both school and early childhood sectors) and the children themselves has been noted by Gallagher (2008) in specific reference to gifted children's transition to school. The literature review on transition from early childhood education to school by Peters (2010) provides valuable considerations for teachers to support transition for all children. Key recommendations of the literature review include that teachers should work with the child, work with the family and share information. These recommendations are not exclusive to gifted education, but then gifted children should not be excluded from the considerations given to every other child either.

According to Peters (2010), key transition strategies include:

- connecting with funds of knowledge that children bring to school
- culturally responsive teaching
- diverse assessment practices
- making links between children's learning in early childhood education and school
- fostering positive children's relationships and friendships
- considering children's whole experience of school
- providing rich, open-ended opportunities for play and learning
- understanding the impact of rules and the way these can support belonging, but can also constrain children's behaviour and create anxiety
- providing information and familiarisation activities for children and families
- learning about children and their families
- developing home–school partnerships.

These strategies can be supported with four key provisions: release time, small class sizes, a flexible curriculum, training and professional development.

Focus on continuity

The need to promote continuity and consistency between early childhood and school educational experiences has been identified as a key feature of effective transition to school practice (Dockett & Perry, 2007; Howie & Timperley, 2001; Peters, 2010). Continuity of experiences helps children to understand the links between their home lives and each of the sectors, and to discover ways in which they can see and use the learning strategies, skills and interests developed during early childhood in the more formal school context. Although the need for continuity is made clear in the curriculum documents for both sectors, which will be further explored shortly, what this looks like in practice can be quite varied. Pedagogical differences were found by Wright (2010, p. 151) to have a direct impact on the "learning continuity children experience as they move from one setting to another", and differences in teachers' practices had the potential to have a significant impact on children's learning.

Continuity does not mean that early childhood and primary settings need to be the same. Instead, shared understanding needs to be cultivated between teachers in order to recognise, value and build on the learning and opportunities that are available in each sector (Cameron, 2010). Given Gallagher's (2008) finding that primary teachers are often reluctant to trust early childhood teachers' judgements in relation to children being gifted, it is critical that teachers in both sectors collaborate to build a better understanding of each other's work. Communication and collaboration between teachers is essential if we want to ensure continuity of learning for young children who are gifted.

Networks are one way that teachers from both sectors can come together and engage collaboratively in professional learning communities specifically focused on effective transition, or on supporting gifted children's learning—or in fact on any mutually agreed purpose. Such networks can support teachers from both sectors to develop relationships and trust, but also to share knowledge, understanding and commitment to ensure effective transition to school processes for all involved (Cameron, 2010). Networks are further discussed in Chapter 11.

Curriculum connections supporting transition
Despite the early childhood and school sectors being guided by two separate curriculum documents, there are many points of alignment. Both curricula are underpinned by sociocultural theories of learning, and the key competencies of *The New Zealand Curriculum* were specifically designed to align with the learning dispositions of *Te Whāriki* (Carr, 2006). As well as these points of connection, both documents make specific reference to the need for collaboration and effective transition processes for all children, as highlighted in the citations below.

The following quotations relating to collaboration and transition are from *Te Whāriki* (Ministry of Education, 1996):

> *Te Whāriki* is designed to be inclusive and appropriate for all children and anticipates that special needs will be met as children learn together in all kinds of early childhood education settings. (p. 11)
>
> Young children experience transitions from home to service, from service to service, and from service to school. They need as much consistency and continuity of experience as possible in order to develop confidence and trust to explore and to establish a secure foundation of remembered and anticipated people, places, things and experiences. (p. 46)
>
> The early childhood curriculum provides a foundation for children to become confident and competent and, during the school years, to be able to build on their previous learning. (p. 93)

The following quotations on transition are from *The New Zealand Curriculum* (Ministry of Education, 2007):

> The curriculum offers all students a broad education that makes links within and across learning areas, provides for coherent transitions, and opens up pathways to further learning. (p. 9)
>
> As students journey from early childhood through secondary school … they should find that each stage of the journey prepares them for and connects well with the next. Schools can design their curriculum so that students find the transitions positive and have a clear sense of continuity and direction. (p. 41)
>
> The transition from early childhood education to school is supported when the school:
>
> - fosters a child's relationships with teachers and other children and affirms their identity
>
> - builds on the learning experiences that the child brings with them; considers the child's whole experiences of school; is welcoming of family and whānau. This new stage in children's learning builds upon and makes connections with early childhood learning experiences. (p. 41)

Conclusion

Communication between all stakeholders—including children, families and teachers—is critical for ensuring that gifted children's unique needs are met in early childhood settings and as they begin school. Effective communication is more likely to occur when there are trusting, respectful and professional relationships between everyone involved. It is therefore important that teachers and families work collaboratively to establish such relationships. The building of such relationships can take time and must involve concerted effort on the part of the adults involved. The benefits of forming and maintaining such relationships are substantial, as together all parties will be better able to support each other and respond to the child in ways that best meet their needs and support their learning.

Further reading

The following text is an easily readable and highly recommended book download (see http://gifted.tki.org.nz/For-schools-and-teachers) which discusses parent–teacher partnership with specific reference to children in Aotearoa New Zealand who are gifted.

J. Bevan-Brown & S. Taylor. (2008). *Nurturing gifted and talented children: A parent–teacher partnership.* Wellington: Ministry of Education.

References

Cameron, M. J. (2010). *Teachers need to talk: The role of cross-sector professional learning communities in promoting effective transition to school practice.* Unpublished critical literature review, Massey University.

Carr, M. (2006). Learning dispositions and key competencies: A new curriculum continuity across the sectors? *Early Childhood Folio, 10,* 21–26.

Dockett, S., & Perry, B. (2003, September). *Children's voices in research on starting school.* Paper presented at the 13th annual conference of the Early Childhood Education Research Association, Quality in Early Childhood Education, Possible Childhoods: Relationships and Choices, Glasgow, Scotland.

Dockett, S., & Perry, B. (2007). *Transitions to school: Perceptions, expectations, experiences.* Sydney, NSW: UNSW Press.

Fabian, H. (2007). Introduction. In A. W. Dunlop & H. Fabian (Eds.), *Informing transitions in the early years: Research, policy and practice* (pp. 3–17). Maidenhead, UK: McGraw-Hill.

Gallagher, G. (2008). *Gifted and talented children in transition to school: What do we need to know and do? To whose voices do we need to listen?* Paper presented at the New Zealand Association for the Gifted Child conference, Auckland.

Grant, A. (2013). Young gifted children transitioning into primary school: What matters? *Australasian Journal of Early Childhood, 38*(2), 23–31.

Howie, L., & Timperley, H. (2001). *Educators' responsibilities for providing for effective transition from early childhood centre to school.* Paper presented at the New Zealand Association for Research in Education Conference, Christchurch.

Margrain, V. (1998). *Young able readers: Parental perceptions regarding their children's literacy learning and transition to school; and parent experiences of school collaboration and consultation.* Unpublished master's project, Massey University.

Margrain, V. (2003). *Already reading in early childhood: Issues of identification, accommodation and collaboration.* Occasional paper no. 15. Wellington: Institute for Early Childhood Studies, Victoria University of Wellington.

Margrain, V. G. (2005). *Precocious readers: Case studies of social support, spontaneous learning and self-regulation in the early years.* Unpublished doctoral thesis, Victoria University of Wellington.

Margrain, V. (2007). Inside the greenhouse: Hothousing, cultivating, tending or nurturing precocious readers? *New Zealand Research in Early Childhood Education Journal, 10*, 33–46.

Margrain, V. (2010). Parent–teacher partnership for gifted early readers in New Zealand. *International Journal about Parents in Education, 4*(1), 39–48.

Ministry of Education. (1996). *Te whāriki: He whāriki matauranga mō ngā mokopuna ō Aotearoa: Early childhood curriculum.* Wellington: Learning Media.

Ministry of Education. (2007). *The New Zealand curriculum for English-medium teaching and learning in years 1–13.* Wellington: Learning Media.

Ministry of Education. (2012). *Gifted and talented students: Meeting their needs in New Zealand schools.* Wellington: Learning Media.

Mirkhil, M. (2010). Important ingredients for a successful transition to school. *International Research in Early Childhood Education, 1*(1), 60–70.

Mitchell, L., Haggarty, M., Hampton, V., & Pairman, A. (2006). *Teachers, parents and whānau working together in early childhood education.* Wellington: NZCER Press.

Needham, V. (2012). Primary teachers' perceptions of the social and emotional aspects of gifted and talented education. *Apex: The New Zealand Journal of Gifted Education*, *17*(1). Retrieved from http://www.giftedchildren.org.nz/apex

Peters, S. (2010). *Literature review: Transition from early childhood education to school: Report to the Ministry of Education*. Wellington: Ministry of Education. Retrieved from http://www.educationcounts.govt.nz/__data/assets/pdf_file/0003/78825/Literature-Review-Transition-from-ECE-to-School.pdf

Peters, S., & Kelly, J. (2011). Exploring children's perspectives: Multiple ways of seeing and knowing children. *Waikato Journal of Education*, *16*(3), 19–30.

Porter, L. (2006). *Twelve myths of gifted education*. Retrieved from http://www.louiseporter.com.au/pdfs/twelve_myths_of_gifted_education_web.pdf

Rogoff, B., Goodman Turkanis, C., & Bartlett, L. (2001). *Learning together: Children and adults in a school community*. New York, NY: Oxford University Press.

Sutherland, M. (2012). *Gifted and talented in the early years: A practical guide for 3-6 year olds* (2nd ed.). SAGE: London.

UNICEF. (2005). *Convention on the rights of the child*. Retrieved from http://www.unicef.org/crc/index_30229.html

United Nations. (1989). *Convention on the rights of the child*. Retrieved from http://www.ohchr.org/Documents/ProfessionalInterest/crc.pdf

Wright, J. (2010). *Schisms and shimmers of hope: Sector difference and the influence on children's learning*. Unpublished master's thesis, University of Canterbury. Retrieved from http://ipac.canterbury.ac.nz/ipac20/ipac.jsp?index=BIB&term=1654057

Yeboah, D. A. (2002). Enhancing transition from early childhood phase to primary education: Evidence from the research literature. *Early Years: Journal of International Research and Development*, *22*(1), 51–68.

Chapter 10: Liam's story: At risk of underachievement

Carola Sampson

Introduction

Many intellectually gifted children underachieve in the regular classroom, their performance not reflecting their true potential. This can have many reasons, an unresponsive school or early childhood environment being just one of them (Clark, 2013; Hodge; 2012, Porter, 2005). This chapter reports a case study of underachievement and misunderstanding of a young gifted child, Liam, and follows his development chronologically from toddler to primary school student, highlighting his outstanding abilities, his educational environments (home, kindergarten, school) and the development of his gifts into talents. The case study was informed by checklists from Cathcart (2005), Allan (2002) and Piechowski (2006), as well as interviews conducted either with Liam or with his parents, work samples, learning stories, school reports and Liam's educational assessment. These all provide insight into his developing outstanding abilities (gifts) and the contributing circumstances to his discontent at school. The case study was undertaken as a Master of Education assignment, and consent from his parents has been obtained for publication; the child's name has been changed to 'Liam' to protect his identity.

Gagné's (2012, 2014) Differentiated Model of Giftedness and Talent (DMGT) was applied to Liam's situation at a certain time in his school life, emphasising the strong interactions and impacts of internal and external influences on Liam's well-being and talent development. Gifts, intrapersonal and environmental catalysts, and talent development are interdependent contributors to the manifestation of fully developed gifts (talents) (Gagné, 2012). Each component influences the others in multifaceted ways; the application of the DMGT to individual cases like Liam's can make these causal influences more visible in an attempt to counteract undesired negative outcomes such as underachievement (Gagné, 2012).

Liam's family

Liam, aged 9 at the time of this study, is the firstborn child of a German mother, fluent in German and English, and an Irish father, fluent in English and Spanish. Both parents are tertiary educated and have siblings with the same or similar education. Like his younger sister, Liam was born overseas. The family moved to New Zealand in 2008 for lifestyle reasons.

Early competencies and interests

Liam was walking and talking at around 14 months and started showing signs of being different around the age of 2 years, when the family found him obsessed with the letters of the alphabet, surprising his mother when he spelled each letter of 'fire extinguisher'. By the age of 3 his mother noticed him beginning to read whole words; shortly after, he was reading street signs, car number plates and roadwork signs. Liam also showed an interest in writing. By age 4 he was reading books at home, such as Geronimo Stilton, the Gruffalo books and one specific book by Roald Dahl. His reading and writing skills became obvious at kindergarten, where he tended to label doors, tables, items and even the Christmas tree, as well as writing notes.

Liam taught himself reading and writing prior to school. He used his self-taught skills to learn about areas of his interests, mainly from books at home. His parents accommodated his interests in LEGO®, science, space and anything related to computers by providing the necessary literature and items needed. They created a nurturing and stimulating learning environment at home. According to his family, Liam spent a great amount of time reading fiction, non-fiction and manuals at home, and took pride in creating his own 'books' and manuals, such as one about circuits; he wrote, illustrated, printed and stapled them.

Moltzen (2011a) has suggested a strong link between early reading and giftedness. This is supported by the research literature, which shows that many highly gifted children are self-taught readers before commencing school (Margrain, 2011). Often they tend to move on from fiction to non-fiction books, encyclopaedias, maps and even instruction manuals to gain more knowledge in the areas of their interests (Harrison, 2005; Porter, 2005). This can be seen very clearly in Liam's case, when he developed a strong interest in parallel and relay circuits and electronics as soon as he could read. He began to build them, following instruction manuals at kindergarten (which he attended from the age of 3 years 5 months), with special construction sets, and at home.

Kindergarten

The kindergarten teachers seem to have been aware of Liam's interests, and throughout his portfolio there was ample evidence of his developing writing skills and his growing passion for electricity and electronics. While going through the portfolio, I, a practising kindergarten teacher myself, also noticed the fast rate of learning and development of these skills, which are examples of characteristics of giftedness highlighted by Gagné (2013). As an example, I asked Liam during his interview if he recalled when and why he had changed very suddenly from writing all words in upper case to the correct form of lower-case writing. Liam remembered that one day at kindergarten a teacher mentioned the correct writing to him while passing by and looking over his shoulder. He had been intrigued at hearing this and wanted to know more, so the teacher obliged and explained it to him. From then on he applied his new-learnt knowledge, which was clearly seen in his early childhood assessment portfolio.

The responsiveness of Liam's kindergarten environment appears to have strongly influenced Liam's learning and the development of his advanced skills, although his teachers didn't seem to know much about his activities at home. However, they accommodated him and offered additional activities that were of interest to him, like the circuitry building set or the old car radio that didn't work, providing him with opportunities for problem solving and higher-order thinking. They also had him write his own learning stories about his research activities, like the one about his 'café', where he 'surveyed' how many children visited; the teachers supported those stories with photos. Their learning stories and other documentation on Liam acknowledged him as a competent and confident learner, encouraging him to meet the next challenge. Liam was very happy at kindergarten because he was free to pursue his interests and felt at ease with the children and adults in this setting.

Liam's kindergarten assessment portfolio contained the voices of several teachers as well as his own, and although his parents and his grandmother were visibly involved in kindergarten life (as documented by the teachers,) there was no parent's voice to be found or other indication that could support a link from the kindergarten to home in which parents would comment on Liam's learning experiences inside and outside kindergarten. Liam's parents were never asked about interests at home, nor were there ever indications made about Liam's advanced abilities. His mother recalled the occasional brief talk with teachers around pickup times, which covered Liam's activities and interests on those days—nothing more. According to Liam's mother, there was only one other reading child at kindergarten at that time, and, to her knowledge, no other child was writing like Liam did. It would have made for a more holistic picture of Liam's learning and development if the parents' and family voices had been included in Liam's portfolio, which would have enabled his teachers to gain more insight into his exceptional abilities and his way of thinking, and to plan extra challenges he might have needed in areas of his advanced learning.

The additional view of Liam's activities outside kindergarten would have made his advanced abilities more obvious. Portfolios as formative assessment tools can reveal interests, exceptional abilities and advanced learning best if shared with all involved— teachers, children, parents and family, caregivers and even student teachers (McLachlan, Edwards, Margrain & McLean, 2013). In Liam's case, his home learning environment was supportive, with many learning opportunities, providing a valuable parallel to the kindergarten environment. It would have been of great advantage for Liam, his family and his teachers to have had a shared and collaborative understanding of both environments, not only for furthering his exceptional abilities but also for supporting his parents' advocacy at school, as described below (Harrison, 2005).

Beginning school

Liam started school, aged 5, in 2010. His new entrant teacher tested his reading skills by handing him the letters of the alphabet to see what he would recognise and was surprised when he formed full sentences with them. She didn't ask the parents any further about his skills, nor did she enquire about his kindergarten portfolio, which would have shown his advanced literacy skills. However, her school report about Liam's learning by the end of Year 1 acknowledged Liam's advanced reading skills as 3 years above his chronological age, as well as his advanced spelling, writing and number skills, and his extensive knowledge in topics of science and technology. I noticed a ceiling in the school's grading system, which had only three different grades, ranging from 'shows strength (SS)' via 'good (G)' to 'is developing (ID)'; this did not leave much room for any performance in between, nor did it provide information about performances higher than the school's expected age-appropriate level.

Liam's school ran a mixed-class system whereby Year 1 and 2 students would be taught in one class, Year 2 and 3 students in another, and Year 3 and 4 students in yet another class. This mixed-class system concluded with Year 7 and 8 students in a mixed class. While Liam was attending his first year of school his passion for technology progressed further at home. He created little animated short films with his camera and his laptop, taking a special interest in editing films. In school he moved up into Year 2 within the Year 2/3 class level, but while his grades were still top within the class, and his next teacher acknowledged his well-above-average performance, Liam had begun to get bored and unhappy, and this was documented in his second school report.

Outside school he was performing at a much higher level of thinking and problem solving, having begun building and programming with Arduino® electronic building kits and learning the computer programming language Python by himself, all the while keeping up with plenty of non-fiction books and manuals, which provided him with even more knowledge in his areas of interest. During his second year of school Liam's mother had begun to work as a parent helper in both her children's classes, and she noticed a difference in Liam's classroom behaviour. She became increasingly concerned about his boredom and his obvious unhappiness in class, which made him just sit there doing nothing.

Assessment

A family friend suggested having Liam assessed by an educational psychologist because she believed him to be gifted. A cognitive and educational assessment was done in 2012; Liam had just turned 7 years old at that time. The applied assessments consisted of the Woodcock Johnson III tests of cognitive abilities, tests of achievement, given information and observations. The results revealed a ranking of Liam's overall intellectual abilities within the top 0.3 percent of his age peers, a very advanced comprehension knowledge, and fluid reasoning for problem solving, as well as very superior language, reading, writing and spelling skills. Liam was, indeed, found to be a highly gifted child. However, the findings in relation to his short-term and working memory, as well as his slower processing speed, being not quite as advanced as his other abilities, were found to be a possible source of frustration. The discrepancy was large enough to create a need for more time to process information and to make decisions.

Liam's parents presented this assessment to his school, but they were ignored. Only after several meetings with the principal did the school finally agree to have Liam accelerated and skip Year 3, going straight into Year 4 in 2013. However, the school's teacher for gifted and talented education (GATE), who had monitored Liam's performance as his class teacher in Year 2, told his parents that she did not believe him to be gifted. A friend of the family, who was a school teacher at a different school, assessed Liam's reading comprehension and found it to be at age level 13.5 years on a reading PROBE assessment, but by then the parents felt too disheartened to show this result to Liam's teacher. They could not understand the school's negative and unsupportive attitude towards their son, especially after he had been assessed.

Frustration, misunderstanding and risk

Liam's parents faced the same difficulties many families do with gifted children in Aotearoa New Zealand, whose children feel under-challenged, misunderstood and bored (Chellapan & Margrain, 2013). A recent study on the perspectives of parents with gifted children in New Zealand found that a lack of knowledge of gifted education could be seen as a main cause for failing to provide for gifted students in mainstream schools, making parent advocacy and knowledge in gifted education vital (Chellapan & Margrain, 2013). Parents with gifted children reported difficulties, hardships and loneliness in being the sole advocates for their children, especially in unresponsive school environments where children increasingly lost motivation and no longer performed (Chellapan & Margrain, 2013).

Although Liam was finally accelerated, he still felt unhappy, bored and misunderstood. He often had questions about tasks that were not clear to him, like on the day when he was asked to write down the feelings one would have winning a gold medal at the Olympic Games. To Liam there were big differences in Winter or Summer Olympic Games, ancient Greek Olympic Games or modern ones, or even Paralympics. He was wondering where those Olympic Games would have taken place, what nationality, what gender he was supposed to imagine for his task. He had many questions, but his teacher remained unresponsive and discouraged Liam from asking further questions. This happened on several occasions until Liam stopped working in class, which in turn was seen by the school as confirmation that Liam could not possibly be gifted. Liam's third school report mentioned his struggle to commence writing tasks and as needing assistance.

Liam's grades began to slip, his unhappiness became more and more apparent, and he became tearful at home, complaining he had "lost his spark". His parents kept trying to seek support and acknowledgement from the school, but to no avail, and also searched for any suitable enrichment outside school. There was no 'One Day School' or any other pull-out programme in the area, but they found Gifted Online, an extension programme run by the New Zealand Centre of Gifted Education, and they enrolled him during the last term of 2013 to give him the needed intellectual challenges the school could not provide. While his school accommodated the 1-hour pull-out per week necessary to join the online community of this programme, allowing his mother to sit with him in the school library during online sessions, there was no interest in this programme or in Liam's progress in it by the school. Liam's school report at the end of the year advised that Liam needed to focus on quick recall of times tables and basic facts, as well as improvement in time management skills, which comes as a surprise given that his cognitive assessment 6 months earlier explicitly stated his need for less time constraints due to his speed processing issues.

When the school refused to have Liam accelerated from Year 4/5 into 5/6 while most of his classmates did go up, his parents began to consider a change in schools. His mother, still parent helper in his class, looked at the learning content her son engaged in and compared class exercises with the activities he did outside school (like developing his own website and blog, story writing, programming and reading books like *The Hobbit*) and found her son under-challenged at school. A non-stimulating school environment with a lack of challenge and acknowledgement, and a strong emphasis on failure and weaknesses, can have a major impact on gifted students, causing underachievement (Clark, 2013; Seeley, 2004). Although Liam's mother was actively involved in her children's school life as parent helper, she and her son felt unheard and unvalued by the school; Liam performed less and less in class and began to underachieve (Clark, 2013).

Unresponsiveness to the parents' and Liam's voices, together with a lack of time to listen and to find out about Liam's extracurricular activities and achievements, contributed to Liam feeling unvalued and not good enough: it led to a decrease in his self-esteem. This affected his motivation, self-awareness and resilience. Liam was at risk of academic underachievement when he began to withdraw from classroom activities. Current research in underachievement has found that a school can be the main cause of underachievement due to a lack of challenge, inflexibility, excessive dwelling on failure or poor performance, a rigid curriculum, non-responsiveness, and a lack of collaboration with students and their families (Clark, 2013; Moltzen, 2011b).

The previous descriptions indicate a mismatch between Liam and his initial school environment, which had put Liam at risk of academic underachievement and not performing to his true potential (Moltzen,

2011b; Siegle, 2013). Intellectually gifted children have the potential to make important contributions to society when acknowledged within a nurturing environment, but they are susceptible to boredom and disengagement in the classroom when unrecognised and unappreciated (Hodge, 2012). The interviews with Liam and his parents, and examination of checklists, revealed a lack of collaboration, acknowledgement and recognition of Liam as a gifted child on the school's part. As part of my case study assignment, I applied Gagné's (2012) Differentiated Model of Gifts and Talents (DMGT) to this child study. The purpose of completing the DMGT model (see Figure 1.1 in Chapter 1) was to have a better understanding of the possible ramifications for Liam if his school situation had remained as it was, and to emphasise the strong influence and interdependence of environmental and intrapersonal catalysts.

Applying Gagné's DMGT model

Gagné (2012, 2014) presents his DMGT as a useful framework that can be applied to various contexts in order to analyse and understand gifts and how these can develop into talents, influenced by intrapersonal and environmental catalysts and (to some extent) by chance. His model is widely recognised and has been applied successfully in the past, even to areas outside academia, such as sport, culture and the arts (Frengley-Vaipuna, Kupu-MacIntyre, & Riley, 2011; Tranckle & Cushion, 2006). The DMGT can provide explanations and give insights into the causes of gifted underachievement, opening up possibilities for teachers and parents to step in and support gifted children to realise their talents (Gagné, 2012). The term 'gift' or 'giftedness' is not without controversy, and attitudes toward giftedness depend on societal, cultural and educational contexts, as well as understanding of what forms it might take, making it a sociocultural concept (Hodge, 2012; Moltzen, 2011a).

Harrison (2005) describes giftedness in children as having the ability to perform at a level considerably higher than their age peers. Gifted children require special provisions and challenges as well as the social and emotional support from the adults around them, which includes educational settings in early childhood and school. Gagné (2012) distinguishes between gifts and talents, describing gifts as outstanding natural abilities in at least one ability domain (intellectual, creative, social, perceptual, muscular and motor control), which positions the owner of this ability among the top 10 percent of their age peers. According to Gagné (2012), these abilities develop over time through maturation and use, gradually becoming talents when systematically nurtured. Talent is described as the sum of those fully developed natural abilities and their skilful use in at least one area of human activity, to the extent of being placed among the top 10 percent of age peers in that area (Gagné, 2012). In explaining what natural abilities are and how they are evident as giftedness, Gagné (2008, 2010, 2013) suggests that gifted individuals are born with a specific genetic potential in certain areas. This potential develops into natural abilities at a faster speed, which can be seen more easily during the early years because of less restrictive environments young children are in. There is a strong risk that, without appropriate support and opportunity, young children who are gifted may not realise talent.

The process of developing outstanding natural abilities or gifts into talents is strongly influenced by intrapersonal catalysts such as personal health, temperament, perseverance and motivation, and environmental catalysts such as home, educational settings, culture and society; chance as a form of fate is considered as an additional influence. Catalysts and chance can support or hinder the talent development process in many ways (Gagné, 2012).

In Liam's case, as shown in Figure 10.1, natural abilities and their development at a fast rate were clearly seen within the intellectual domain through his strong interest in letters of the alphabet as a toddler, which progressed into self-taught reading by the age of 3, and went from there to self-taught writing, enabling him to gain more knowledge in the areas of his interests and communicating his newfound insights to others in writing. His educational assessment recognised and attested to his very advanced intellectual skills in reading, writing, comprehension, fluid reasoning, cognitive efficiency, working memory and long-term retrieval, as well as spelling, writing and reading fluency and maths calculation.

Chapter 10: Liam's story: At risk of underachievement

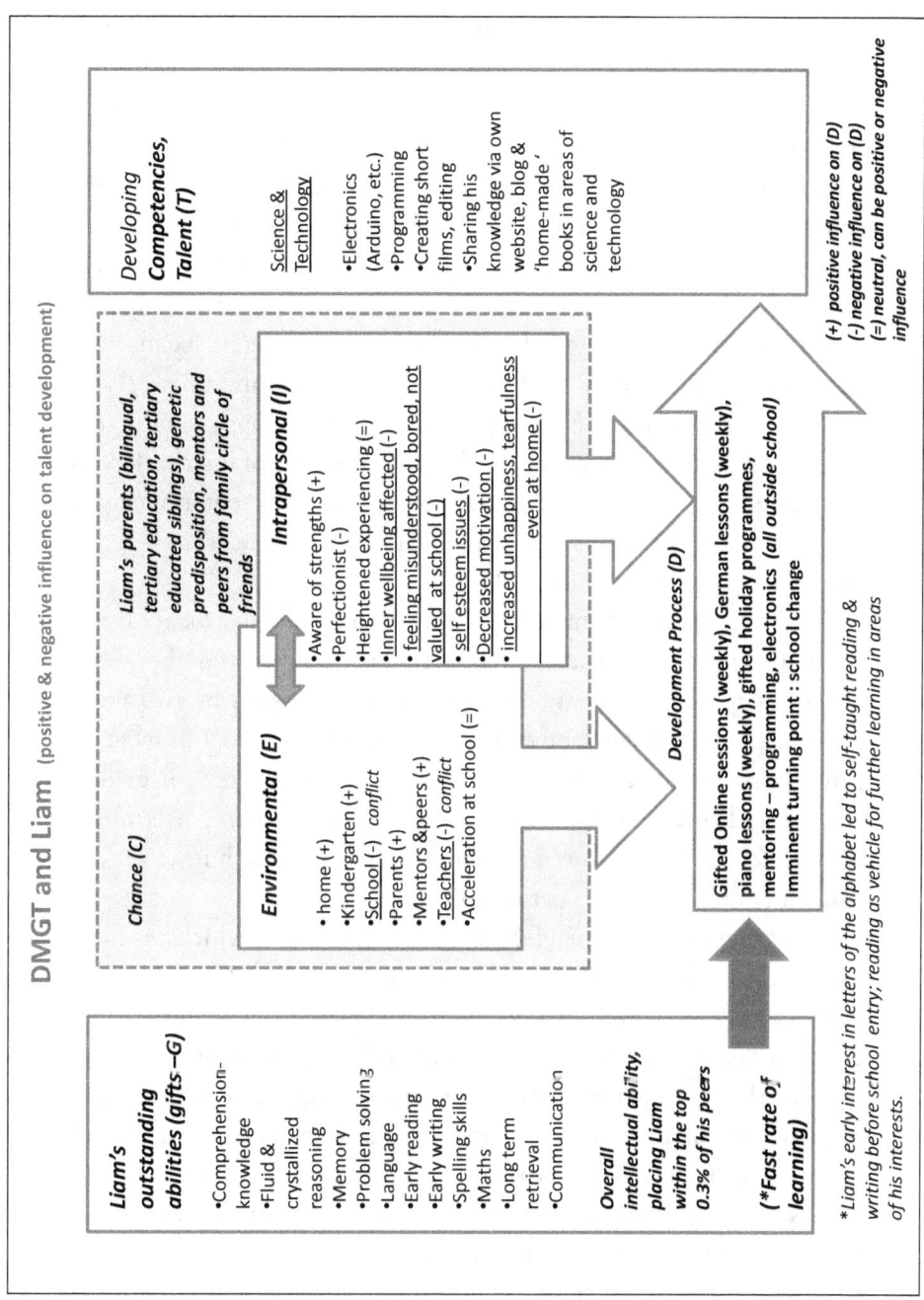

Figure 10.1. Gagné's Differentiated Model of Giftedness and Talent applied to Liam.

For natural abilities (gifts) to become talents, they need to be developed, nurtured and supported, which can be seen as a talent development process. This process is mainly a systematic progression of extra courses, training, enrichment programmes, differentiated curriculum, and so forth (Gagné, 2012). Gagné (2008) divides these ideas into three sub-components of activities, investments and progress. Liam's development process is currently defined by his enrolment in the Gifted Online programme once a week, holiday enrichment programmes, extra language lessons in German once a week, piano lessons, the time he spends with his mentors on his passion of electronics and programming, as well as the turning point in changing schools. Liam was born to bilingual parents with tertiary education, both very supportive of their children's interests and actively involved in their education. His mentors emerged from the family's circle of friends, which can be allocated to Gagné's chance aspect within the DMGT.

Liam's talent development process was (and still is) strongly influenced by intrapersonal and environmental catalysts and the above chance factor. Intrapersonal catalysts are distinguished by two main features, physical and mental qualities being one of them. This includes general appearance and health, as well as temperament, personality and the resilience to bounce back from failures and staying determined (Gagné, 2012). Liam knew his strengths and abilities, but he was, at times, in doubt due to his perfectionism.

The second intrapersonal facet is goal management, which has three sub-aspects: self-awareness, motivation and volition (Gagné, 2012). Self-awareness supports the setting of individual goals in strong areas of ability and fosters talent development in those areas. Motivation and volition, the two other subcomponents of goal management, determine the ambition or pursuit, the desire to achieve in the specific area of talent, and the personal approach or strategy to do so (Gagné, 2012). Liam's learning stories from kindergarten, along with the interviews with him and his parents, showed an intrinsic need for learning, so the learned knowledge could be put to use in learning even more in areas of his passion, such as science, electronics and technology. Each achievement was experienced as pleasure, feeding the need to move on and learn more. Rather than following this path for any extrinsic reasons, such as awards or prestige or peer pressure, Liam's motivation at the time of this study appeared to be intrinsic (Gagné, 2010).

Heightened intensities were obvious through excitement, like hopping, nail biting and getting very upset when interrupted in his projects, indicating a deeper experiencing of events (Piechowski, 2006). Liam's intellectual, psychomotor, emotional and sensual intensities were evident throughout the interviews and checklists of this study, corroborating that Liam's strong interests and activities were his own and, as part of his self-expression, intrinsically motivated (Garrett & Moltzen, 2011; Piechowski, 2006). He was able to follow his passion and pursue his self-developing goals due to the nurturing and accommodating support of his parents, family and mentors.

Gagné (2012) would allocate such support to the area of environmental catalysts, which affirms the interdependence and close interactions between all the components of his talent development model, the DMGT. Environments of key influence may include society, culture, early childhood setting, school and home. Catalytic individuals within these environments include parents, siblings, teachers, peers and mentors. Provisions may also be catalysts; for example, enrichment classes, class acceleration and pull-out programmes such as One Day School (ODS) (Gagné, 2012).

Liam's extracurricular activities (which accommodated his interests), his class acceleration after Year 2, and his support from family, peers and mentors (like the engineer and the programming psychologist) are all within this area of the DMGT (Gagné, 2010). It also includes environments such as home, educational settings and the relationships of everyone involved. All those environmental aspects can be contributors to or inhibitors of the talent development process, directly and indirectly, through their impact on intrapersonal qualities (Gagné, 2010, 2012).

Liam's responsive home and kindergarten environment, relatively free of a restricting curriculum, had certainly contributed to his fast-developing skills in reading, writing and making sense of literature, which enhanced his knowledge and expertise in science and technology (Ministry of Education, 1996). As mentioned previously, his kindergarten teachers did not appear to have had much insight into his learning at home, but both learning environments (kindergarten and home) had fuelled his motivation and his own awareness of what he was capable of regardless. They encouraged him to persevere in his pursuit of knowledge and implementation of what he had learnt with pleasure. School life brought changes for Liam, and with it more restriction, like time constraints, often inflexible learning content, paired with an increase in conflicting relationships with teachers. Liam's special educational needs for more challenging learning content and an adaptation to his learning style were not acknowledged, and his outstanding abilities were not acknowledged even after his parents presented an educational assessment that attested to these (Gagné, 2010).

Collaborative partnerships

Collaborative partnerships between parents and educational settings, early childhood and schools alike, foster children's well-being and academic achievement as they take the various perspectives of the child—in this case Liam—and his learning in various environments into account (Clark, 2013; Ministry of Education, 1996, 2008; Moltzen, 2011a; Porter, 2005). These relationships, strongly encouraged by the Ministry of Education, provide additional information on children's interests, abilities and their way of learning. They enhance gifted children's achievement because they feel more at ease and understood in a triadic partnership of child, teachers and parents (Ministry of Education, 2008; Porter, 2005).

Liam's case demonstrates how this lack of collaboration and the unresponsiveness to his needs in the classroom affected his inner well-being and became negatively influential on his academic talent development, which was seen in his unhappiness, loss of motivation, and decreased performance at school and in his school report. It shows clearly the interdependent relationships of natural abilities (G), environmental catalysts (E), intrapersonal catalysts (I) and talent development (D); and provides a useful insight into Liam's progress in developing his outstanding abilities (gifts) into talents (Gagné, 2012). Liam's outstanding natural abilities were evident through parent interviews and checklists, interviews and checklists with Liam, work samples, learning stories and school reports, and through his educational assessment with the applied Woodcock Johnson III achievement tests. Also evident were his own intrapersonal influences and those from the various environments he was in at the time (Allan, 2002; Cathcart, 2005; Piechowski, 2006). The impacts of those environments were clearly seen in his gradually declining academic performance at school, and while the school issue appeared to be the primary reason for Liam's difficulties, it was also the one Liam's parents could handle more readily and make amends for (Clark, 2013).

Making a positive change

Liam's parents decided to go ahead and change Liam's school environment. After researching and visiting several schools in the area, they found one that had a principal "who really listened". The new school encourages close parent–teacher relationships and is interested in and supportive of gifted programmes that can be included in the classroom. On finding out about Liam's expertise in programming and computer software, the headmaster has given Liam the leading role in a special project, involving the whole school, by running a survey on student's transport to and from school over a longer timeframe. He can create his own way of presenting the results, which will be published on the local council website. It would be interesting to re-apply the DMGT at a later stage, as things are now looking up for him at school.

While conducting this study, I showed Liam a student checklist on how to get more out of school (Cathcart, 2005). His choices clearly revealed his longing for peers, and his need for differentiated learning and being allowed to ask questions, for acceptance and positive feedback when asking questions, for less repetition, and for being allowed to be more creative in class (Cathcart, 2005). Outside school Liam is busy with his interests and hobbies, feeling supported by his family and two community mentors. These mentors are a psychologist who shares Liam's passion for programming, and an engineer who shares Liam's passion for electronics.

Conclusion

Liam's case study highlights the strong impact school environments have on young children's well-being and development. It demonstrates the importance of collaborative relationships between teachers and parents, and the need for education sectors to work together (McLachlan, et al, 2013). Liam's school experiences could have been different if his new entrant teacher had seen his kindergarten portfolio, which attested to his advanced literacy and problem-solving skills. A shared understanding about gifted children's outstanding abilities, their interests and their way of learning in and outside school will have a positive impact on these children's overall happiness and make the development of their gifts into talents achievable.

Gagné's DMGT has been applied to Liam's case study to shed light on his unhappiness and declining performance at school, exhibiting clearly how strongly environmental catalysts can influence intrapersonal aspects. As a flexible framework, this model supports a deeper understanding of giftedness and its development into talent (Gagné, 2012). It also makes potential inhibitors to talent development visible, which then makes it possible for involved adults, such as teachers and parents, to act on these in an attempt to prevent underachievement of gifted children and students (Gagné, 2012).

References

Allan, B. (2002). *Identifying and providing for giftedness in the early years*. Palmerston North: Kanuka Grove Press.

Cathcart, R. (2005). *They're not bringing my brain out: Understanding and working with gifted and talented learners* (3rd ed.). Auckland: Hodder Education, Hachette Livre.

Chellapan, L., & Margrain V. (2013). "If you talk, you are just talking. If I talk is that bragging?": Perspectives of parents with young gifted children in New Zealand. *Apex: The New Zealand Journal of Gifted Education, 18(1)*. Retrieved from http://www.giftedchildren.org.nz/apex.

Clark, B. (2013). *Growing up gifted: Developing the potential of children at school and at home*. Upper Saddle River, NJ: Pearson.

Frengley-Vaipuna, I., Kupu-MacIntyre, L., & Riley, T. (2011). Successful Tongan students in New Zealand secondary schools: Default or design? *Kairaranga, 12*(2), 42–51.

Gagné, F. (2008). *Building gifts into talent: Brief overview of the DMGT 2.0*. Retrieved from http://gagnefrancoys.wix.com/dmgt-mddt

Gagné, F. (2010). Motivation within the DMGT 2.0 framework. *High Ability Studies, 21*(2), 81–99.

Gagné, F. (2012). Differentiated model of giftedness and talent. In T. L. Cross & J. R. Cross , (Eds.), *Handbook for counsellors: Serving students with gifts and talents* (pp. 3–19). Waco, TX: Prufrock Press.

Gagné, F. (2013). The DMGT: Changes within, beneath and beyond. *Talent Development & Excellence, 5*(1), 5–19.

Gagné, F. (2014). Differentiated model of giftedness and talent (DMGT). Retrieved from http://www.gagnefrancoys.wix.com/dmgt-mddt

Garrett, L., & Moltzen, R. (2011). Writing because I want to, not because I have to: Young gifted writers' perspectives on the factors that 'matter' in developing exercise. *English Teaching: Practice and Critique, 10*(1), 165–180.

Harrison, C. (2005). *Young gifted children: Their search for complexity and connection*. Exeter, NSW: Inscript Publishing.

Hodge, K. (2012). Giftedness. In J. Bowes, R. Grace, & K. Hodge (Eds.), *Children, families and communities: Contexts and consequences* (4th ed., pp. 58–68). Melbourne, VIC: Oxford University Press.

Margrain, V. (2011). Assessment for learning with young gifted children. *Apex: The New Zealand Journal of Gifted Education,16,*(1). Retrieved from http://www.giftedchildren.org.nz/apex/

McLachlan, C., Edwards, S., Margrain, V., & McLean, K. (2013). *Children's learning and development: Contemporary assessment in the early years*. Melbourne, VIC: Palgrave Macmillan.

Ministry of Education. (1996). *Te whāriki: He whāriki mātauranga mō ngā mokopuna o Aotearoa: Early childhood curriculum*. Wellington: Learning Media.

Ministry of Education. (2008). *Nurturing gifted and talented children: A parent–teacher partnership*. Wellington: Learning Media.

Moltzen, R. (2011a). Characteristics of gifted children. In R. Moltzen (Ed.), *Gifted and talented: New Zealand perspectives* (3rd ed., pp. 54–81). Auckland: Pearson.

Moltzen, R. (2011b). Underachievement. In R. Moltzen (Ed.), *Gifted and talented: New Zealand perspectives* (3rd ed., pp. 404–433). Auckland: Pearson.

Piechowski, M. (2006). *"Mellow out," they say. If I only could: Intensities and sensitivities of the young and bright*. Madison, WI: Yunasa Books.

Porter, L. (2005). *Gifted young children: A guide for teachers and parents* (2nd ed.). Crow's Nest, NSW: Allen & Unwin.

Seeley, K. (2004). Gifted and talented students at risk. *Focus on Exceptional Children, 37*(4), 1–8.

Siegle, D. (2013). *The underachieving gifted child: Recognising, understanding & reversing underachievement*. Waco, TX: Prufrock Press.

Tranckle, P., & Cushion, C. (2006). Rethinking giftedness and talent in sport. *Quest, 58*(2), 265–282.

Part 4: Possibilities for Change

Chapter 11: Supporting the advocates of young gifted children: Weaving connections and inspiration

Valerie Margrain and Jo Dean

Introduction

This book, *Giftedness in the Early Years: Informing, Learning and Teaching*, has discussed a number of important aspects of giftedness, learning and teaching, including ways to provide support for young children who are gifted. This support includes assessment for learning and its accompanying exemplar documentation. Although there are many individuals who know little about giftedness and continue to question whether they need to know, there are also many who provide essential support and deserve recognition. This chapter builds on recommendations throughout the book to affirm and empower supportive parents, teachers and community advocates.

Continuing advocacy is important to ensure that giftedness is profiled constructively, well connected to children's rights and addressed within curriculum delivery. In Chapter 6 Wong and Margrain discussed a number of myths and misconceptions affecting young gifted children. As a society we have much yet to achieve to ensure that all children are accepted, valued and understood. However, it is also a myth that no one cares: every person who reads this book has invested time to learn more about giftedness in the early years. As noted in Chapter 6, teachers and parents have the opportunity to become fearless advocates. In this final chapter we provide additional examples of how such advocacy can be curriculum-connected, using the metaphor of weaving. As we conclude, we also provide constructive examples of leadership and networking to ensure we continue to support our young gifted children, and each other.

Curriculum for adults as change agents

We often think of the curriculum as being a document that guides our planning for children. However, a broader definition of curriculum is expressed in New Zealand's early childhood curriculum document, *Te Whāriki*, which refers to curriculum as describing "the sum total of the experiences, activities, and events, whether direct or indirect, which occur within an environment designed to foster children's learning and development" (Ministry of Education, 1996, p. 10). This holistic interpretation of curriculum positions teachers as part of the curriculum rather than merely a means of delivery. It addresses both the child as a learner, and the early childhood settings and the communities to which the child belongs.

The early childhood curriculum

The metaphor of *Te Whāriki* (Ministry of Education, 1996) as a woven mat is significant. It honours diversity by symbolising the integration of differing but equally valuable threads. It also represents inclusion through providing a place for all to stand (May, 2001). This inclusion not only represents children, but also staff, services, families and communities. When we consider the range of early childhood teachers, each and every one of them brings a uniqueness that has been shaped by their own background and culture.

> The early childhood curriculum has been envisaged as a whāriki, or mat, woven from the principles, strands, and goals defined in this document. The whāriki concept recognises the diversity of early childhood education in New Zealand. Different programmes, philosophies, structures, and environments will contribute to the distinctive patterns of the whāriki. (Ministry of Education, 1996, p. 11)

Te Whāriki acknowledges the influence of Bronfenbrenner (1979), including an image of nested Russian dolls to illustrate ecological systems theory (see Ministry of Education, 1996, p. 19). This theory of social interaction and influence acknowledges that, in addition to considering the learner and the microsystem (immediate learning environment), relationships between them are important. Other levels in the ecological system also have a powerful influence on the child's well-being and capacity to learn; in Bronfenbrenner's model these elements are termed 'exosystem' and 'macrosystem'. *Te Whāriki* notes that these levels are an important influence in terms of the leverage adults can bring to their direct work and broader advocacy:

> the quality of children's experiences, encompasses the world of work, the neighbourhood, the mass media, and informal social networks. It also includes the conditions that influence the well-being and support of the adults in the children's lives: the demands, the stresses, and the opportunities for development experienced by significant adults in each child's life. There is a further national level—the nation's beliefs about the value of early childhood care and education and about the rights and responsibilities of children (Ministry of Education, 1996, p. 10).

These aspects of social network and interaction can be seen as providing an ecological whāriki. Contextual factors both weave and nest within each other.

The school curriculum

The New Zealand Curriculum (Ministry of Education, 2007) is also holistic, with very broad aims. In addition to the seven learning areas (English, Social sciences, the arts, and so forth), essential elements of the curriculum include values, key competencies and principles. Although written with consideration as to how these elements support students to become "confident, connected, actively involved, life-long learners" (Ministry of Education, 2007, p. 7), the vision, and the values, key competencies and principles can also form the basis of important professional self-reflection for adults working with children and students:

- *values:* excellence; innovation, inquiry and curiosity; diversity; equity; community and participation; ecological sustainability; integrity; respect

- *key competencies:* thinking; using language, symbols and texts; managing self; relating to others; participating and contributing
- *principles:* high expectations; Treaty of Waitangi; cultural diversity; inclusion; learning to learn, community engagement, coherence; future focus. (Ministry of Education, 2007, p. 7)

The curriculum competences and principles noted above have relevance for all learners, including gifted education and advocacy. For example, advocating for equity occurs on behalf of children; teachers and parents relate to others when facilitating home–school partnerships; and advocates of gifted education argue for the importance of future focus. Self-reflection might lead to adults developing their own areas of innovation, enquiry and curiosity, participating and contributing to networks, and maintaining high expectations for their own work.

Self-determination

New Zealand curricula reflect principles of self-determination. The influence of indigenous self-determination—rangatiratanga—is connected by Reedy (1995) to *Te Whāriki* (Ministry of Education, 1996) when stating, "Toko Rangatiratanga na te mana-matauranga— knowledge and power set me free" (p. 21). Self-determination is also more broadly acknowledged by Reedy (1995): "Our rights are recognised and so are the rights of everyone else ... *Te Whāriki* recognises my right to choose, and your right to choose too" (p. 13). It also represents the right that teachers and child advocates have to their own professional learning.

If we reflect on assessment and strengths-based practices in the early years (see Chapters 4 and 5), we can see how these practices could support gifted children if teachers have a solid understanding of giftedness. Learning stories are a common form of assessment in early childhood, but we could more often document "teaching stories" (Podmore, May & Carr, 2001) to support professional reflection. Rights, reflection and responsibility extend beyond early childhood, and those working with young gifted children can draw on both *Te Whāriki* (Ministry of Education, 1996) and *The New Zealand Curriculum* (Ministry of Education, 2007) to justify and support their own advocacy, development and learning.

Professional reflection and evaluation are a critical element of practice in both early childhood (Ministry of Education, 2009) and gifted education (REACH Education Consultancy, 2006). We can draw on professional models to not only remind us of what we *should* be doing, but what we *may* do, what is possible, and what inspires us to be the best practitioners and parents we can be.

Podmore, May and Carr (2001) created "the child's questions" as a mechanism for programme evaluation which connected to *Te Whāriki* (Ministry of Education, 1996). These questions were not written exclusively for gifted children, but they can be utilised to reflect on the quality of provisions for gifted children. The questions remind us that children's perspectives should inform our professional reflection.

Table 11.1. The child's questions connected to considerations for gifted education in the early years (Margrain & Dean)

Child's Questions (Podmore, May & Carr, 2001)	Te Whāriki curriculum strands (Ministry of Education, 1996)	Young gifted children need to believe that ...	Advocates of gifted education need to know that they ...
Do you know me?	Belonging	Their individuality is valued	Can draw on knowledge and evidence
Can I trust you?	Well-being	They are respected	Make a critical difference
Do you let me fly?	Exploration	They are free to achieve highly, to fulfil their potential	Need not limit their own or others potential
Do you hear me?	Communication	They have a voice	Can listen and learn
Is this place fair for us?	Contribution	Equity exits	Can create change

Clustering and networking

As advocates for gifted children, teachers and others who work with children benefit from collective sharing of research and innovation. In this section, examples of clustering and network groups are provided as examples of collegial support systems. To be strong advocates and agents of change, adults need opportunities for professional support and engagement with like-minded colleagues. These opportunities enable adults to weave valuable community connections.

Clustering

'Clustering' refers to grouping educators so that they can share skills, knowledge and resources (Giordano, 2008) beyond their specific institutions. For example, a cluster might involve several small rural schools in a specific region, or it might involve both schools and early childhood centres. Support professionals, such as Resource Teachers: Learning and Behaviour (RTLB), and special education services often use a cluster model so that specific personnel are allocated a 'patch'. Clustering addresses issues of isolation, consistency, motivation, professional support and engagement:

> Change takes place in the classrooms behind thousands of doors and depends on the motivation and the qualifications of teachers, who may or may not adopt the teaching strategy most adapted to the needs and the level of their pupils, and who may or may not implement policy recommendations. Teachers, however, need support to accomplish their tasks, to reflect on their day-to-day experiences and to improve their skills; they also need to exchange with others. (Giordano, 2008, p. 11)

One New Zealand application of clustering and networking, the Cluster Model (Bush, 2011b), was specifically utilised to support gifted and talented education in a region of New Zealand. This model supported teachers from both rural and urban schools in their intention to provide a quality learning environment for children through enhanced collegial and collaborative support of, and for, teachers. One participant remarked that the cluster focus on child outcomes was a key element in developing an approach that could be sustained over time: "Whenever we came to an impasse or something, we would always come back, to hey, 'what's best for the kids?' " (Bush, 2011a).

Network learning communities

Cluster groups are often—though not exclusively—formed in particular regions or physical communities. However, network learning communities (NLCs) offer the opportunity to create communities of interest that supersede geography. The online learning community TKI (Te Kete Ipurangi) has shared the results of research in NLCs as a mechanism for teacher professional learning. These show that not one single participant found there to be *no* value from engaging in a network learning community (Ward & Henderson, 2011). Ward and Henderson found that NLCs increased the knowledge and/or expertise of school participants in the following three outcome areas:

- leadership practices for facilitating change
- engaging students in decisions about their learning
- effective pedagogies, as described in *The New Zealand Curriculum*.

Thus, NLCs can support teachers—and others—in their own learning (as adults), to effect positive societal change and to ensure quality outcomes for children and students. NLCs can enable those adults most passionate about gifted education—whether teachers, leaders or other advocates—to find each other, regardless of where they live. In the same way that gifted children need like-minded peers, so too do adults, as well as mechanisms to support finding one another.

Special interest group

The cluster and NLC initiatives described in the preceding paragraphs report on school-based initiatives for quality teaching and learning. However, the approaches are not exclusive to school settings; they provide a valuable model which could be utilised in to the early childhood sector also, enabling like-minded teachers who share a passion for advocacy to collaborate. giftEDnz, the professional association for gifted education in New Zealand, has a special interest group for early years (see http://www.giftednz.org). Strengthening links between diverse early childhood education services encourages "a growing appreciation of each other's differences and similarities" (Ministry of Education, 1996, p. 17). This giftEDnz early years special interest group has been a valuable source of support for teachers, researchers and parents. It has also provided a strong network platform for like-minded adults to come together and gain strength, encouragement and motivation from each other to continue to advocate for gifted children. From a personal perspective, although all the members have had experience working with gifted children, there were varied levels of experience as researchers. Within the special interest group, leadership and mentoring supported emerging researchers and writers, which enabled more people to join the group as time went by. This book has in part developed through the support of the giftEDnz special interest group.

Additional special interest groups have focused on 'twice exceptional' learners, while the giftEDnz special interest group He Kāhui Pūmanawa (see http://www.giftednz.org) focuses on Māori gifted learners. The purpose of He Kāhui Pūmanawa is to advocate for multiple perspective of Māori giftedness; share stories of Māori gifted learners; share effective practices for identifying and/or providing for Māori gifted learners across a range of settings; and promote/enhance relationships within the whānau, iwi and communities of gifted Māori learners.

Table 11.2. Four national gifted education organisations and selected aims

Organisation	Examples of aims to support adult professional learning
Gifted and Talented Online (via the Ministry of Education online platform Te Kete Ipurangi, TKI) http://gifted.tki.org.nz/	"This site ... provides ongoing professional learning and support for gifted and talented communities" (Ministry of Education, n.d.).
New Zealand Association for Gifted Children (NZAGC) http://www.giftedchildren.org.nz	"Goal 3: To support families belonging to the organisation to empower them in their decision making and family life, in relation to their gifted child" (NZAGC, 2011). "Goal 4: To support educators belonging to the organisation to empower them in their decision making and family life and teaching of the gifted child" (NZAGC, 2011). "Goal 5: To provide and promote access to information and resources regarding giftedness and gifted children to relevant individuals and groups" (NZAGC, 2011).
giftEDnz, the Professional Association for Gifted Education http://giftednz.org.nz (including the Early Years special interest group)	"To create a professional community for networking, supporting and learning. To encourage the pursuit and sharing of best practice in gifted and talented education. To provide liaison with international organizations and other national associations for gifted and talented education."
New Zealand Centre for Gifted Education http://www.nzcge.co.nz	"Maximising gifted young New Zealanders' potential through recognition, access and support." - *MindPlus*, 1-day programme - *Small Poppies*, for gifted children 2-6 years old - *Gifted Online*, for students Years 4-10 - *Consult*, professional learning and development (NZCGE, 2014)

Key organisations that support advocacy for young children who are gifted

Although new clusters and networks may serve particular purposes, building on the work undertaken by existing organisations is also important. Four key national organisations must surely be:

- Gifted and Talented Online, via the Ministry of Education
- giftEDnz, the professional association for gifted education
- NZAGC, the New Zealand Association for Gifted Children.
- New Zealand Centre for Gifted Education (established 2014)

From their websites, links and connections to a range of other organisations can be found, including regional networks and associations, and providers of professional learning, for example REACH Education www.giftedreach.org.nz. Table 11.1 provides website contact details and excerpts from each organisation's published aims, illustrating examples of the contribution made to adult professional learning. A range of other organisations exist to support specific aspects of professional development.

Distributed leadership

As the examples discussed above show, good leadership doesn't always need to come from the top. Distributed (non-hierarchical) and collective leadership models of leadership are particularly valued in early childhood contexts, empowering and providing a voice for all (Heikka & Waniganayake, 2011). A number of these groups are led by teachers, parents and researchers. Everyone can be leaders concurrently, so long as everyone is striving for the same vision. In this case, the shared goal is ensuring our gifted children reach their potential. Consider the metaphor of weaving the whāriki within cluster groups or other professional groups. Each member can be seen as a single strand, bringing knowledge and experience to weave the whāriki. Over time the whāriki will take shape, and like any whāriki some parts will be smooth and others will be a bit uneven. As an individual it can take considerable time and effort to achieve progress when advocating for gifted children, but if we can weave collectively, strengthening and building partnerships, then our whāriki will have greater resilience and strength.

Another example of distributed innovation and critical thinking across communities is given in an interesting blog from Bill Gates. Gates is well known as a philanthropist, investor, computer programmer and inventor. Although not a teacher, Gates (2014) suggests connecting the importance of support for teachers with child outcomes: "Getting great tools into teachers' hands is one of the keys to delivering on the promise of a great education for every child". This applies equally to other adults who support children, especially parents. We have countless opportunities to reach out beyond our immediate family, friendship group, school, centre or community in order to work with others who can support and facilitate effective outcomes for children. Thus, there is the potential for clusters to include wider community and industry partnership.

Finding inspiration

Children may well look to adults—and occasionally youths such as Malala Yousafzai (a Pakistani activist for female education, who was shot in the head for espousing her beliefs)—as role models. But who do adults look to for inspiration? We look to historical and mythical figures such as the Greek goddess Athena; we look to contemporary figures prominent in the media; we look to colleagues or important people in our lives; and most likely we draw on inspiration from a combination of all of these sources. For many of us, a particular teacher or family member will have been of profound influence in helping us to realise our potential. Fictional characters, though at times whimsical or fantastical, can also be inspiring. Even the story of Peter Parker (aka Spiderman) reminds us that "with great power comes great responsibility". In the early years sector the workforce is predominantly women, and thus we should to draw on the inspiration of notable women leaders.

Malala

Although aimed at advocating for peace and against illiteracy, the words of Malala are broad: "One child, one teacher, one pen and one book can change the world" (Yousafzai, 2013). Malala is a gifted young woman who started speaking out about injustice at a young age, including television interviews from the age of 11 (A World at School,

2014). At age 17, in 2014, Malala was awarded the Nobel Peace Prize, the youngest recipient ever.

One child can, like Malala, change the world, and that child realises their potential more readily with the support and opportunity provided by key adults. Gagné's (2014) Differentiated Model of Giftedness and Talent (DMGT) (see Chapter 1) illustrates a range of catalysts that have an impact on the opportunity gifted children have to become talented individuals, and this was illustrated in the Chapter 10 case study of Liam. These catalysts include three aspects of learning environment: milieu, individuals and provisions. By positively influencing any or all of these aspects of the environment, adults, too, can change the world. That is, they can change it themselves, and they can change the conditions so that gifted children can in turn change the world. In this way, every adult that facilitates opportunity is a teacher and a facilitator.

Malala thanks her father for 'not clipping her wings' (A Word at School, 2014) and acknowledges inspiration from a range of notable people:

> This is the compassion that I have learnt from Muhammad—the prophet of mercy, Jesus Christ and Lord Buddha. This is the legacy of change that I have inherited from Martin Luther King, Nelson Mandela and Muhammad Ali Jinnah. This is the philosophy of non-violence that I have learnt from Gandhi Jee, Bacha Khan and Mother Teresa. And this is the forgiveness that I have learnt from my mother and father. (Yousafzai, 2013)

Athena

Another strong female leader, but one from antiquity, is Athena. The daughter of Zeus, Athena is the Greek goddess of wisdom, known as Minerva in Roman mythology. She is also the goddess of war strategy, and arts and crafts. As such, she exercises leadership, creativity and intelligence. Athena is an armed warrior goddess, and appears in Greek mythology as a helper of many heroes, including Heracles, Jason and Odysseus.

Athena's role as the goddess of wisdom has a strong connection to the work of early years teachers. Any teaching decision requires us to draw on reserves of professional experience and specific knowledge and competence, but also acknowledges the importance of ethical reflection and uncertainty. Goodfellow (2001) challenges the existence of best practice and developmentally appropriate practice, and instead urges "wise practice", which includes ethical, philosophical and reflective judgement-making. We need to apply these elements of wisdom in our advocacy for young children who are gifted. A key element of this advocacy is to become an Athena-like warrior as we fight for recognition, for understanding, for resources, and for the value of our work. Yet we also have to choose our battles wisely and determine where to most effectively invest our energy.

Athena's own gifts include being a talented artist and weaver. In the early years we draw on a range of skills, knowledge, competencies, networks, resources and opportunities and weave these together in our daily practice. In the same way that curriculum provides a woven mat for all to stand on (May, 2001), the outcomes of our weaving create opportunity, connection and outcomes. May our work supporting young children who are gifted do the same.

Inspiration from the arts

We can also look more locally, to people who have made inspirational changes in New Zealand education. Although not a female leader, Elwyn Richardson was one of the educational pioneers who was "driven by a belief in the creative power of children" in primary school (Richardson, 2012, p. v). He demonstrated innovative teaching well before its time. Recognising children as young artists and scientists, he encouraged his students to follow their curiosity, and through exploration they explored the natural world together. Arts practices became the basis for the curriculum. Rather than separate subject areas, Richardson integrated environmental study through the arts and sciences. The thing that is so attractive about Richardson's approach is that he gave each child "the opportunity to reach their full height as artists, as craftsmen, as scientists" (cited in Richardson, Melser, 2012, p. xiii). This allowed children to follow their interests and be active learners through hands on learning and exploration through the arts and sciences. We need teachers to be creative, enthused and adventurous, to ensure children dare to imagine, ask questions and feel free to create. As Torrance (1995) points out, "No one's potential can be achieved by 'holding back'" (p. 16).

If we look at exemplars of the arts within early childhood, these are well documented. The arts support children's holistic learning in many different ways, and they are particularly appealing for gifted children.

An example of using the arts to holistically support children's learning potential is found in one study undertaken in a kindergarten, where the second author of this chapter researched the use of textiles in the environment (Dean, 2011). Children thrived in this environment through hands-on experiences, embodied learning and meaningful interactions with the teachers. The children expressed their imagination and creativity through many uses of textiles. Beautifully coloured scarves were used to bridge block construction on the mat, long lengths of fabric were formed into water, and a bridge and stepping stones were made to enhance dramatic play. "Exploring textiles creatively supports a child to express their thoughts, comprehend, respond and represent perceptions and understanding of the world, such as dressing up with textiles through role-play" (Dean, 2011). In Figure 11.1 we can see children engaged in role-playing the story of "The three Billy goats gruff." The costumes and fabric props used in this role play encouraged embodied learning through different characters. Figure 11.12 documents that children were able to express their creativity using different medium as they experimenting with spatial awareness, textures and shapes while creating textile boards. Teachers in Dean's research were observed to scaffold the children to freely access the resources (textiles in this case), and encouraged children to transfer the textiles to different areas of the setting. Such open-ended and creative experiences form part of the environmental support and catalysts integral to Gagné's (2014) Developmental Model of Giftedness and Talent. Creative environments are motivating for adults as well as for children. The teachers in Dean's (2011) study were remarkable, vibrant and creative thinkers, who truly encouraged the children to be the same. The aspirations of all the children, family/whānau and the community were met through the diverse range of the arts.

Chapter 11: Supporting the advocates of young gifted children:
Weaving connections and inspiration

Figure 11.1. Children role-playing the story of *The Three Billy Goats Gruff*

Figure 11.2. Textile board created by children in a kindergarten

Conclusion

As advocates for gifted children, we may have many mats to stand on, but it is through collective endeavours that we can most effectively weave our whāriki to support all of our children. Making connections and weaving the whāriki are strengthened by the use of cluster groups and professional groups to ensure people's strengths and abilities are tightly woven together to build strong and resilient leaders and to continue supporting our young gifted children. When adults take the time to see and visualise the world through a child's lens, and also from colleagues, then so much more can be discovered. Children should feel like they can 'fly', and we need to provide them with these opportunities. However, we also need to 'fly' as teachers and advocates: we need professional support and we need inspiration. We too may experience the intensity of being "quiveringly alive" (Piechowski, 1991). Please be adventurous, creative and joyful, to inspire children and each other.

References

A World at School. (2014). *Malala Yousafzai and Kailash Satyarthi win Nobel Peace Prize for children's rights campaigning.* Retrieved from http://www.aworldatschool.org/news/entry/malala-yousafzai-and-kailash-satyarthi-win-nobel-peace-prize

Bronfenbrenner, U. (1979). *The ecology of human development.* Cambridge, MA: Harvard.

Bush, K. (2011a). *Story: Turanga-Gisborne cluster model.* Retrieved from http://gifted.tki.org.nz/For-schools-and-teachers/Stories/Story-Turanga-Gisborne-Cluster-Model

Bush, K. (2011b). *'The Cluster Team': A model of collaboration and collegiality in New Zealand gifted and talented education 2003–2008.* Unpublished master's thesis, Massey University, Palmerston North.

Dean, J. (2011). Textiles can stimulate children's creativity and imagination. *Art Educators Journal,* 21(2). Retrieved from http://www.arteducatorsJournal2011

Gagné, F. (2014). *Differentiated model of giftedness and talent* (DMGT). Retrieved from http://www.gagnefrancoys.wix.com/dmgt-mddt

Gates, B. (2014). *Gates notes: The blog of Bill Gates.* Retrieved from http://www.gatesnotes.com/Education/Breakthrough-Tools-for-Teachers

giftEDnz. (2013). *Goals.* Retrieved from http://giftednz.org.nz/goals/

Giordano, E. A. (2008). *School clusters and teacher resource centres*. Paris, France: UNESCO International Institute for Educational Planning. Retrieved from http://unesdoc.unesco.org/images/0015/001597/159776e.pdf

Goodfellow, J. (2001). Wise practice: The need to move beyond 'best practice' in early childhood education. *Australian Journal of Early Childhood, 26*(3), 1–6.

Heikka, J., & Waniganayake, M. (2011). Pedagogical leadership from a distributed perspective within the context of early childhood education. *International Journal of Leadership in Education: Theory and Practice, 14*(4), 499–512.

May, H. (2001). *Politics in the playground: The world of early childhood policy in postwar New Zealand*. Wellington: Bridget Williams Books and New Zealand Council for Educational Research.

Ministry of Education. (1996). *Te whāriki: He whāriki matauranga mō ngā mokopuna ō Aotearoa*. Wellington: Learning Media.

Ministry of Education. (2007). *The New Zealand curriculum*. Wellington: Learning Media.

Ministry of Education. (2009). *Ngā arohaehae whai hua: Self-review guidelines for early childhood education*. Wellington: Learning Media.

Ministry of Education. (n.d.). *Gifted and talented online: Realising potential*. Retrieved from http://gifted.tki.org.nz/

New Zealand Centre for Gifted Children [NZGCE] (2014). About us. Retrieved from www.nzcge.co.nz

NZAGC (New Zealand Association for Gifted Children). (2011). *NZAGC constitution*. Retrieved from http://www.giftedchildren.org.nz/national/constitution.pdf

Piechowski, M. M. (1991). Emotional development and emotional giftedness. In N. Colangelo & G. A. Davis (Eds.), *Handbook of gifted education* (pp. 285-306). Boston: Allyn and Bacon.

Podmore, V., May, H., & Carr, M. (2001). The "child's questions": Program evaluation with Te Whāriki using "Teaching Stories." *Early Childhood Folio, 5*, 6–9.

REACH Education Consultancy. (2006). *The REACH Model*. Retrieved March 2nd, 2015, from http://www.giftedreach.org.nz/reach_model.htm

Reedy, T. (1995). I have a dream. In *Proceedings of the Sixth Early Childhood Convention, Volume one* (pp. 13–32). Auckland: Convention Committee.

Richardson, E. S. (2012). *In the early world* (3rd ed.). Wellington: NZCER Press.

Torrance, E. P. (1995). *Why fly? A philosophy of creativity.* New York, NY: Ablex Publishing Corporation.

Ward, L., & Henderson, A. (2011). *An evaluation of network learning communities: Main report.* Wellington: Ministry of Education. Retrieved from http://www.educationcounts.govt.nz/publications/curriculum/100828/executive-summary

Yousafzai, M. (2013). *Speech at the youth takeover of the United Nations, July 12, 2013.* Retrieved from https://secure.aworldatschool.org/page/content/the-text-of-malala-yousafzais-speech-at-the-united-nations/

Biographies

Editors

Dr Valerie Margrain

Valerie is a senior lecturer working at the Australian Catholic University (ACU) in Melbourne, and currently ACU National Director, Early Childhood. She values the diverse range of opportunities her educational career has provided, including Playcentre, early childhood centres, primary classrooms, special education, Reading Recovery, polytechnic and university. Valerie's research interests include assessment, early literacy, and inclusive and gifted education.

Dr Caterina Murphy

Caterina first became interested in gifted education as a means to understand how best to parent her children. She completed her Master of Education (Hons) at Massey University in 2005, which investigated the play patterns and behaviours of young children in an early childhood setting who are gifted. She is a 'grassroots' early childhood professional, who ran an enrichment programme for many years at her early childhood centre and introduced the concept of peer nomination with 3- and 4-year-olds. She has published and presented on many occasions about giftedness in early childhood. Her 12-year career in tertiary education over a range of academic roles offered countless opportunities to guide student teachers in understanding the phenomenon of giftedness.

Jo Dean

Jo currently works at Massey University, teaching a range of papers in the Early Years and Primary programmes. Jo was formerly a kindergarten teacher and has been involved in working with gifted children. Jo's research interests are creative and critical thinking, visual arts, and supporting young gifted learners. Her doctoral research is based on quality interactions through visual art practices within early childhood. Jo has been part of the Early Years Special Interest Group since it was established in 2010.

Authors

Sue Breen

Sue has been working with gifted children for nearly 40 years. She is the lead teacher, Small Poppies, for the New Zealand Centre for Gifted Education. She is a board member of giftEDnz and is a life member of the New Zealand Association for Gifted Children and their Auckland branch. Sue has presented at conferences on numerous occasions, has presented and organised subject-specific workshops for teachers, parents and students, and is still working with young gifted children. She brings a great deal of experience, enthusiasm and passion to the field of gifted education, especially within the New Zealand early years environment.

Monica Cameron

Monica is a former kindergarten teacher and professional development facilitator who now teaches in the Institute of Education at Massey University. Her particular interests are assessment, transition, supporting children's learning and working with student teachers. Her doctoral research is focused on the assessment of 4-year-old children's learning, and in particular, teachers' understanding, beliefs and practices with regard to this.

Annette Preston

Annette has been involved in early childhood education in Dunedin for 28 years. Her experience includes early childhood education, and leadership and management experience in early childhood education and care centres. She is currently head teacher of the Otago University Childcare Association College Centre—Rōpu Tiaki Tamaiti, a mixed-age centre in Dunedin. Annette has a special interest in gifted education in early childhood, and has completed an undergraduate and graduate paper on Teaching Children with Special Abilities. She is part of a giftEDnz special interest group of early childhood teachers supported by the Todd Foundation to research narrative assessment for gifted children under 5 years.

Carola Sampson

Carola is a kindergarten teacher and postgraduate student in early years with Massey University. She is a member of the New Zealand Association for Gifted Children and a contributing member to giftEDnz and their interest group, Early Years. Through working in New Zealand and Australian kindergartens, she is advocating for gifted young children and their families in both countries, and has presented in New Zealand and Melbourne.

Deborah Walker

With a background in classroom teaching and senior management experience in the mainstream teaching Year 1 through to 8, Deborah began working in gifted education in 2002. She is passionate about leading positive change, and as a result of this has played an integral part in the development of programmes offered by the New Zealand Centre for Gifted Education, where she is currently CEO. Deb has a Master of Education degree from Massey University, specialising in gifted education, and a graduate Diploma in Not-For-Profit Business Management from Unitec. Although her CEO role is one of leadership, management and advocacy, working primarily with adults, she still jumps at the chance to work with students. Deb was a founding member of giftEDnz and has been a member of the Early Years subcommittee since its establishment.

Emma Wallace

Emma Wallace has been an early childhood teacher for 7 years, working at the OUCA College Centre—Rōpu Tiaki Tamaiti, primarily with 2- to 5-year-olds. Early in 2014 she was appointed to the position of assistant head teacher. Emma has completed a 2-year Early Childhood Diploma and has a Bachelor of Arts, majoring in English. During her teaching practice she was fascinated with the different ways children learn. Through her own learning journey she has been discovering ways to be responsive to children's individual strengths, experiences and knowledge, celebrating children's gifts and extending their learning in meaningful ways. Emma has been involved in the narrative assessment for gifted children research project though the preparation of a case study.

Melanie Wong

Melanie is a research co-ordinator at the Faculty of Education and Social Sciences, Manukau Institute of Technology. Melanie is also a PhD candidate at the University of Canterbury. Melanie's research interests include gifted education, inclusive education and initial teacher education.

Jo Dean

Valerie Margrain

Caterina Murphy

(see p 217 for biographies)

Appendices

The following Appendices are provided in photocopyable format to support professional development.

Appendix A: Two models of giftedness
Appendix B: Characteristics of giftedness in the early years
Appendix C: Peer nomination form for use with 3- and 4-year-old children
Appendix D: Parent reflection prompts
Appendix E: Play patterns of young children who are gifted
Appendix F: Myths and responses for giftedness in the early years
Appendix G: 'Excitabilities' and strategies
Appendix H: Differentiation, metaphor and practice
Appendix I: Applying a taxonomy to differentiation in the early years
Appendix J: Teacher reflective questions
Appendix K: School communication strategies valued by parents

Appendices

Appendix A: Two models of giftedness

Chapter 1, by Murphy and Walker, provides a summary of these two well-known models of giftedness that are relevant to the early years.

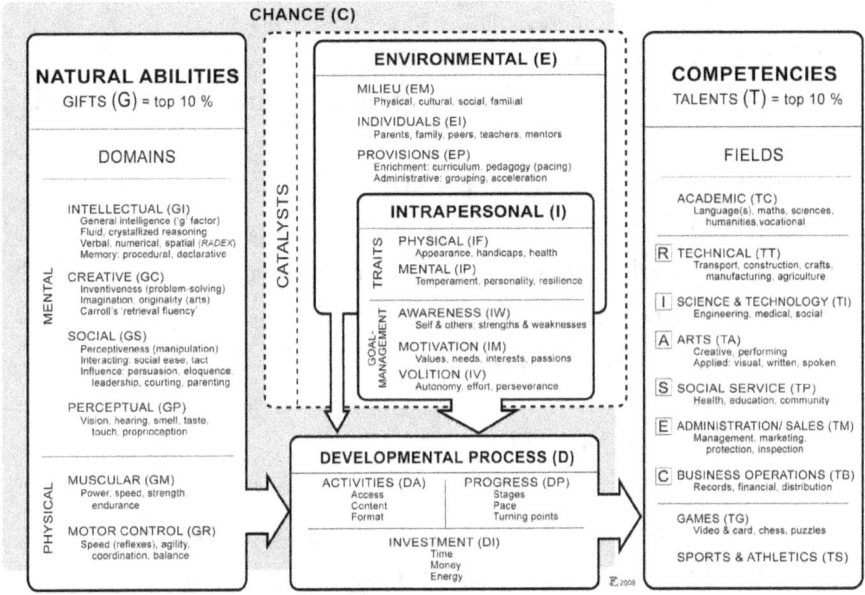

Figure A.1. Gagné's Differentiated Model of Giftedness and Talent (DMGT)
Source: Gagné, 2014, downloaded, with permission from Gagné, from his website: http://www.gagnefrancoys.wix.com/dmgt-mddt

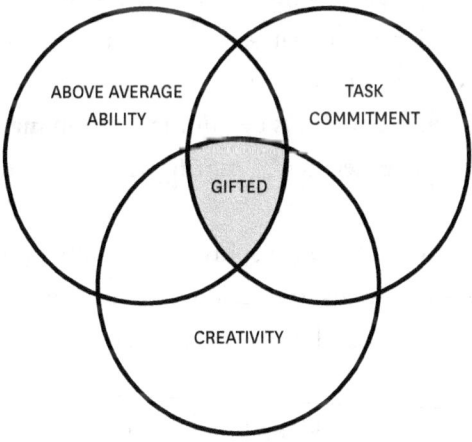

Figure A.2. Three-Ring Conception of Giftedness
Source: Reproduced with permission of J. S. Renzulli.

Appendix B: Characteristics of giftedness in the early years

The following helpful lists of characteristics has been provided, with permission, by the New Zealand Centre for Gifted Education (see Chapter 2).

- Needs very little sleep
- Began to talk very early or was very late in talking but then learned fast.
- Has a large vocabulary; uses unusual or 'big' words.
- Talks very fluently; uses language easily and correctly.
- Generally reached physical milestones earlier than most,
- Demands attention constantly; is persistent,
- Is intensely curious; is always asking "Why?"; really wants to know the answer.
- Is very observant of detail.
- Has an excellent memory.
- Is very independent; insists on doing things for him/herself.
- Loves being read to; follows story closely.
- Is beginning to read / is reading / has asked to be taught to read.
- Is quickly bored with simple or repetitive games and toys.
- Shows impatience with tasks that seem meaningless.
- Can concentrate for long periods when interested.
- Creates make-believe playmates, invents games, makes up lots of stories (often complicated).
- Can not only count but also is beginning to grasp maths concepts.
- Arranges toys and other items, putting the same kinds of things together.
- Has a highly developed, quite sophisticated, sense of humour.
- Learns easily—only needs to be told things once or twice.
- Is very sensitive; distressed by hurts experienced by other people or creatures.
- Is generally the leader in any group of children.
- Seems to prefer the company of older children or adults.
- Doesn't seem to fit in with other children.

- Can be impatient with others who don't think as fast or do things as well as s/he does.
- Often seems frustrated when ideas outreach ability to perform.

A gifted child often:
- achieves milestones much earlier
- has a heightened sensitivity
- has a good sense of humour
- has a high degree of creativity
- has a high degree of energy
- has a long attention span
- has a preference for older friends or adults
- has a sense of justice and moral sensitivity
- has a variety of interests
- has a vivid imagination
- has above average ability with numbers
- has above average language development
- has an advanced vocabulary
- has an excellent memory
- has apparent maturity in judgement
- has keen powers of observation
- has good problem-solving and reasoning abilities
- has leadership qualities
- has non-conformist behaviour
- has unusual curiosity
- has unusual emotional depth and intensity
- is a rapid learner
- is able to master more complex jigsaw puzzles
- is an early and avid reader
- is persistent
- is very alert
- is very curious
- is very observant
- shows perfectionism traits.

Appendix C: Peer nomination form for use with 3- and 4-year-old children

Developed by Murphy (2001) (see Chapter 2).

Who would be the best organiser if the teacher was away?
_____
_____

Who has the most unusual ideas?
_____
_____

Who is best at making things?
_____
_____

Who is a good leader in the group?
_____
_____

Who is the funniest person in the group?
_____
_____

Who is best at doing difficult things?
_____
_____

Who is the first person to suggest new games to play?
_____
_____

If you needed help, who would you ask?
_____
_____

Appendix D: Parent reflection statements

Developed by Breen, see Chapter 2

The information shared below provides useful information to contribute to discussions on the potential identification of giftedness.

- To bring out the best in my child ……….
- The ways my child shows values and emotions are ……….
- My child struggles with ……….
- Evidence of my child's abilities ……….
- Something amazing my child did was ……….
- If only ……….
- People don't realise ………. about my child.
- The balancing act in parenting my child is ……….
- Something I don't understand about my child is ……….
- Other people have told me my child is absolutely passionate about ……….
- I worry about my child because ……….
- My child combines ……….
- My child 'comes alive' when ……….

Appendix E: Play patterns of young children who are gifted

This content is drawn from the research by Murphy (2005). See Chapter 3.

Characteristics of giftedness evident during play
advanced language and knowledge
perfectionism/frustration
highly imaginative, abstract, conceptual thinking
heightened interpersonal awareness
ambidexterity
advanced sense of humour
boredom
love of learning
curiosity

Play preferences
open-ended play
solitary play
pretend play
undisrupted play
rules-oriented play

Interactions
teacher/adult preference
repelling and ignoring peers
dominating and leading peers
self-perception as teacher's peer and helper

Reference
Murphy, C. L. (2005). *Play patterns and behaviours of young children who are gifted in an early childhood setting.* Unpublished master's thesis, Massey University.

Reflective questions on play
The following questions have been adapted from my earlier interview questions with teachers (Murphy, 2004), but they generated so much discussion at the time of that research I think they will continue to be of value. I suggest taking a team approach—every teacher could consider these questions individually, thinking of a specific child who you have noticed plays

differently to other children, then discuss your answers as a team and consider how best to respond in order to enrich the child's learning.

1. What specific aspects come to mind when you think of the play you have observed this child engaging in?
2. Have you observed this child utilising resources in ways that differ from their peers?
3. Have you observed this child seeking out or repelling adults during their play?
4. Have you observed this child seeking out or repelling peers during their play?
5. Are requests for help during play similar to that of their peers, or does this child demonstrate a need for more or less assistance?
6. When you observe this child playing in a specific learning area (e.g., dramatic/fantasy play), do you find the games created by him or her to be more imaginative, less imaginative or similar to those of their peers?
7. Have you observed this child engaged in play for longer periods than their peers, despite distractions? If so, what do you think determines this?
8. Which areas of play or aspects of learning appear to be of most interest to this child?
9. Have you found that questions generated from play and during play are different to their peers? If yes, then in what way?
10. Have you observed any direct links between the types of learning experiences this child chooses to engage in and the types of thinking that these learning experiences generate?
11. In your experience, what types of play experiences does this child most often engage in?
12. Do you think this child chooses these experiences for particular reasons; for example, the people participating with them, the challenge of resources?
13. What sort of games do you see this child generating?
14. Why do you think he/she engages in these experiences more so than others?

Appendix F: Myths and responses: Giftedness in the early years

These myths and responses are a summary of the content in Chapter 6, by Wong and Margrain. Information will give teachers and child advocates the opportunity to reframe their ideas about giftedness.

Table F.1. Common myths about giftedness in the early years, with suggested responses

Myth	Response
Myth 1: Teachers 'know it all'.	Learning is lifelong and information is being updated all the time.
Myth 2: Preschoolers and new entrants are too young to be gifted.	Giftedness is evident in early childhood, and teachers should expect to find young gifted children across a range of domains.
Myth 3: Teachers get adequate training.	Teachers deserve to receive professional development, support and resources to enable them to make a positive difference, but not all teacher education providers cover gifted education in their courses.
Myth 4: Very bright children don't need to be taught—they know everything already.	Gifted children may know more than their peers but they don't know everything. They still need teachers to teach and guide them, and deserve enrichment and extension. Their passion for learning means they want to learn new things.
Myth 5: Parents who think their children are gifted usually aren't right.	Parents are far more effective than teachers at correctly identifying giftedness.
Myth 6: Every parent wants their child to be gifted.	Parents are proud of their child and they want their child to do well at school, but this doesn't mean they want their child to be gifted.
Myth 7: Every child is gifted.	All children have areas of strength and competency but these do not necessarily mean the child is gifted. All children are unique, and all are able to learn, but some are born with a predisposition towards exceptional performance in one area or another.
Myth 8: Gifted children have social problems and can't make friends.	Like-minded peers do not need to be the same chronological age. Gifted children often form strong relationships with adults and older children.

Myth 9: Gifted children's needs can be met by giving them more challenging resources.	Responding to gifted children requires engagement as well as resources.
Myth 10: Gifted children are difficult and challenging to teach.	Gifted children are no more difficult or easier to teach than others. All children need to be able to learn at their own pace and level. When young children engage in their learning they are likely to operate more autonomously.
Myth 11: The parents of gifted children are usually challenging and demanding.	Parents are their children's advocates, but asking for an appropriate education for their child is often interpreted as being demanding.
Myth 12: Early years teachers know how to respond to children's strengths and interests.	Early years teachers need continued professional learning to understand the phenomenon of giftedness, and be exposed to current research in order to strengthen their teaching.
Myth 13: Children in junior primary can't be accelerated.	There are many valid ways of appropriately accelerating children's at any age.
Myth 14: Gifted children have to do the basics in case they miss out on something important.	Gifted learners learn faster and make connections in ways that others don't. Learning 'the basics' should be part of complex conceptual thinking, not the focus of the learning.
Myth 15: Giftedness only relates to academic success.	Giftedness is manifested across many areas, including physical, spiritual, cultural, the arts and interpersonal domains.
Myth 16: Young children should be playing and having fun, not being 'hot-housed'.	When young gifted children are able to acquire early and advanced knowledge without this being induced by adults, this is not hot-housing

Appendix G: 'Excitabilities' and strategies

This table summarises the five areas of excitability, based on Piechowski (2014). See Chapter 7 by Sampson.

Table G.1. 'Excitabilities', behavioural indicators and useful support strategies

Social–emotional focus	Behavioural indicators	Useful support strategies
Psychomotor intensity: oversupply of energy	Busy, restless, moving while thinking, difficulty sitting still on the mat, chatting, talking out of turn, nail biting, picking	Give children something to hold (e.g., a bean bag or soft toy). Fill a balloon with rice or corn flour. Include outside and physical learning. Limit the time for sitting still.
Sensual intensity: heightened sensory and sensual expression of emotional tension	Intense seeing, hearing, smelling, touching and tasting: either beautiful, soothing and pleasing, or offensive, disturbing, hurting and distasteful. Dislikes clothing labels and tight clothing.	Support self-help skills and strategies. Create aesthetically pleasing environments and positive sensory experiences. Provide comfort and discussion, help children identify likes and dislikes, remove clothing labels and scratchy fabric.
Intellectual intensity: superior activity of the mind	Passion for problem solving, hunger for knowledge, avid reading, voracious curiosity, keen observation, high concentration, perfectionism, fear of failure, avoidance, anxiety, frustration	Give children time and space to complete projects, discuss mistakes, share own experiences of mistake making. Arrange meeting with like-minded peers, extra-curricular activities such as chess, or join gifted support groups.
Imaginational intensity: spontaneous imagery as an expression of emotional tension	Immense ability to be immersed in imaginary worlds, create imaginary friends and pets. Differentiates between imagination and reality. Able to involve others in play and amuse self.	Talk through stories the child has created. Record learning stories. Document examples of creativity. Use imaginative skills to problem solve real-life situations. Involve other children in play activities.
Emotional intensity: strongly intensified feelings and emotions.	Aware of own and others' feelings. Rollercoaster emotions (extreme): anguish, despair, anger, compassion, misery. Deep relationships, though not necessarily with age peers. Strong attachments, rituals. Change is challenging. Blushing, sweating, heart racing, 'knot' in stomach.	Accept that adults can be friends. Help children recognise and understand feelings and physical reactions. Help children learn self-control and manage anger and behaviour. Respond to behaviour calmly. Teach empathy

References

Daniels, S., & Meckstroth, E. (2009). Nurturing the sensitivity, intensity, and developmental potential of gifted young children. In S. Daniels & M. Piechowski (Eds.), *Living with intensity* (pp. 33–56). Scottsdale, AZ: Great Potential Press.

Probst, B., & Piechowski, M. (2011). Handbook for counsellors serving students with gifts and talents. In T. Cross & J. Cross (Eds.), *Development, relationships, school issues, and counseling needs/interventions* (pp. 53–71). Waco, TX: Prufrock Press Inc.

Appendix H: Differentiation, metaphor and practice

The terms below are explained through the metaphor of a multi-storey home, and with application to a typical early years activity, play dough, from Chapter 8 by Murphy. When reflecting on this activity, consider the following questions.

- What about the child who is bored at the play dough table?
- What about the 3-year-old who is tired of the same old equipment?
- Some children quickly lose interest, and activities soon lack novelty and challenge. What about the ones who want to do something different with materials? Do we 'extend' the play? If so, how?

These considerations are reflected in Table H.1, which connects approaches to differentiation with a metaphor of a home and the practice example of using play dough.

Table H.1. Differentiation, metaphor and practice connections

Term	Explanation	Metaphor of a house	Practice example: play dough
Core curriculum	Content that teachers routinely cover	Exploring a room on the ground-floor level of a home	Talk, roll, pat and pound, sing, add glitter, cut shapes, share tools, add water, stick things into the dough, mould it, laugh about it, smell it, taste it and squeeze it.
Quantitative differentiation	More of the same thing	Exploring the room next door	
Extension	Application to new areas of activity	Finding out how you can use downstairs belongings in new ways in second-floor discoveries.	Make play dough, grate it, bake it, paint it, stamp on it, glue with it, add more to it, print with it and build with it.
Complex curriculum	Ensuring that learning opportunities are deeper, richer and more complex	Climbing up to the loft, where there is a bottomless treasure chest. The content on the ground floor is still there, but the journey has moved on.	Find out how flour is made, experiment with dyes, test the salt in science experiments, visit a bakery, bake bread, design new printing materials, make new cutters, compare it to clay, analyse it, try to move it, break it down, boil it, find out what else can be done with it, read about salt lakes, try and squeeze oil out of things, examine the shapes of oil bottles, draw the shapes find out what happens when we make it without oil, examine wet and dry, microwave it, sun dry it, and much more!
Qualitative differentiation	Open-ended adaptation and application	The treasure chest in the loft is used in diverse and novel ways that capture interest. Wings are made and the child may choose to fly beyond the loft.	

Appendix I: Applying a taxonomy to differentiation in the early years

Bloom's Taxonomy (Bloom, 1956) provides a mechanism to apply the higher-level thinking skills, critical thinking skills and creative thinking skills advocated in gifted education literature. Table I.1 provides an illustration of Bloom's taxonomy applied to the content area of zebras for young children; see Chapter 8 by Murphy.

Table I.1. Bloom's Taxonomy applied to young children and zebra learning

Stage	Explanation of stage	Zebra Example
Knowledge	Young children acquire knowledge, through play, exploration, manipulation and with the assistance or guidance of the teacher or others in their environment	"This animal is called a zebra" (a teacher reading from a book).
Comprehension	Young children gain an understanding of the information they have acquired.	"I know that is a zebra because it has black and white stripes and looks like a horse."
Application	Young children apply their understanding of the information they have acquired.	"I can draw and paint zebras on my own".
Analysis	Young children break a concept or idea etc. down into components, elements or parts.	"Do zebras look like any other animal? Where do zebras live? What do they eat? Do we have them in New Zealand? Why don't we? Are there any other animals in the world with black and white stripes? How will we know if they are zebras?"
Synthesis	Young children put the parts together again and create something new, or adapt an idea to suit their needs or to answer their initial questions.	"Let's create our own black and white striped animals! What shall we call them? Where will they live? What will they eat?"
Evaluation	Young children make judgements about the value or purpose of something and make connections with internal or external evidence.	"What do zebras offer to our world? What do we need to do to conserve them? Should we care about them? How can we learn more about them?"

Appendix J: Teacher reflective questions

(See Chapter 8 by Murphy). Opportunities for supporting young children can be enhanced when professional reflection is applied. Anyone working with young children may find it helpful to think of a particular child who is gifted and then ponder over the following points of reflection which evaluate programme differentiation:

- What did the child learn?
- How did I facilitate and support their learning?
- How can I help the child to find the right level of challenge?
- In what ways does the learning environment need adapting in order to maximise learning opportunity?
- Were the experiences I planned for and provided of quality and at varying levels?
- Were the learning outcomes planned for? Realised? If not, why not?
- How challenged and supported am I feeling?
- Have I encouraged growth in all developmental domains?

Appendix K: School communication strategies valued by parents

Chapter 9, by Cameron and Margrain, reports school communication strategies valued by parents, from a study by Margrain (2003).

Table K.1. Categorised school communication strategies valued by parents

Category	Strategy
Informal interpersonal	Informal comments, personal contact, questions, email
	Parent involvement in school, class or centre
	Teacher actively approachable
	Listening, acknowledgment and reassurance
Formal interpersonal	Formal parent–teacher interviews
	Meetings regarding an 'issue': 'awesome' or 'intense' meetings
	Individual education plan (IEP) or education plan (EP)
	Parent education evenings
Written communication	Written reports
	Portfolios or work samples
	General newsletter
	Certificates
	Comments notebook
	Homework
Systems-level communication	Open-door policy—parents able to observe
	Support for 1-day school for gifted students
	Principal/manager supportive
	Websites
	Advising parents of child's reading age or level, test results or grades

Index

A

A Nation Deceived, 110
abilities (gifts), 4–6, 21, 23–4, 112, 189–90, 192
Absolum, M., 59
abstract thinking *see* thinking
accelerated learning, 111, 146
   case study, 185
agency *see* children's voice
Allan, Barbara, 59, 71, 181
   Giftedness in Early Childhood Scale, 29, 68–9, 97
Amy (case study), 155
Andrew (case study), 174
artefacts, 66–7
assessment, 31–2, 57–60, 61–3, 69–70, 71–2
   case studies, 32–3, 83, 186
   formal, 31–2
   partnerships, 70–1, 164
assessment *see also* learning notes, learning stories
assessment tools *see also* observation scales, 30–2, 68–9
asynchronous development, 23–4, 60
Athena, role model, 210–1

B

Barry, S, 71
Beresford, L, 32, 109
Bevan-Brown, J, 7, 21, 61, 85, 115
Blaiklock, K, 66
Bloom's taxonomy, 157, 158
Breen, Sue, 109, 110
British Picture Vocabulary Scale, 69
Bronfenbrenner, U, 202
Burt Word Reading Test, 69

C

Carr, M., 64, 65
case studies, 132, 165, 169, 174
   individual, 76–84, 84–90, 90–9, 113, 122, 130, 134, 135, 137, 148, 155, 181–9
Cathcart, R, 142, 158, 181
checklists and scales, 68–9
children's voice, 59, 67–8, 170–1, 204
   case study, 172
Clark, B., 14, 156
clustering, networking, 204–5
   Cluster Model, 205
Code of Ethical Conduct for Research, 75
Code of Ethics for Registered Teachers, 107
Colangelo, N., 110
collaborative relationships, 163, 176, 194
Coloured Progressive Matrices, 69
communication, 163–4, 164, 165–7
   case studies, 165, 169
   strategies, 168
competencies (talents), 4–5, 60, 65, 69, 176, 203
computer activity *see* technology
conceptual themes, 151
Consult, 207
convergent thinking, 50, 152
creativity, 6, 64, 211–3
   case studies, 92–5, 92–6
critical thinking *see* thinking
curriculum, 115–6, 176–7, 201–3
   differentiation, 144–52, 159–60
      case studies, 149, 155
      process differentiation, 152–4
      product differentiation, 154–5
   and dispositions, 65
curriculum see also *Te Whāriki; The New Zealand Curriculum*

D

Dabrowski, Kazimierz, 129, 130
David (case studies), 113, 169
Dean, Jo, 68, 212
Dereck (case study), 84–90
Differentiated Model of Giftedness and Talent (DMGT) *see* Gagné
differentiation *see* curriculum differentiation
Discovery Time, 39
dispositions, 24, 63–5, 65, 176
dispositions *see also* learning stories
divergent thinking, 152
Dockett, S., 170
drama, 47, 48, 51, 92, 212
drawing, 67, 95, 134, 155
Drummond, M. J., 57, 61, 67
Dunn, L., 71
Dweck, C. S., 24

E

early childhood curriculum *see* Te Whāriki
early years, 2
  core principles, 8, 107
education specialists, 71
Emily (case study), 134
Emma (case study), 90–9
emotional intensity, 135–6, 137
enrichment, 145–6, 151, 154–5
environment *see* learning environment
ethics, 75
  Code of Ethics for Registered Teachers, 107
  Massey University Committee of Ethics, 75
Explorer camps, 133

F

families *see* whānau

Fisher, J., 38
Fisher, R., 39

G

Gagné, F., 4–5
  Differentiated Model of Giftedness and Talent (DMGT), 5, 107, 108, 109, 118, 210, 212
    application, 182, 183, 189–93, 191, 196
Gallagher, G., 173, 174, 176
Gallagher, J. J., 25
Gates, Bill, 209
genetics, 14
Gifted and Talented Education (GATE), 2, 169, 186
Gifted and Talented Online, 207–8
Gifted and Talented Students: Meeting Their Needs in New Zealand Schools, 7
gifted children, 2–3
  characteristics, 15–6, 18–20, 22, 41
  denied, overlooked, 16–7, 106
  myths about, 107–112
gifted education, 8–11, 204
  organisations, 207–8
  teacher roles, 9–10, 49, 109, 118–121, 119
  terminology, 145–7
Gifted Online, 187, 207
giftedness definitions, 2, 4, 7–9, 108–9, 111–2, 128, 189, 190
  Māori perspective, 7, 89
Giftedness in Early Childhood Scale, 29, 68–9
giftedness *see also* identification
Giftedness, Three-Ring Concept, 6
giftEDnz, xiv, 206, 207, 208
gifts (natural abilities), 4–5
goal management, 192–3

Goodfellow, J., 211
Grant, A., 47
Greenman, J., 155
Gross, M. U. M., 46

H
Harrison, C., 17, 47, 67, 70, 95, 150
  giftedness definitions, 7, 128, 189
He Kāhui Pūmanawa, 207
Hollingworth, L. S., 46, 49, 111
hot-housing, 112, 113
Hubbard (1929), 46

I
identification of giftedness, 3, 10, 15, 24–5, 40, 51
  core principles, 25–7
  observation scales, 29–30
  parties to, 25, 27–8, 30–1
  recommendations, 30
Identifying and Providing for Giftedness in the Early Years, 29, 69, 97
imaginational intensity, 134–5
inclusion, 17, 106, 114–8, 122
Individual Education Plan (IEP), 168, 169
individual plan (IP), 71
information sharing, 3, 30, 70–1, 164–6
  case studies, 165, 174
initial teacher education (ITE), 114–5
intellectual intensity, 132–4
IQ and giftedness, 9, 26
  tests, 31–2, 69

J
Jackson (case study), 76–84

K
kaitiakitanga, 89

Kane, R. G., 107
kaupapa Māori *see* Māori
Kulik, J. and C. C., 148

L
language development, 16, 67–8, 92
leadership, 172, 208–10
learning dispositions, 24, 64, 65
learning environment, 9, 14, 131, 143, 155–6, 210
  case studies, 183–4, 193, 195
learning notes, 66
learning stories, 29, 59, 63–5, 89
  case studies, 78, 82, 86, 88, 91, 93, 94, 96, 98
Liam (case study), 181–9
Lily (case study), 172
literacy, 23–4
literacy skills, 22–4, 67, 167, 209
  case studies, 81, 182–3
  tests, 69

M
Maker, C. J., 50, 152
Māori giftedness, 7, 17, 39, 61, 207
  kaupapa Māori, 21–2, 27, 144
  case studies, 85–9
Margrain, Valerie, 5, 110, 112, 167, 168, 173
  early readers, 24, 29, 64–5, 68–9, 108, 111, 112, 166
  case study, 113
Martin, B., 39
Massey University Committee of Ethics, 75
Meade, A., 49, 156
MindPlus, 207
Ministry of Education, 21, 25–7, 107, 194
  Gifted and Talented Advisory Group, 7

Gifted and Talented Online, 207
Te Kete Ipurangi, 29
Moltzen, R., 183
Morelock, M. J., 151
Murphy, Caterina, 14, 22, 23, 28, 29, 116
myths and responses, 106–12

N

narrative assessment *see* learning stories
National Administration Guidelines (NAGs), 3, 116
National Education Guidelines (NEGs), 3, 116
Neale Analysis of Reading, 69
Nelson, R L, 48
networks, 176, 204
    network learning communities (NLCs), 205–6
New Zealand Association for Gifted Children (NZAGC), 105, 207, 208
New Zealand Centre for Gifted Education, 18–20, 32–3, 187, 207, 208
New Zealand Curriculum *see The New Zealand Curriculum*
New Zealand Teachers Council, 107
NLCs *see* network learning
Nutall, E. V., 9

O

O'Day, S., 47
observation methodology, 29–30, 61–3, 62–3, 97
observations *see* case studies
Oliver (case study), 130
One Day School (ODS), 193
open-ended activity, 38–9, 42, 50, 152–3
Oscar (case study), 137

overexcitabilities (intensities), 85 129-36
    case study, 193
    overview, 138

P

parents, 20–21, 27–8, 70–1, 108, 121, 163
    case studies, 80–3, 81, 113, 165, 184
    communication, 26, 30–1, 110, 163–6, 194–5
    experiences, 166–8, 173
parents *see* whānau
partnerships, 70–1, 121, 163, 170, 174, 194
passion, 64
Patterson, K., 144
peers, 22–3, 28, 45, 109, 133
Perkins, D. N., 64, 65
Perry, B., 170
Peters, S., 174–5
photos *see* technology
Piechowski, M., 130, 181
play, 38–9
    giftedness characteristics, 22, 41, 45–6
    teacher strategies, 49–51
play patterns, 41–5
    drama, role play, 47, 51, 80, 212–3
    open-ended, 38–9, 42, 50–1
Podmore, V, 204
Poppy Peek *see also* Small Poppies, 32–3
Porter, L., 68, 83, 108, 144, 154
process differentiation, 152–4
product differentiation, 154–5
professional learning, 110, 120–1, 176, 205–6, 207
psychometric testing *see* IQ
psychomotor intensity, 129–30

R

Radue, L., 15
rangatiratanga, 203
REACH Education, 207
reading *see* literacy
Reedy, T., 203
Reese (case study), 135
reflection, 64
    parents', 30–1, 33
    professional, 107, 120, 204
reflective questions, 51–2, 159–60
Renzulli, J. S., 4, 6, 6, 7
Resource Teachers: Learning and Behaviour (RTLB), 205
Richardson, Elwyn, 211
Riley, T. L., 9, 107, 151, 156
Ritchhart, R., 64
Roberts, J. and R., 147

S

school *see* transition to school
self-determination (rangatiratanga), 203
sensory learning, 92
sensual intensity, 130–2
six-year net, 69–70
Small Poppies, 32–3, 133, 207
social integration, 48–9, 109, 128–9
SPELD, 169
Stamford-Binet test, 32
supporting gifted children, 118–121, 119

T

talents (competencies), 2, 4–5, 190, 192–3
Te Kete Ipurangi, 29, 205
Te Tiriti o Waitangi, 7, 21
Te Whāriki, 17, 40, 59, 64, 65, 111, 170, 204
and giftedness, 3, 115
philosophy, 201–2, 203, 208
and transition, 173, 176–7
teacher education, 116, 205–6
    initial teacher education (ITE), 114
    professional development, 107, 110, 113–4, 117–8, 120
Teacher Observation Scales for Identifying Children with Special Abilities, 30
teachers, 9–10, 44–5, 49, 108, 109, 210–1
    and giftedness identification, 16–7, 25, 28, 51–2
    case study, 122
    and learning environment, 156
technology, 66–7, 154, 209
    case studies, 113, 174, 195
temperament, 138
terminology, 2, 145–7
tests, standardised, 69–70
The Battle of the Mountains, 86
The New Zealand Curriculum, 17, 59, 65, 115–6, 170, 173, 177
    philosophy, 202–3
thinking, 47, 64, 157, 209
    abstract, 40, 45, 48, 95, 150
    convergent, divergent, 50–1
    dispositions, 64
Three-Ring Concept of Giftedness, 6
Toby (case study), 149–51
Torrance, E. P., 211
Townsend, M. A. R., 145, 146
transition to school, 172–6
    case study, 174

U

underachievement, 188–9
United Nations Convention on the Rights of the Child, 59, 171

V
Van Tassel-Baska, J., 144
video *see* technology
Vygotsky, L. S., 49

W
Walker, B., 151
Walters, Peter, 105
Ward, L., 206
Weschler intelligence scales, 32
whakapapa, 17, 89
whānau relationships, 26, 27–8, 59, 70–1, 172–3
Wong, Melanie, 106, 107, 109, 110, 113, 114, 119, 123
Woodcock-Johnson tests, 32, 186, 194
Working Party on Gifted Education, 7, 8
Wright, J, 176

Y
Yousafzai, Malala, 209–10

www.ingramcontent.com/pod-product-compliance
Lightning Source LLC
Chambersburg PA
CBHW051148290426
44108CB00019B/2647